# New Wine,
# New Wineskins

# New Wine,
# New Wineskins

## A Next Generation Reflects on Key Issues in Catholic Moral Theology

Edited by
William C. Mattison III

A SHEED & WARD BOOK

ROWMAN & LITTLEFIELD PUBLISHERS, INC.
*Lanham • Boulder • New York • Toronto • Oxford*

A SHEED & WARD BOOK

ROWMAN & LITTLEFIELD PUBLISHERS, INC.

Published in the United States of America
by Rowman & Littlefield Publishers, Inc.
A wholly owned subsidiary of The Rowman & Littlefield Publishing Group, Inc.
4501 Forbes Boulevard, Suite 200, Lanham, Maryland 20706
www.rowmanlittlefield.com

PO Box 317
Oxford
OX2 9RU, UK

British Library Cataloguing in Publication Information Available

**Library of Congress Cataloging-in-Publication Data**

New wine, new wineskins : a next generation reflects on key issues in Catholic
moral theology / edited by William C. Mattison III.
    p. cm.
Includes bibliographical references and index.
ISBN 0-7425-3245-3 (alk. paper) — ISBN 0-7425-3246-1 (pbk. : alk. paper)
    1. Christian ethics—Catholic authors. 2. Catholic Church—Doctrines. I. Mattison,
William C., III, 1971–
BJ1249.N49 2005
241'.042—dc22                                                                        2004029284

Printed in the United States of America

∞™ The paper used in this publication meets the minimum requirements of
American National Standard for Information Sciences—Permanence of Paper
for Printed Library Materials, ANSI/NISO Z39.48-1992.

For
**Fr. Timothy R. Scully, C.S.C.,**
a true model of a Catholic intellectual,
with gratitude for your friendship,
your dedication and service to Catholic education,
and your mentorship over the years,
particularly with New Wine, New Wineskins

# Contents

# Foreword

Likewise, no one pours new wine into old wineskins. Otherwise, the wine will burst the skins, and both the wine and the skins are ruined. Rather, new wine is poured into fresh wineskins (Mk 2.22 and parallels).

At first sight, *New Wine, New Wineskins* looks like a brash appropriation of this synoptic parable. One might even hear an implied warning in the bursting ruin of wineskins that are not new. Such a title could give an "old guy" flashbacks to the days of "The Times They Are 'A Changin.'"

But then the subtitle is more respectful. It takes the edge, though not all of it, off the title. Some edge is good. The essays in this book represent, the subtitle tells the reader, *A Next Generation in Catholic Moral Theology*. This intriguing juxtaposition of the brash and the respectful captures the tone of the book.

We have neither the triumphal "A New Generation" nor the definitive "The Next Generation," but the more merely chronological and indeterminate *A Next Generation*. "A Next Generation" brings some welcome irony to a polarized landscape. It suggests people who believe in the communion of saints, who are not out to slay or even to show up their teachers, and who want to walk forward faithfully on the path worn by the moral theologians who have gone before them. One contributor invokes the wisdom of Monika Hellwig that it is the vocation of the theologian to disappear.

And most strikingly, according to the subtitle, this is a next generation of "Catholic moral theologians." At an uneasy moment in Catholic intellectual life, these authors self-identify without apology as theologians, and even as "Catholic moral theologians." Twenty-five years ago, a comparable group might have subtitled their book "A New Generation in Christian Ethics." But these authors reclaim for themselves the time-honored name that modern Catholics have given to their discipline.

This juxtaposition of the brash and the respectful promises something different. And that promise is cast in generational terms. Two examples convey how the importance of generational difference crystallized during the discussions of the *mandatum* that led up to the full implementation in 2001 of *Ex Corde Ecclesiae* in this country.

In June 2000, the College Theology Society held its annual meeting at Villanova University. By this time, it was clear to many young people that they had become unwilling stakes in the battle over the *mandatum*. In the middle of a heated discussion following a plenary session, a young moral theologian, Timothy Muldoon, stood up to speak. A 1998 Duquesne Ph.D., he was teaching at Mount Aloysius College in Cresson, Pennsylvania. Most striking about his intervention was his claim to speak for a generation. He reminded the audience that their discussions of theology's future had to make room for a new cohort that hadn't been born in 1968. As the fifty-somethings descended on him at session's end, the significance of Muldoon's intervention was clear. Jesus teaching in the temple would be a stretch, but I had to admit with the early Bob Dylan that the waters around me had grown.

The second example is Christopher Ruddy's "Young Theologians," an article that appeared in *Commonweal* a few weeks before the 2000 CTS meeting. Perhaps Muldoon read it. Or perhaps he and Ruddy were just drinking from the same wells. A doctoral student in theology at Notre Dame, Ruddy tried to reconfigure contemporary discussions to include his concerns about Catholic theology's "increasing captivity to the mores of the academy and its concurrent ecclesial deracination." Like Muldoon's, Ruddy's intervention drew immediate responses, but they tended to force him back into the confines of a discussion he was trying to get beyond. Ruddy brought to the fore two issues that are at the center of New Wine, New Wineskins: the spiritual formation of theologians and their day-to-day rootedness in the life of the local church.[1] It would not surprise me if the New Wine, New Wineskins initiative that first brought young moral theologians together at Notre Dame in the summer of 2002, and eventually issued in this book, percolated from some of the same sources that inspired Ruddy's article. Archbishop Daniel Pilarczyk's wise handling of the implementation of Canon 812 in 2001, along with the awful disclosures that followed in 2002, have pushed the *mandatum* to the theological periphery and cleared a space for concerns such as Ruddy's to gain a more serious hearing.

## DOING MORAL THEOLOGY WITHOUT A SUBCULTURE

But why do young theologians care about spiritual formation and ecclesial roots? In the introduction to *A People Adrift*, Peter Steinfels identifies two key transitions that will be completed over the next two decades in the Catholic Church in the United States. The first is a "passage in generations" from the "leadership formed in the dense subculture that characterized American Catholicism before the Second Vatican Council." The second is a "passage from clergy to laity." The young moral theologians who have contributed to *New Wine, New Wineskins* are living these two passages. Among the book's contributors, only one belongs to a religious order. The rest are lay people. As university-trained theologians, they have not necessarily received any serious spiritual formation. Nor does their training in theology necessarily entail any formal role in the ecclesial structures in which they participate with the rest of the baptized.

No wonder that spiritual formation and ecclesial connectedness are central themes in these essays. Called to a theological vocation in the church through the dynamics of American pluralism rather than from Steinfels's "dense subculture," this next generation of Catholic moral theologians looks a lot like the "Evangelical Catholics" I have been meeting and trying to figure out over the past five years.[2]

My guess is that the contributors to *New Wine, New Wineskins* might resist the label "evangelical Catholics," especially if they thought this designation came to them from and forced them back into contemporary ecclesial battlefields. But they might well resonate with David McCarthy's recent account of "Catholic moral theology in an evangelical key," where *evangelical* means primarily "engaging the world through witness." Whether individual authors would accept the term or not, the difference between them and my own generational cohort can be described in terms of the two settings McCarthy contrasts, the subculture, now passed or dissolved, and pluralism.[3]

My fifty-or-sixty-something colleagues, along with our seventy-something and older professors, were formed in a clearly bounded Catholic world. We still carry it around inside us. Sometimes we need to get some distance from it. These authors, by contrast, come from the heart of American pluralism and religious voluntarism. Being Catholic is something they enjoy working at.

In their essays, the undergraduate classroom replaces the confessional as the practical site of moral theology. Taking theology's hard won academic legitimacy as a given and presuming the rigor with which their elders trained them, these authors are in a strong position to take subjectivity seriously, their own as well as their students'. They dare to thematize their care for the holiness of theologians and the faith of students. With an epistemologically sophisticated emphasis on the moral formation and ecclesial location of theologians, these essays evade positioning by polarized arguments from the past. Church authority doesn't get a free pass, nor is it ignored as external to theology. The authors have a strong sense of where they stand in the history of moral theology. But they are "wayfaring strangers" and their book is neither a movement manifesto nor a youthfully pretentious scold. As theologians should but too often fail to do, it speaks easily and modestly, of God and the things of God.

Almost forty years ago, Pope Paul VI published his birth control encycli-cal, *Humanae Vitae*. The response to it determined the terrain of moral the-ology for the next two generations. As with the Vietnam War, young theolo-gians had to choose. In this contentious atmosphere, I began my own study of moral theology in the fall of 1968. Many in my generational cohort would eventually disappear from moral theology, abandoning it as a hopelessly contested field. But as with aging presidential candidates, the question of where we were in 1968 continues to dog and define us.

But the generation of New Wine, New Wineskins has no such history. As Timothy Muldoon reminded that CTS audience in June 2000, they weren't born in 1968. Their essays make me want to read moral theology again. Their book is one that "old guys" like me can read with hope for the future of Catholic theology in the United States.

William L. Portier
Mary Ann Spearin Chair of Catholic Theology
University of Dayton

## NOTES

1. Christopher Ruddy, "Young Theologians" *Commonweal* April 21, 2000: 17–19, citation at 17, and the responses in June 2, 2000: 11–14, 4, 29–30.

2. Peter Steinfels, *A People Adrift, The Crisis of the Roman Catholic Church in America* (New York: Simon & Schuster, 2003), 11. On Evangelical Catholics, see William L. Portier, "Here Come the Evangelical Catholics." *Communio* 31 no. 1 (Spring 2004): 35–66 and "In Defense of Mount Saint Mary's," *Commonweal* February 11, 2000: 31–33.

3. David M. McCarthy, "Shifting Settings From Subculture to Pluralism: Catholic Moral Theology in an Evangelical Key," *Communio* 31 no. 1 (Spring 2004): 85–110, at 110.

# Acknowledgments

This volume, and the annual conference out of which it grew, simply would not have been possible without the institutional support of the University of Notre Dame, and in particular the generous administrators who saw the value in supporting a gathering of young intellectuals to reflect on their work in the discipline of Catholic moral theology as a vocation in service to the Church and the academy. Provost Nathan Hatch has been especially supportive of this project. He has generously agreed to provide funding for this project for four years now, and his own work on religious identity in higher education has helped inspire this project. John Cavadini, chair of the Department of Theology, has been equally unwavering in his support both institutionally and personally, greeting and challenging the symposium participants at each annual meeting. Finally, without Fr. Timothy Scully, C.S.C. this volume and New Wineskins in general would not exist. Throughout a decade of friendship he has shared with me his extraordinary dedication to Catholic education and the intellectual life. He has provided invaluable advice since the very beginning of the group and this volume. He so understood and inspired this project that he literally gave it its name. To the University of Notre Dame, and in particular these friends, I am most grateful.

The contributors to this volume (myself included) also owe a debt of gratitude to their fellow participants at New Wine, New Wineskins, whose friendship and conversations have so vitally shaped the essays herein. In particular, special thanks are due to Maria Malkiewicz (who co-founded this group in 2002) and to Margaret Pfeil, David McCarthy, David Cloutier, and Patricia Powers, all of whom have helped steer the *New Wines, New Wineskins* project during the past three years. Special thanks to David Cloutier, whose agreement to co-write the introduction to this collection jumpstarted a stalled project, and provided the occasion for deepened friendship and a better introduction because of it.

Many Catholic moral theologians with more experience in the discipline have been most supportive of this project as well. In particular I would like to thank Cathleen Kaveny (another person whose friendship is a source for this project), William Werpehowski, and an anonymous reviewer, all of whom read the manuscript and provided helpful suggestions. At the 2002 symposium, several established Catholic moral theologians were generous enough to share with our participants, by letter, their thoughts on the field and advice, for which we were grateful and edified in our discussions: Bernard Bardy, Lisa Sowle Cahill, Mary Jo Iozzio, Mark Johnson, Cathleen Kaveny, John Langan, S.J., Daniel Maguire, William O'Neil, S.J., Philip Rossi, S.J., Thomas Shannon, William Spohn, Cristina Traina, and Todd David Whitmore. Though not Catholic, Stanley Hauerwas was kind enough to review the manuscript, submit a letter of encouragement and advice with those above, and generously support this project over the past three years. For the contributions these gracious mentors made, all *New Wine, New Wineskins* participants and I are grateful.

Since this is my first foray into the world of editing, I was in need of publishing guidance and was fortunate enough to receive it. Thanks to Jeff Gainey, whose support and enthusiasm for this project helped get it off the ground. Thanks especially to Jeremy Langford at Sheed & Ward. One couldn't ask for a more conscientious publisher, and I am grateful not only for his guidance but also his friendship, as well as that of his wife Liz.

And lastly, thanks especially to my wife Courtney for all she has done and all she is. Her support for my work is beyond generous. And every day she manages to teach me through example more about the Christian life.

# Introduction

*David Cloutier and William C. Mattison III*

Given changes in the Roman Catholic Church in America over the past three or four decades, it is unsurprising that the field of moral theology has undergone enormous change as well. This is especially evident and well documented, as it concerns the issues addressed in the discipline and how they are addressed. But what have received less attention are the changes in Catholic moral theologians themselves as practitioners of their discipline and the resulting impact of these changes on the discipline they practice. This collection includes chapters that address traditional moral issues and methodological questions. What makes this work distinctive is its attention to the second question, to changes in moral theologians themselves and how those changes affect the discipline. It is that shift that this introduction comments on, placing the contributions to Catholic moral theology in the context of a changing church and changing world.

## A CHANGING AMERICAN CATHOLIC CHURCH

There is no shortage of books describing the current state of the Catholic Church in the United States.[1] Many focus on the impact of Vatican II as a watershed event in the church as a whole and trace changes in the American church directly to the renewal sought by the council.[2] Others have focused on social, historical, and institutional developments in the American church.[3] Recently, of course, this has prompted several examinations of the sex abuse scandal and how that scandal reveals and/or affects life in the church.[4] Even

1

the attacks of September 11, 2001, have been examined as a cause of turn-ing to faith among the young.[5] Yet before the scandal or September 11 seized our attention, scholars had already begun to discuss changes in the Ameri-can Catholic Church by observing and identifying certain changes in the identity of young Catholics. The portrait these works paint of young Ameri-can Catholics is by no means univocal. Yet there are several common fea-tures that may be identified. These distinctive characteristics are best under-stood when presented as part of a larger schema that compares and contrasts generational cohorts.

In recent scholarship on the American Catholic Church in the late twenti-eth century, three such cohorts are readily identifiable. They are commonly labeled in reference to the Second Vatican Council. For instance, James Davidson and his colleagues label their three generational cohorts "pre–Vatican II, Vatican II, and post–Vatican II" Catholics. Though Davidson and colleagues' threefold schema is largely adopted here and though the impor-tance of changes brought about by the council is of course accepted, we fol-low William Portier's recent work that emphasizes social changes in the American church, and not just the council, as explanatory of generational distinctions. Portier has argued that the most important change driving dif-ferences in young American Catholics is the dissolution of the Catholic sub-culture in the United States over the last half-century.[6] Cohorts may be la-beled in reference to the Second Vatican Council, and naturally the changes initiated by the council contributed to the dissolution of the American Catholic subculture; but it is the presence, dissolution of, or absence of that subculture that best differentiates recent generations of American Catholics.[7]

What characterizes a Catholic subculture? The subculture generation, by definition, grew up in social settings that were decidedly Catholic.[8] Atten-dance in Catholic school was more common than it is today. The parish served as a neighborhood gathering place in a manner uncommon today. Catechesis, devotional practices, and other such factors combined to enve-lope these folks in a thoroughly Catholic vision of life.[9] Their stance toward the outside world, even if engaged with that world, was more guarded. Given this tendency toward insularity, it is unsurprising that people have labeled the Second Vatican Council—with its focus on *aggiornimento*, or openness to the world—as the decisive factor in initiating the changes to come. Yet Portier rightly calls attention to the impact of the dissolution of the subculture in America as a too-often-neglected driving force behind changes to come.

To better understand the distinction between pre–Vatican II Catholics, who were immersed in the Catholic subculture, and the Vatican II Catholics who began the transition out of that subculture, consider a 1965 volume ed-ited by Daniel Callahan and entitled *Generation of the Third Eye*.[10] Calla-han's volume is in many ways similar to this one. He gathers approximately twenty Catholic "young intellectuals" from his own generation to speak about themselves and the church. He did not ask them to speak explicitly about the distinctiveness of their generation but rather hoped the volume as a whole would do that on its own. Indeed it does.

What most clearly marks this American Vatican II (or what we ethnocentrically call here "transitional") generation is a sense of liberating engagement with the world outside the church. Consider Callahan's own contribution in which he describes his own undergraduate studies. That this Catholic young man went to Yale at all is significant in representing this generation's increased engagement with the world beyond Catholicism. He recognizes its significance when he speaks of how the "basically tidy inner world I had carried with me from a Catholic high school . . . was breaking down" (6). It was here that he became more aware of the "cultural differences" separating Catholics from other Americans (7). Overall he found this engagement with the world outside Catholicism positive. There were previously untapped resources out there waiting to be marshaled in his generation's quest for wisdom. He speaks of studying under John Courtney Murray, SJ, while at Yale and learning to "relate Thomism to modern philosophical currents," including the thought of Hume, Gide, and Russell (8–9). This engagement enabled Callahan not only to understand his Catholicism from a broader perspective but also to "speak directly" without "vouching for . . . orthodoxy every time we have something to say" (4–5). He explicitly eschews the language of affirming his "commitment to the Church" because it seems often to function as an implicit "signed loyalty oath" guarding one from accusations of "harboring secularist ideas for daring to raise questions about this or that point of Catholicism" (5, 10).

Yet despite this spirit of liberating engagement during his years at Yale, Callahan notes at times that he surprised himself in his reaction against much outside of the Catholic subculture in which he was formed. He speaks of joining and soon quitting a fraternity. He devotes extensive intellectual energies into providing a rational defense of the Catholic faith in conversation with non-Catholic philosophers. This twofold stance toward the world seems to perfectly encapsulate the stance of a Vatican II Catholic living at the time of transition from Catholic subculture to postsubculture Catholicism. Though he found that engagement liberating and positive, he was still sufficiently formed within the subculture to ground that engagement with the extra-Catholic world. At one point Callahan casually mentions that at the time of his study of the "rational basis of the Catholic faith," which he undertook in conversation with modern philosophy, he "fortified this quest with daily Mass" as well as strict arguments (8). Extraordinary! He later claims with obvious sincerity that despite all his criticisms of the church, "I love the Church [and] could not imagine being anything but Catholic" (13).[11]

Callahan's book perfectly illustrates the differences and similarities between his own generation and that which preceded him. Callahan's group of

Catholic intellectuals were representative of the signs of their times. Larger changes in the church as a whole and in American society are reflected in their concerns, projects, and formation. His own generation was the first to engage the world beyond the subculture in a sustained manner and in large numbers, and they bear the "joy and hopes, the grief and anguish" of that engagement.[12] Nevertheless, what they share in common with the previous generation is their formation in that subculture, even though they spent later years moving outside of it. It is precisely this formative period that distinguishes the generation of Catholics represented in this volume from their immediate predecessors, including folks like Callahan.

The signs of the times for today's younger Catholics are not the same as those described by Callahan in his work. This is why so many of the aforementioned works on the Catholic church in America today include attention to generational differences. Young American Catholics have been formed in a different church than that which formed Callahan and his generation. As noted, characterizing young Catholics is a contested endeavor. Yet the works examined here do agree on three interrelated features.

First, while recent accounts of young Catholics today differ sharply in many of their assessments, all acknowledge that this generation regards itself as having been poorly formed in the Catholic faith.[13] What marks a subculture is the formation of its denizens with a cohesive vision of life. Parenting, education, religious practices, and extrafamilial relationships all combine to reinforce, in this case, a Catholic lens through which those in the subculture see themselves and the world around them. Such formation does not necessarily preclude encounters with others or conversions to alternate ways of life. But it does provide one a stable Catholic identity that grounds such encounters. We saw in Callahan's own autobiographical account how engagement with the world beyond Catholicism was grounded by a formation that engendered a "tidy little world" and by practices such as daily Mass. This is why so many folks of that generation were and are unable to imagine not being Catholic.

Yet the collapse of the Catholic subculture generally occasions the loss of such a thoroughgoing formation and identity. Most young Catholics of the current generation simply did not grow up "unable to imagine not being Catholic." On the contrary, they lack a cohesive Catholic vision—or Greeley's "Catholic imagination"—provided by the subculture.[14] Two reasons are suggested to explain this lack of formation and identity. First, each of the aforementioned treatments of poor formation in young Catholics attends to poor catechesis in the years following the Second Vatican Council. Second, it was easy to "imagine not being Catholic" when, in the postsubculture world, non-Catholics were all around! David McCarthy speaks of how young Catholics were formed in the culture of pluralism.[15] No one in this volume would wish to withdraw from engagement with those outside the Catholic

Church or return to re-create Catholic subculture. Such a move is unimaginable to this generation. Yet in the absence of more thoroughgoing formation in the Catholic faith, young Catholics increasingly disregard their Catholicism as irrelevant or, at best, do not fully understand the practices and norms that structure a life of discipleship.[16]

Second, and deriving from the first point, young Catholics are notably different in their disposition toward "the world" outside the church. On the one hand, their parents (Callahan's generation) were raised in the church and engaged with the world. On the other hand, young Catholics, largely devoid of the Catholic lens through which to comprehensively view their lives and the world around them, have lived primarily in the world. Young Catholics feel no need to "engage the world"; they are immersed in the world from the beginning and grope to understand better their Catholic identity. It should come as no surprise, then, that young Catholics who want to make their faith a central part of their identity seek to better understand their own Catholic tradition by turning to the Church. From this renewed appreciated of their own tradition, they engage secular culture in which they have been imbued their whole lives. Rather than fleeing the table of pluralistic dialogue (*that* would be nearly unimaginable to this generation!), this typically reflects an ardent desire to bring something to that table of dialogue with the world outside the church.[17] They are looking for the sort of identity that drove Callahan and Greeley to say that they could not imagine not being Catholic. Thus, while the previous generation was marked by a trajectory from the church outward toward the world, this younger generation of American Catholics exhibits a turn from the world toward the church in search of wisdom. Once nourished by that wisdom, they then turn back toward the world in witness and service.

This trajectory helps explain a common charge directed toward such young Catholics from those raised in earlier times—namely, that such younger folks are sectarian. The young "orthodox" described by Colleen Carroll in her *The New Faithful* seem to be precisely the folks who would receive such an accusation. Carroll responds to this charge:

> Rather than believing the Church needs to be more like the world, these young adults decided long ago that the world needs to be more like the Church—at its best. And most of them have seen enough of the secular world to be wary of its seductions. Most also are more focused on transforming the culture for Christ than finding a safe niche where they can hide.[18]

Carroll acknowledges that some such young folks can indeed opt out of dialogue with others and become smug, defensive, and isolationist.[19] Others simply spend so much time with like-minded folks that they fail to see how others perceive them. Yet for most she claims this is not the case. Most simply try to walk the fine line between "selling out" on their religious convictions and "opting out" of dialogue with those in wider society. When successfully walking this fine line, these young Catholics generally engage in ecumenical and interreligious dialogue more effectively than others due to their stronger sense of identity regarding their own tradition.

Regardless of what one makes of Carroll's "new faithful,"[20] there is wider recognition that many young adult Catholics turn back toward the church in search of a more solid understanding of their tradition before then turning back toward the world in witness and service, having been nourished by that wisdom.[21] As Peter Steinfels notes, knowledge of American religious history is rewarded with two key insights for this discussion.[22] First, it is the religious groups with a strong sense of identity that flourish. Second, religious groups that last are those ones that engage large social transmutations directly. Young adult Catholics who seek a better knowledge of their tradition in order to then turn back toward the world fortified by such an identity seem to heed Steinfels's prognosticating insight.

Third, the faith of young adult Catholics, particularly those mentioned here who actively seek to learn more about their religious tradition in compensation for their own lack of formation, takes on a voluntaristic character. This term requires explanation since it is so variously used. At a most basic level, *religious voluntarism* means that religious belief is freely chosen rather than adopted more or less automatically as a result of upbringing or culture.[23] In terms of this discussion of late-twentieth-century Catholicism, it means that individual choice, rather than ethnic or cultural identity such as that generated by a subculture, is the primary source of religious conviction.[24] There is something genuinely good about this sort of voluntarism. The faith of young Catholics is generally an authentic commitment that has been personally chosen and appropriated by one's own self. As Carroll notes, "the strongest attribute of today's young believers is that they are choosing their religious beliefs with enthusiasm rather than simply inheriting them with indifference."[25] Anyone who teaches theology to undergraduates today knows that one of the things they hate most is identifying one's self with a religious tradition simply because of one's parents or cultural background rather than one's own choosing. This does not mean, of course, that one cannot have an authentic, personal faith commitment that is the same as that of, say, one's parents. But it must be appropriated for one's self.

Again, this voluntarism is generally a good thing, the sort of mature faith that serves as an antidote to a religious identity generated solely by one's membership in a subculture. But it is not without problems. As noted by Carroll, a faith that is sustained primarily by individual choice may be more authentic in some ways, but it is also more easily tossed aside. She quotes one Catholic youth minister as saying that today's youth are "conversion-prone" but find it difficult to maintain commitment. "Today's culture makes it easy to evangelize and very difficult to make disciples."[26] Related to issues regarding sustaining commitments, voluntaristic faith is also more individualistic and prone to problems inherent to consumerism.[27] One challenge for young Catholics is to understand that

> they embody a Catholic ecclesiology in which the Church is the body of Christ to which we are called by God rather than a voluntary association that religious consumers choose to join.[28]

Each of these three features of the current generation of young American Catholics holds promise and poses challenges. Young Catholics frequently recognize their poor formation and then seek to rectify this lack. They fully understand the riches available from growing up in a pluralistic environment but then seek to better grasp their own tradition to bring its wisdom to the table of dialogue. Finally, their faith commitments are more manifestly "their own," though the more individualized commitment that engenders such authenticity commonly lacks the social and institutional support to both sustain the commitment and keep it in ongoing continuity with the tradition. Most especially for the purposes of this volume, these characteristics shape who young American Catholics today are and thus their ways of being Catholic.

## MORAL THEOLOGY IN THESE WINDS OF CHANGE

It should thus be no shock that the dynamics briefly outlined here have shaped today's young Catholic moral theologians as well as the practice of their discipline. The formation and ongoing professional life of today's Catholic moral theologians is markedly different from that of predecessors both in the time of the Catholic subculture and in the period where theologians (such as Callahan) saw the dissolution of that subculture even while they themselves were largely formed by it in their early years.

But how is this shift in Catholic culture actually reflected in the substance of moral theology? Often, it is not noted, as if theoretical debates went on oblivious to the actual changing life of the church. But John Mahoney, in his renowned history of moral theology, describes the importance of the church community in his concluding chapter: "Catholic moral theology has characteristically been the reflection upon Christian behaviour as developed, and, indeed, controlled, within the context of the Church." He goes on to say that the moral theology of the future should provide "an enriched awareness of the *locus* of moral theologizing."[29] The locus of Mahoney's own book, and most other books of moral theology in the period of and subsequent to the council, is a move away from the context of the church as subculture as narrated here.[30] This is not merely a "revisionist" position—figures such as Germain Grisez and Servais Pinckaers, critical of revisionist methods and positions, share with revisionists the desire to overcome the type of moral theology that was associated with the earlier Catholic subculture.[31] They name that way of doing moral theology as "legalism," or perhaps more appropriately, the moral theology "of the manuals." The standard criticisms assume (rightly) that Vatican II marked a move out of the subculture mentality and therefore necessitated a move toward a different sort of moral theology.

But what sort? Let us use Mahoney's final chapter as a model for the trajectory anticipated by the transitional generation.[32] An analysis of its predictions concerning the future of moral theology indicates the way in which postsubculture moral theology both *fulfills* and yet *revises* the directions he offers.[33] Because of this continuity with and critique of revisionist directions, postsubculture moral theology can appear frustrating to those who wish to map positions onto the standard liberal–conservative schema. However, that schema is as historically conditioned as any other, as we have argued. The work of the present authors demands a different schema.

Mahoney offers three directions for moral theology, which he indicated were in their ascendancy in the mid-1980s—a drive toward totality, a recognition of diversity, and a recovery of mystery.[34] When Mahoney wrote of a "drive toward totality," he meant that the act-centered moral theology of the manuals, which fragmented human action into "atomic elements," was being overcome by "a refusal to ignore the relationship of the parts to each other."[35] Surely the same rejection of the atomism of the manuals is present in this collection; however, when Mahoney speaks of "the totality of the human person," he makes it clear that such a move toward totality underlies "the breaching of absolutes and the incorporation of consequences."[36] According to Mahoney, the future belongs to Rahnerian fundamental option theory and proportionalist moral theory. In contrast to Mahoney's vision, what characterizes the moral theology of the present volume is a far richer account of the complexity of human action than either the proportionalist or the fundamental option school of moral theology seems to have achieved. Mahoney's prognosis misses the already-nascent revival of virtue ethics and concomitant renewal in studies of Aquinas, both of which offer a more holistic account of human action than the manuals but neither of which are products of the sort of analysis proposed by revisionists of Mahoney's generation.[37]

Members of the postsubculture generation of Catholic moral theologians, far more aware of their somewhat alien status in the larger culture, also characteristically place their descriptions of actions within a thicker context of the distinctive Christian narrative and tradition. Yet a recognition of "totality" by postsubculture moral theology means a more self-conscious and intentional recognition of Christian action within the distinctive life of discipleship. The rising interest in the methodological significance of the saints as moral exemplars, in the importance of ecclesial practices for Catholic moral formation, and in the import accorded to adoption of a personal vocation all point in this intentionally Christian direction.[38] Yet these post–Vatican II Catholics are misinterpreted if the transitional generation of Catholic moral theologians assume that the post–Vatican II generation are seeking to retreat from the world back into a no longer existing subculture. Rather, we would argue that this new generation reflects an accurate sense of the "signs of the times" for their generation in a way similar to that of the transitional generation.

When Mahoney recognizes a move toward "diversity," he oddly bases his observation on the modern achievement of "the ability to stand outside history and see it precisely as history, rather than being completely immersed in its stream."[39] Hence, he claims that the "totality" of his first point can be viewed from a variety of perspectives. Because we know that change characterizes history (as opposed to those "static" theories of nature in the manuals), he argues that none of these perspectives can be hegemonic. He grounds his assumption about "historical change" in Teilhard's evolutionary theory or *Gaudium et spes'* "signs of the times," thus insisting that moral theology must come to grips with a pluralism of perspectives, both social and personal.

While this collection of chapters is characterized by a methodological eclecticism, it is grounded in a postmodern sensibility, a sensibility that escapes Mahoney. For example, one of his central claims—that is, that our characteristic ability is the ability to stand outside history (and presumably, our historic social roles)—is precisely the reverse of the postmodern appreciation for the tradition-constituted and contextual character of knowledge. Having imbibed the view that all perspectives are necessarily tradition constituted, the post–Vatican II generation of moral theologians seek not an escape from their tradition but a deeper immersion in it. This phenomenon has been commented on at the popular level in Catholicism, but it is no less true in theological fields. This "traditionalism," however, is not (at least here) monolithic and static but is rather reflective of the richness of its history and its resources over and against a postmodern world whose dizzying pace of change masks a reality of global uniformity and cultural emptiness.

Here lies the particular irony of the moral theology of the transitional generation: while harshly critiquing the "static" view of the previous moral theology, its own theology threatens to become a view just as ahistorical, just as oblivious to its own rootedness in a cultural context. For example, Mahoney comments (quite ahistorically) that the 1960s and 1970s were "not an uncharacteristic or exceptional period" but rather that "change is here to stay and that every age is an age of transition."[40] It is difficult to imagine a more transparent attempt to turn one's own period into a universal and "static" truth. In the aforementioned claim, we find expressed in moral theology what we earlier argued: that the transitional generation is enchanted with the world outside the subculture and does not share the need of the present generation of the intentional cultivation of a Catholic sensibility. The claim reflects a view that someone raised in a postmodern culture might even consider naïve.

Thus, the diversity of the collection is marked not so much by a static appeal to "the diversity of human and moral experience"[41] but rather by attempts to find linguistic and ecclesial resources to incorporate and understand diverse experiences in the context of the Catholic tradition. In a postmodern world where diversity is so obvious and dominant that it can become a blur, how might the Christian find language and practices that allow him or her to sort through, appreciate, and order energy and experience? As we noted, pluralism is a given now; the challenge is a recovery of ways and means to live sanely and faithfully amidst it.[42]

Similarly, Mahoney's final point, a recovery of mystery, risks offering a monolithic perspective (in his case, a Rahnerian cosmology) in the guise of diversity. However, overlooking some of the particulars of his exposition, Mahoney clearly wants to overcome some of the frustrating impasses of the "distinctiveness of Christian ethics" debates and reconnect moral theology to the living Spirit of God, particularly as it is active in human relationships. This refusal to disconnect moral teaching from human and divine relationships is characteristic of a larger move to reconnect spirituality and moral theology, a connection now all but taken for granted by writers in our field. Mahoney quotes Joseph Fuchs as indicating the primary task of post–Vatican II moral theology is "to explain that man is called personally in Christ by the personal God."[43]

But here again, the tendency to read such a call in an existential, athematic fashion as somehow underneath all human behavior (apparently what Fuchs and Mahoney have in mind) is now being transformed into a moral theology of lived discipleship or of witness, in which the concrete, costly, biblical call of Christ challenges worldly pictures of happiness or fulfillment. Here, of course, the post–Vatican II generation of moral theologians are more likely to take up the call of the council for a more scriptural moral theology, as well as *Veritatis Splendor*'s use of the story of the rich young man (Matthew 19:16–22) as a paradigmatic description of the Christian moral life. This focus on personal, more voluntaristic discipleship and witness does not (at least in these cases) mean a return to legalism, but it does reflect a high level of seriousness about the worthy challenges presented by some of the "rules" of the tradition. But even these rules it subsumes under a larger vision of holiness of life, a holiness only possible by connection with a life of prayer and community, in communion with the mystery of God and of others.

Mahoney, following Fuchs's classic assessment of the significance of the council for moral theology, indicates that, above all, the new moral theology "should be Christocentric, focusing on the response of the individual Christian to the call of Christ."[44] This is in contrast with the "abstract" approach of law and, particularly, natural law. It would be difficult to find a moral theologian, in this collection or elsewhere, who would dispute this claim as it stands.

However, the interpretation of this claim would be disputed, for Mahoney and Fuchs narrate "faith" and "Christ" in a very distinctive way, as existential claims about the human condition—a narration perfectly understandable given their generational place as moving out of a suffocating subculture. Christ becomes a symbol for a belief in becoming "fully human" and thus is a claim that can connect transitional Catholics to the larger world.[45] However, Christocentric morality as referring to explicit faith in the Jesus of the scriptures and as demanding lived and visible discipleship is absent from their analysis. Yet it is central to those of the postsubculture generation, who recognize discipleship as a challenging and perplexing proposition in a secularized society. The postsubculture generation does not need a conception of Christ-centeredness that connects them to the larger human world but one that helps them sort through the larger world for what is and is not fully human.

Mahoney and Fuchs rightly note that the renewed moral theology must be fully enriched by both dogmatic theology and biblical studies. This movement seems to be exactly what has happened—but again, not with the outcome foreseen by Mahoney, simply because he offers a view of these other fields and their possible contributions that is constrained by his own cultural context. There is a desire on the part of revisionists to reconnect moral theology with spirituality, imbued with the aforementioned voluntary character, and that seems entirely consonant with the chapters collected here.

The work in this collection therefore both fulfills and contradicts some of the predictions made about moral theology in the decades following the council. Ideally, such an understanding will enable all those working in the field to avoid facile oppositions and stereotypes when regarding the work of younger scholars. An appreciation of the sort of Christocentrism exemplified by *Veritatis Splendor* does not necessarily indicate a desire to return to the "bad old days." Nor does a refusal to place natural law and moral absolutes at the center of one's moral theology necessarily indicate that one has essentially sold out to proportionalism. Instead of totality, diversity, and mystery, one might suggest that the moral theology in this collection is characterized by (1) attention to virtue, character, and moral psychology; (2) methodological critique and eclecticism shaped by a desire to order diverse experiences within the Christian tradition; and (3) a longing for lives of Christoform holiness and witness.

The battle lines of American Catholic moral theology of the previous generation can be seen as having been drawn by the move out of the subculture. These battle lines—most notably characterized by a debate over moral absolutes and their continuity validity—have shifted because the historical context of the church has shifted.[46] Obviously, the preoccupation with norms—characteristic of both revisionists and some of their opponents—reflects the experience of being formed in a dissatisfactory (or satisfactory!) subculture very much shaped by a focus on these norms. It is not as if post-subculture Catholics have grown up in a church without norms. But their experience of these norms was never the experience one often hears from sub-culture Catholics, of terror or certainty of the punishment of God if they get run over before Saturday. Thus, their moral theology does not involve the same allegiance to or flight from rules. Rather, it shifts the concerns to a life of witness in a rather chaotic society, the sustaining of which rules, and everything else, ought to serve.

## ENTER NEW WINE, NEW WINESKINS

Given the changes discussed here in young American Catholics and the im-pact of these changes on how young Catholic moral theologians practice their discipline, we should already expect to see tangible signs of such change in the discipline. This volume is clearly one such sign. An even more obvious sign is the annual gathering out of which this volume grew. In the spring of 2002, two Notre Dame doctoral students in moral theology organ-ized a weekend symposium for "young Catholic moral theologians" that was eventually held in the summer of 2002, corresponding to the feast of St. Alphonsus Ligouri (August 1), patron of moral theology.[47] The conference was the first of what has become an annual event entitled New Wine, New Wineskins. According to the promotional material of the weekend,

> New Wine, New Wineskins is an annual symposium convened at the University of Notre Dame by Catholic moral theologians at the beginning stages of their ca-reers. We engage in scholarly activities relevant to the field of moral theology and devote particular attention to the vocational meaning of being a moral the-ologian in today's Church and academy. Since strong collegial bonds will nour-ish and inform our intellectual activities, the symposium is structured around scholarly pursuits complemented by shared meals, prayer, and social events. It is hoped that the incipient friendships nourished at the conference will con-tribute to greater collegiality in our field and engender further scholarly projects.

What drove the organization of this symposium was a sense that some-thing distinctive marked younger moral theologians in the field, a sense that despite differences in doctoral training programs or positions on contested issues, these folks at similar stages in their careers shared something in com-mon besides being trained in roughly the same decade. This was a rather in-choate sense. In fact, one main purpose of the gathering was to reflect on whether or not this was indeed the case and if so, how it might be articulated. Speakers (either invited or those submitting proposals) were given two broad themes for their presentations: the vocation of the Catholic moral theologian in today's church and academy, and pressing issues in contemporary moral theology. The themes examined here were readily evident in both the papers themselves (examined in the following) and the interests of those thirty folks who attended New Wine, New Wineskins that first summer.[48]

What drew this group of young Catholic moral theologians together that first summer and each summer since then? In one sense this was just another conference where scholars with similar interests could gather to present and debate their research. Yet most participants would later say that something else attracted them to this distinctive group. First, they were drawn to a symposium that asked them to explicitly reflect on their work in the context of "vocation." The language of vocation suggests a certain sort of formation. Years of training in rigorous doctoral programs had equipped them with the academic skills needed to succeed in their careers. Yet those gathered sensed that their particular paths of discipleship required more formation and nourishment than that provided by academic training alone. They came to explore how that could be done and to actually do it in the context of a group of friends who share similar callings. The language of vocation also suggests a relationship with a community of believers, the church. Invitational literature made it quite clear that participants would be explicitly exploring what it meant to be called to be a moral theologian in today's church. There were differences over what this means today. But there was a unanimous desire among participants to be more explicitly in service to the church in their work. There was a sense that their relationship to the church was, far from accidental, actually central to their call to be Catholic moral theologians. Thus, the first participants, and those since 2002, came to New Wineskins to reflect on and nourish their vocation, with particular attention to their formation and how their work was in service to the church. The language of vocation naturally led to common prayer as well as formal and informal discussions and debates over what it means to be a moral theologian in the Catholic Church today.

"Friendship" suggests the second reason why they came. Without exception, the participants lamented how divisive the field of Catholic moral theology had become in the United States. There was a widespread hope that they could embark on a career in this field without ending up in the encamped divisions that were so evident and stifling in many of their predecessors. Thus the symposium's explicit attempts to nurture collegiality and friendship were particularly attractive to those gathered. The symposium was held in Moreau Seminary, where it was easy to host common meals, pray together, and find space to socialize and have (often heated!) discussions long into the night. This sense of collegiality did not lead them to resist debating difficult issues in the field. To the contrary, in a setting of those who shared a common understanding of their work as vocation, participants actually spoke of further freedom to argue and debate difficult issues. Yet the tenor of this debate took on a more charitable character. Participants saw an opportunity not to run from dividing questions but rather to model a charitable discourse in addressing them. The chapters in this collection are the fruit of those discussions as much as the more formal scheduled presentation times.

## A NEXT GENERATION OF AMERICAN
## CATHOLIC MORAL THEOLOGIANS

What thematically unites the enclosed chapters on a variety of topics is the recognition of how the particular American Catholic Church in which this younger generation has been raised shapes how these moral theologians practice their discipline. Distinctive here is the interweaving of serious and sustained attention to ongoing methodological issues with self-reflective concerns over questions of formation, ecclesial identity, and ongoing Christian practice. The specific generational features elaborated here are particularly evident in three important arenas for the practice of Catholic moral theology: formation of moral theologians, the classroom, and engagement in methodological debates in the discipline.

### Formation

Consider first the formation of young Catholic moral theologians. Few would be willing to sacrifice the rigorous academic training programs won by our predecessors. And a flight away from conversations with non-Catholic Christians and non-Christians is unimaginable. Rather, it is assumed to be a present and important part of one's formation. But there is also a yearning for more demonstrable formation within the church. There is a niggling sense that their formation as moral theologians, while intellectually rigorous and employing the benefits of contemporary academia, should be more than simply academic.

It is precisely this sense that drives the first three contributions to the volume. The chapter by Christopher Steck, SJ, starts the collection largely due to his incisive diagnosis of the culture of professionalism that dominates academic theology, marked primarily by a lack of attention to the personal qualities of the practitioner of the discipline. He argues that contemporary Catholic moral theology would benefit from a method he calls "discipleship casuistry," or "saintly voyeurism." His proposed moral methodology, looking to concrete models of Christian holiness, attends both to the personal formation of Catholic moral theologians and to the ways that this translates into a different methodological approach to the discipline itself. For Steck, saintliness is both a topic for scholarly reflection and the scholar's goal for herself or himself.

Christopher Vogt shares Steck's diagnosis of the culture of professionalism in the field and laments certain inadequacies in the formation of (particularly lay) Catholic moral theologians today. After an account of his own formation, Vogt concludes, "In the absence of such [formative] practices, I am becoming a professional academic, but one with only loose, informal connections with the Church." Like Steck, Vogt is not content simply to criticize. He offers a bold proposal to place Catholic moralists closer to "the heart of the Church": preaching by lay theologians at the invitation of their local ordinary. Though seemingly rash, Vogt is persuasive that his proposal, or something akin to it, is needed for lay theologians to be better formed within the church.

Margaret Pfeil's contextualization of the vocation of the moral theologian within a life of discipleship similarly disrupts a purely professionalized understanding of the vocation. Pfeil claims that the particular role of the theologian is to mediate between faith and culture in both the church and the larger society. This mediating role is grounded in the theologian's own call to follow Christ and thus is "intensely personal but always ecclesially oriented." She argues that one best serves this role by "transparently" mediating God's love to the world in a manner shorn of the ego attachments that inhibit the theologian's capacity as a conduit of the divine love. Again we see the theologian's own personal formation at the level of character as quite relevant for her practice of moral theology.

## Teaching

A concern for formation does not extend solely to moral theologians themselves. As members of the postsubculture generation, they are acutely aware that their students generally lack adequate formation in how to live a life of moral wisdom or even in how to name their desire to do so. Recognizing this situation, young moral theologians are more conscious of their call to help form their students in their faith, to help equip them with the practical reasoning skills they will need to live their lives while recognizing that such reasoning is intricately connected to broader substantive claims about God, humanity, and the meaning of life. To previous generations this may appear to be a setback, a reversion to "catechesis rather than theology." Yet the goal here is not the rote memorization of doctrine from a catechism. Rather it is to engage students through the discipline of theology presented not simply as a technical exercise but primarily as an occasion for developing moral wisdom.

Several chapters in this volume emphasize this theme. The two that focus primarily on it are those of William Mattison and William Bolan. Mattison's provocative title question, "Dare we hope our students believe?" reflects a desire on the part of young Catholic moral theologians to engage students at the level of their faith commitments. Acknowledging the challenges of this task, given diversity in the classroom and respect for student freedom, he turns to patristic saints Augustine and Gregory of Nazianzen for guidance on formulating a "Christian rhetoric" for the classroom today. He also identifies an example of this method in C. S. Lewis's *Mere Christianity*.

Continuing on the topic of teaching, William Bolan examines a popular teaching methodology in Catholic institutions (and elsewhere) today—namely, that of community-based learning (CBL), or service learning. It seems particularly appropriate for moral theologians, who explore how the gospel is lived, to employ pedagogical techniques that target the experiences of students as material for, and a source of, learning. Bolan's endorsement of CBL, however, is conditional. He claims that CBL is best done, and most in line with its own historical genesis, when grounded in a substantive model for social change, such as Catholic social teaching. He further argues that Catholic social teaching and CBL employ comparable models of practical moral reasoning, making their conjunctive use not only possible but mutually reinforcing.

Though concerned with the formation of theologians and moral methodology, Steck's piece is additionally attentive to how his "saintly voyeurism" can better serve students in his classroom. David Cloutier and Darlene Weaver, whose chapters look at debates in moral methodology and are further discussed here, are also concerned with the extent to which moral theologians who teach about methodological debates on intrinsic evils and the fundamental option are actually attending to the practical reasoning formation of their students. Finally, Kelly Johnson's piece, also examined here, explicitly recognizes that her role in the classroom is to not only teach about, but help students learn to live, economic justice.

What all these authors have in common is a concern for formation that extends beyond the teacher of moral theology to the students themselves. These theologians recognize that their students come from various faith traditions or no tradition at all. Far from a threat to their project, they have experienced no other climate in which to teach and do moral theology. They have lived in no other culture. Having been reared in a pluralistic society rather than one dominated by the lens of the Catholic imagination, they are also aware of the distinctive vision of the moral life to be found in the Catholic faith. They recognize their vocation to teach precisely as an opportunity to share, in a manner respectful of students' freedom, the wisdom of the Catholic moral tradition.

## Methodology

With the undergraduate classroom as the main forum of "pastoral" engagement, the moral theologians in this volume also raise the "what to teach" question. More specifically, there is a consistent recognition that the methodological problems over which the discipline has been hamstrung for decades can be unhelpful or even harmful for teaching in a manner that addresses the actual needs of students. Hence both the identity and the task of young moral theologians converge in work that reorients the methodological questions of the discipline.

The young moral theologians represented here are less likely to champion one side or the other of the controversies that dominated the discipline from 1968 to 1993—the sorts of issues addressed in part II of *Veritatis Splendor*. That is not at all to say that their recent methodological work does not *engage* these debates. Indeed, in this collection, chapters substantively engage and build on discussions of proportionalism, moral absolutes, and the fundamental option. However, rather than forward one side or the other, young Catholic moral theologians generally take altogether different approaches to these questions. Such approaches are themselves often driven by pastoral and/or pedagogical concerns. Perhaps the greatest advantage to this recent work is that, by and large, it appreciates the insights driving both sides of past debates yet manages to avoid their impasses. Rather than approach these methodological controversies with a "you're for us or you're against us" mentality, there is an attempt to make sense of the concerns underlying both sides of the argument, coupled with a willingness to be critical of both sides as well.

David Cloutier's piece is a fine example of how this generation tries to incorporate contributions from both sides of a heated debate and how methodological research can be more attentive to students' formation in practical reasoning. He laments that much post–Vatican II methodological debate between proportionalists and antiproportionalists has failed to provide concrete practical reasoning guidance to today's students for two reasons. First, participants on both sides of this debate remain fixated on rules, either in affirming the existence of intrinsic evils or in attempting to justify certain exceptions. Second, each of these sides attacks what turn out to be straw man caricatures of the other side rather than accurate assessments of genuine threats to virtuous practical reasoning among everyday Catholics today. Cloutier uses his students as examples to demonstrate that neither the specter of relativism (target of antiproportionalists) nor that of legalism (target of the proportionalists) threatens the practical reasoning abilities of college students today. Instead, the students' problems arise out of a more complex set of factors, including their inability to name and understand their own desires, their incapacity to articulate how their actions serve an ultimate end, and the absence of social contexts needed to support wise, practical decision making. Cloutier argues that teachers and researchers of Catholic moral theology should attend closely to these factors in order to best serve their self-stated goal of empowering people in their practical reasoning skills.

Darlene Fozard Weaver addresses another methodological dispute that the new generation of moral theologians has inherited from their forebears: the relationship between persons and particular actions as depicted by fundamental option adherents and their detractors. After pointing out the strengths and weaknesses of each position, she offers a path for transcending this quagmire by examining a person's self-relation in the context of a call to intimacy with the living God as the "juncture of transcendental and categorical freedom." Weaver insists that a proper understanding of prudential reasoning is attained only through attending to the agent's relationship with God: "Reflection on intimacy with God permits a more dialectical account of the person as an acting subject responding to God in and through her involvement in the world."

A revision of practical reasoning is also the goal of Kelly Johnson's contribution. Johnson targets Christian economic ethics. Her analysis of Adam Smith reveals that the belief in a scarcity of goods in society, and an inherent "strangerliness" among individuals, characterizes much modern economic thought. The Christian story, however, is primarily one of plenitude lived out in Eucharistic solidarity. The challenge for Catholics today is living out that story while residing within a world marked by strangerliness and scarcity. "We need to know how, in the face of both astounding cruelty and ostensibly neutral systems that lead good people to participate in evil, to continue to speak of and witness to resurrection and plenty, without glossing over the details or making light of the blood shed."

Johnson's piece is a most fitting conclusion to this volume. She approaches her study by attending both to the vocation of the Catholic moral theologian and to the practices that will form the faithful in their virtuous reasoning concerning the problem at hand.

> If then Christian ethics and classical economic anthropology are at odds in the respects I've mentioned, if the Eucharistic commonality I am pointing toward is rarely articulated and rarely embodied, and if the job of the moral theologian is to assist the Christian community in understanding its calling and following it more faithfully, then we who are called to teach about economic ethics have two closely linked problems: how to teach and how to live. The two are closely linked because our ability to speak well about Eucharistic solidarity is distinguishable but not entirely separable from our living (albeit imperfectly) in that solidarity so that we understand it from the inside.

Johnson exemplifies the intimate connection between the work and the lives of Catholic moral theologians. She asks "what kind of life would we have to lead" in order to acquire the prudence needed to live in an economically just manner and (in the case of moral theologians) to teach economic justice. After suggesting some "ground rules" to guide debate on this often divisive topic, Johnson explores several practices that would equip

Christian individuals and the church to better witness to the delight and plenitude of the Christian message, in solidarity with those experiencing the suffering that makes the Christian proclamation such good news.

Johnson's piece exhibits several of the marks that characterize a young generation of Catholic moral theologians as represented in this volume. She knows well that how we live affects how we practice our discipline. This includes attention to both formation and ongoing practice. She addresses a moral question of enduring import while attending to how her research can help form her students' practical-reasoning skills. Finally, she takes on a contested moral question in a manner that eschews a "for or against us" posture, favoring instead some ground rules aimed toward enabling discussants to progress in their debate without resting facilely in polarized camps that preclude constructive conversation. It is surely too much to adduce one collection of chapters, let alone one chapter, as encapsulating the character of a next generation of Catholic moral theologians. Yet it is hoped that this introduction makes a substantive contribution to characterizing current trends in Catholic moral theology and that the chapters it introduces can serve as evidence for consideration by others in our field who wish to further comment on the changes examined in this collection.

## NOTES

Thank you to John Berkman, David McCarthy, Julie Rubio, and Angela Senander, all of whom read earlier versions of this chapter and provided helpful comments.

1. See Peter Steinfels, *A People Adrift: The Crisis of the Roman Catholic Church in America* (New York: Simon & Schuster, 2003); Dean Hoge et al., *Young Adult Catholics: Religion in the Culture of Choice* (Notre Dame, Ind.: University of Notre Dame Press, 2001); Colleen Carroll, *The New Faithful: Why Young Adults Are Embracing Orthodoxy* (Chicago: Loyola Press, 2002); William Portier, "Here Come the Evangelical Catholics," *Communio* 31, no. 1 (Spring 2004): 35–66; Andrew Greeley, *The Catholic Revolution: New Wine, Old Wineskins, and the Second Vatican Council* (Berkeley: University of California Press, 2004); James Davidson et al., *The Search for Common Ground* (Huntington, Ind.: Our Sunday Visitor Publishing, 1997); David Gibson, *The Coming Catholic Church: How the Faithful Are Shaping a New Catholicism* (San Francisco: HarperSanFrancisco, 2003); Tom Beaudoin, *Virtual Faith: The Irreverent Spiritual Quest of Generation X* (San Francisco: Jossey-Bass, 1998). For a recent piece on "Gen-Y" Catholics, see Mark Massa, "Both Gen-Y and Catholic," *America* 191, no. 7 (September 20, 2004): 8–11.

2. Greeley is the most obvious example of this, calling Vatican II "revolutionary" in the true sense of the word. Davidson's generational categories also reflect this perspective, as he labels his three cohorts "pre–Vatican II Catholics, Vatican II Catholics, and post–Vatican II Catholics" (*Search for Common Ground*, 111ff.). See also, Gibson, *Coming Catholic Church,* 12ff.

3. Steinfels is a fine example of this approach. See *People Adrift,* 12–14.

4. See, for example, Steinfels, *People Adrift*, 40ff., and Gibson, *Coming Catholic Church*.

5. See, for example, Carroll, *New Faithful*, 21–22.

6. See Portier, "Evangelical Catholics," 45–46, 51–54.

7. Besides Portier's work ("Evangelical Catholics"), see Steinfels, *People Adrift*, 11, for an acknowledgement of the importance of the subculture in generational change. As for the role of the Second Vatican Council, he claims, "American Catholicism . . . would not have escaped change even if there had been no Second Vatican Council. . . . But the Council magnified the theological repercussions of these developments" (5).

8. See Portier, "Evangelical Catholics," 45.

9. An excellent, entirely nontheological example is given in Alan Ehrenhalt's *The Lost City: Discovering the Forgotten Virtues of Community in the Chicago of the 1950s* (New York: Basic Books, 1995). Among Ehrenhalt's profiles is a look at St. Nicholas of Tolentine parish on Chicago's southwest side, in which he suggests that, whether in a stance of embrace or of opposition, those who grew up in such parishes could not avoid being shaped by the thick practices of the community.

10. Daniel Callahan, ed., *Generation of the Third Eye* (New York: Sheed & Ward, 1965). References to this book in the following two paragraphs are given parenthetically.

11. For a similar such claim of someone in this generation "not being able to imagine not being Catholic," see Ivor Shapiro, *What God Allows* (New York: Doubleday, 1996), 186. See also, Greeley's recent book, *Catholic Revolution,* where he claims "after absorbing the stories of Catholicism and the parish that told the stories there was no way I could ever be anything but Catholic" (107).

12. See *Gaudium et spes* 1. Though these title words are not referring to the encounter with the world outside the Church at this exact reference, that theme dominates the document as a whole. See "Pastoral Constitution on the Church in the Modern World," in *Vatican Council II: The Conciliar and Post-Conciliar Documents*, ed. Austin Flannery, OP (Collegeville, Minn.: Liturgical Press, 1975), 903–1014.

13. Steinfels, *People Adrift*, 204ff. A failure of formation also helps drive Steinfels's claim that this current period is so crucial for the Catholic Church (11). His first reason is explicitly formative, where he acknowledges the dissolution of the subculture. See also, Davidson et al., *Search for Common Ground*, 117; Hoge et al., *Young Adult Catholics*, 14–16, 148; and Carroll, *New Faithful*, 26. Though Greeley (*Catholic Revolution*, 111–13) claims Catholicism is flourishing in young Catholics (replying primarily on the findings of Hoge and colleagues regarding what Greeley labels the "core" of Catholicism), he also laments the decreasing nourishment of the "Catholic imagination" through formative stories, art, and devotions (cf. Hoge et al., *Young Adult Catholics*, 200). See also Gibson, *Coming Catholic Church,* 82–108, esp. 94–97.

14. Note that for those who are raised in subculture Catholicism, formation is generally assumed. It is provided not simply by religion classes but also by a whole set of family, parish, neighborhood, and educational experiences that combine to provide one with a cohesive vision of life. In a postsubculture world, this formation cannot be taken for granted. Nonetheless it would be wrong to presume that better faith formation for Catholics has to mean a return to the particular subculture of pre–

Vatican II U.S. Catholicism. One of the challenges for today's Church is discerning how to form people in a manifestly postsubculture U.S. Church.

15. David McCarthy, "Shifting Settings from Subculture to Pluralism: Catholic Moral Theology in an Evangelical Key," *Communio* 31, no. 1 (Spring 2004): 85–110.

16. There is an interesting difference of opinion in the works cited here on young Catholics over whether this young generation is "in trouble" concerning the Catholic faith. Is religious faith and practice on the decline? Hoge and colleagues suggest that it is. But they acknowledge that others disagree (*Young Adult Catholics*, 18). Greeley claims that adherence to the "core" of Catholic teaching is as strong as ever (*Catholic Revolution*, 111–13). Hoge and colleagues note that sociologist John Coleman offers a "life cycle" explanation for surveys suggesting decline in young Catholics' belief and practice (18). James Fisher questions (though at times recapitulates) such studies' strong reliance on ascertaining young Catholics' attitudes toward authority and sexuality. See his "Young Adult Catholics: Who Are They and What Do They Want?" *Commonweal* 128, no. 20 (November 23, 2001). The questions one uses to ascertain whether the faith of young Catholics is in decline do indeed seem to make a difference. Other authors, such as Portier ("Evangelical Catholics") and Carroll (*New Faithful*), seem to emphasize *growing* faithfulness among young Catholics. It is suggested here that both may be true. Longitudinal studies such as that by Hoge and colleagues include all who call themselves Catholic. Portier and Carroll focus on those most actively involved in their faith. Portier and Carroll find the latter group more interesting, even while acknowledging that this group is not a majority (see, e.g., Portier, "Evangelical Catholics," 37).

17. For this language of bringing something to the table of pluralistic dialogue, see McCarthy, "Shifting Settings," 86.

18. Carroll, *New Faithful*, 268.

19. Carroll's analysis is on Christians in general and not just Catholics. But on this point she claims that Catholics are particularly prone to err (*New Faithful*, 268)! Thus there is reason to be wary of sectarian flight from the world among young Catholics. But Carroll is equally emphatic that this charge is, in general, too quickly leveled, since the turn back toward the Church is usually not a sectarian flight.

20. For a scathing review of this book, see Tom Beaudoin, "In Need of Absolutes," *America* 187, no. 15 (November 11, 2002): 35–37.

21. See Portier, "Evangelical Catholics," 56–61, for his discussion of the charge of sectarianism.

22. See Steinfels, *People Adrift*, 354.

23. See Portier, "Evangelical Catholics," 41–44.

24. For more on this, see also Hoge et al., *Young Adult Catholics*, 16.

25. Carroll, *New Faithful*, 49.

26. Carroll, *New Faithful*, 50.

27. For more on this, see Portier, "Evangelical Catholics," 44–45.

28. Portier, "Evangelical Catholics," 58.

29. John Mahoney, *The Making of Moral Theology: A Study of the Roman Catholic Tradition* (Oxford: Clarendon Press, 1987), 344.

30. The importance of *Humanae Vitae* and the subsequent reaction can, in some sense, be seen within this subculture context, since the prohibition on contraception had such large and everyday implications for the transitioning of Catholic families

into a different sociocultural milieu with a different set of practices (in this case, sexual). For more on this, see McCarthy, "Shifting Settings," 86.

31. For example, see Germain Grisez, *The Way of the Lord Jesus*, vol. 1, *Christian Moral Principles* (Quincy, Ill.: Franciscan Herald Press, 1984); Servais Pinckaers, OP, *The Sources of Christian Ethics*, trans. Sr. Mary Thomas Noble (Washington, D.C.: Catholic University of America Press, 1995), 254–79; and Pinckaers, "The Recovery of the New Law in Moral Theology," *Irish Theological Quarterly* 64 (1999): 3–15.

32. While Mahoney is a British moral theologian, he reflects the same theological dynamics present in the transitional generation in America, and his history has broadly influenced American moral theology. John A. Gallagher treats moral theology in the American context directly, but without the synthesis Mahoney provides. See Gallagher's *Time Past, Time Future: A Historical Study of Catholic Moral Theology* (New York: Paulist Press, 1990), esp. page 184–202.

33. Other such predictions for the future of moral theology can be found in Richard McCormick, SJ, "Moral Theology from 1940 to 1989: An Overview" and "Moral Theology in the Year 2000," both in *Corrective Vision: Explorations in Moral Theology* (Kansas City, Mo.: Sheed & Ward, 1994). For a more recent set of predictions that nicely meshes with our thesis here, see Michael S. Sherwin, OP, "Four Challenges for Moral Theology in the New Century," *Logos* 6, no. 1 (2004): 1–9.

34. Mahoney, *Making of Moral Theology*, 302.

35. Mahoney, *Making of Moral Theology*, 310.

36. Mahoney, *Making of Moral Theology*, 311.

37. For examples of works already reflecting the recovery of a richer action theory, see Stanley Hauerwas, *Character and the Christian Life: A Study in Theological Ethics* (San Antonio, Tex.: Trinity University Press, 1975); Servais Pinckaers, OP, "Le rôle de la fin dans l'action morale selon saint Thomas," in *Le Renouveau de la morale: Études pour une morale fidèle à ses sources et à sa mission présente* (n.p.: Casterman, 1964), 114–43; Herbert McCabe, OP, *What Is Ethics All About?* (Washington, D.C.: Corpus Books, 1969); and for a somewhat later work but one reflecting earlier interests in its sources, see Jean Porter, *The Recovery of Virtue: The Relevance of Aquinas for Christian Ethics* (Louisville, Ky.: Westminster John Knox Press, 1990). The retrieval of the Aquinas "behind" the manuals continued at an incredible and fruitful rate in the 1990s.

38. For example, William Spohn, *Go and Do Likewise: Jesus and Ethics* (New York: Continuum, 1999); Anthony J. Ciorra and James Keating, *Moral Formation in the Parish: With Your Whole Heart Turn to God* (New York: Alba House, 1998); Timothy O'Connell, *Making Disciples: A Handbook of Christian Moral Formation* (New York: Crossroad, 1998); Germain Grisez and Russell Shaw, *Personal Vocation: God Calls Everyone by Name* (Huntington, Ind.: Our Sunday Visitor Books, 2003); and Robert Barron, *The Strangest Way: Walking the Christian Path* (Maryknoll, N.Y.: Orbis Books, 2002). These examples include writers who, generationally speaking, would belong in the transitional group but who have moved into these three areas (for various reasons that they themselves explain).

39. Mahoney, *Making of Moral Theology*, 322.

40. Mahoney, *Making of Moral Theology*, 326.

41. Mahoney, *Making of Moral Theology*, 324.

42. A very popular example of this is Ronald Rolheiser's *The Holy Longing: The Search for a Christian Spirituality* (New York: Doubleday, 1998). Rolheiser consistently recognizes that the postmodern world presents a pluralism of experiences that is thrilling but ultimately destructive. Yet in addressing these issues, Rolheiser always avoids appealing to some golden age past or some outright rejection of the secular. A moral theology consistent with Rolheiser's book is badly needed.

43. Mahoney, *Making of Moral Theology*, 339.

44. Mahoney, *Making of Moral Theology*, 304.

45. For example, see the moral theologian who teaches the lay ministers in Shapiro, *What God Allows*, by urging them that the basic idea of moral theology is that "God expects them to be human" (166). Fuchs is considerably richer and more subtle but still reduces the difference between Christian morality and human morality to "intentionality." Both have the same goal, however, which is love. See Josef Fuchs, SJ, *Human Values and Christian Morality* (Dublin: Gill and Macmillan, 1970), 112–47.

46. See McCarthy, "Shifting Settings," 86.

47. The moniker "young" has prompted jokes for three years. It is primarily a reference not to age but to years in the field of moral theology. For the purposes of the symposium that first year, the line was set at tenure; all participants were pretenure. Of course, given the larger argument of this introduction, chronological age is indeed a factor, but it was not understood as such at the time.

48. Thirty participants have gathered for each of the first three years of this gathering. This is nearly 50 percent of the total number of pretenure (and post-ABD [all but disseration]) Catholic moral theologians identified over the past few years for the sake of inviting them to participate. Participants have come from all over the country (and even two from abroad). A dozen doctoral programs are represented, though the majority of participants come from Boston College, Duke, and Notre Dame (due primarily to the number of Catholic moral theologians those programs graduate). It is noteworthy that nearly half the participants each year have been women. It is unfortunately noteworthy as well that racial and ethnic diversity is only minimally present. Both of these observations on group representation at New Wineskins seem commensurate with such representation in the field of Catholic moral theology for this generation.

# 1

# Saintly Voyeurism: A Methodological Necessity for the Christian Ethicist?

*Christopher Steck, SJ*

While growth and development are standard features of any flourishing academic discipline, the transformation that the discipline of Catholic moral theology has undergone over the last several decades is extraordinary. And yet most Catholic ethicists would agree that significant as this development is, the task laid upon the discipline by Vatican II's call for reform remains a work in progress.[1] One particularly unsettled area of ongoing exploration appears in the endeavor to integrate Catholicism's natural law tradition and the theological and Christological particularity implicit in the call for reform. How we achieve this integration has implications for how we understand the methodology of the discipline. The more that a Christian specificity is allowed to tutor or qualify the traditional natural law approach, the more important will it be for scholars to be learned in Christian theology, belief, and practices.

One component of this shift toward Christian particularity is a reconfiguration of the Christian moral life around themes of holiness and discipleship.[2] The Christian's calling as a follower of Christ shapes the kind of moral goodness that is to be the norm of every Christian life; thus, that goodness cannot be properly understood through an ethical reflection which simply brackets its Christian context or its eschatological endpoint. Since discipleship and the pursuit of holiness are integral to all Christian life, they are also integral concerns of ethics. Scholars who seek to address issues relating to Christian life would correspondingly need a deep understanding of and familiarity with ideas of Christian perfection and sanctity (i.e., something more than a bookish knowledge) in order to understand well the complex ways they bear on

Christian moral existence. "Holiness" is part of the ethicist's required area of expertise.

I want to explore what competencies are now required of contemporary Catholic moral theologians in light of this focus on Christian discipleship and related developments in the circumstances of Catholic ethicists. My belief is that changes in the discipline of Catholic moral theology have increased the need for ethicists to be rooted in the Christian story and transformed by its message. My concern is that there may be insufficient support for such rootedness within the academic and ecclesial contexts that the moral theologian occupies. Achieving such a Christian vision is complicated in the academic culture in which Catholic ethicists practice their trade. That culture is given shape by a constellation of values whose form does not align well with that of the field of Christian ethics, especially insofar as it is concerned with questions of what constitutes the holy life. This misalignment, I argue, is due in part to the dominance of rationalistic and acutely critical modes of contemporary research, along with a lack of concern for the personal moral character of the one engaging in research. The adverse influence of the secular side of the academy is all the more problematic because there are, I contend, insufficient forces within the discipline of Catholic moral theology to counterbalance these external pressures. More thought, therefore, needs to be given to how Catholic moral theologians can "form" themselves into Christian ethicists and address issues of Christian discipleship and the holy life. I argue that one important way of doing so is through scholarly reflection on the lives of the saints. I refer to this as *saintly voyeurism*, not to advocate a professional disengagement from saintly ideals, but only to call our attention to the fact that such disengagement often exists. We do not occupy the same moral space as the saints, hence the need to learn from them.

There are two overlapping contexts in which Catholic ethicists practice their trade. The first is the academy, with its particular expectations of scholarship and groundbreaking research. The second is the Christian community, which includes the institutional and cultural life of Catholicism and the theological commitments that give normative shape to the particular way ethicists of a Catholic stripe do their work. In recognized and unrecognized ways, these contexts inform ethicists' understanding of the discipline and their responsibilities within it. I examine the academic context first and then turn to the ecclesial context in the following section.

## THE ACADEMIC CONTEXT

We could begin by enumerating the various qualities that are characteristic of academic work. However, I want first to step back and begin with the broader context of American professional life. The culture of professionalism acts as a framework for much of white-collar work in this country, and it also shapes the academic disciplines. Since the turn of the century, the number of professionals in our country has risen dramatically;[3] but more important than sheer number is the influential role that the professional has come to have in our society qua professional (that is, as member of a caste with special expertise). The position of importance that professions occupy in our society is, as the sociologist Talcott Parsons points out, "unique in history."[4] And in subtle ways this cultural climate informs our vision of what constitutes good (i.e., virtuous, honorable, praiseworthy) work in whatever professional field we occupy and, correspondingly, what type of persons we need to be in order to do our work well. What is striking about the culture of professionalism for our discussion is that there is within it only a selective concern about the personal qualities of the practitioner (i.e., personality, moral character, personal incentives, worldviews). That is, it focuses narrowly on those character traits that directly contribute to one's ability to perform the professional task well. Indeed, part of the esteem for the professions is that they hold the professional to universal and objective standards that are not dependent on contentious or subjective judgments, such as those dealing with moral qualities, but instead center on skills and practices that the professional's training allows him or her to perform successfully. To be a good lawyer, doctor, or English professor, one need not be a comprehensively virtuous person; one need only attain those virtues or, better, skills associated with one's profession.

A kind of intensification of some aspects of the professional ideal occurs in its incarnation within university life. Not only did the university give birth to modern professional life,[5] but it is also the institution that continues to preserve the core characteristics associated with it: altruistic ideals, objective procedures, the accomplishment of distinctive skills, and, most important, the cultivation of specialized knowledge that grounds a distinction between the professional and the lay person and justifies the former's claim to authority in matters of its select expertise. Thus the values and standards that characterize much of professional life are particularly ingrained in the standards that shape the culture of university life. At the same time, however, the influential presence in American culture of a version of those same values, by way of the professional ethos, works to reinforce selectively their presence within university life. The professionalism of the wider culture returns back to the university an objectivity stripped of passion, a skillfulness reduced to efficiency, and a concern for truthfulness equated with correction of errors. Such eclipsed values are not always consonant with the broader ideals of the university (e.g., a richly interpreted and energetically pursued quest for truth). This neoprofessionalization has rationalized university life in the sense described by Richard Posner: it has become "businesslike, rule-bound, disenchanted."[6]

Pressures from within the university's own tradition and from without encourage a truncated, narrowly rationalistic understanding of how insight into the world is attained. One element of this truncation is the rather limited set of personal virtues and qualities of character that the university community considers necessary for the scholar. The dominant understanding of scholarly work holds, not without reason, the personal development of one's moral and affective character as marginal to the scholarly enterprise. A "conversion" of an intellectual nature suffices. Each age, of course, views the pursuit of human knowledge differently. Classical thought linked increase in knowledge to the full development of the human person (i.e., to moral and spiritual growth). For the Middle Ages, *eruditio* was tied to *religio*; only through religion could scholars "fulfill their restless yearning to know."[7] For the contemporary academic world, an increase in one's understanding of the world still depends on the virtues of the individual scholar; that is, it is not merely a matter of some external "thing" one does but also about who one is. However, those virtues are no longer tied to traditional themes of morality. The particular virtues that dominate in the contemporary academic pursuit are instead bound up with the professional role of the academic as it is understood by the academic community. These select virtues of the scholarly life are not at all at odds with the discipline of Catholic ethics, but their dominance and the rather exclusive regard given to them are.

Two groups of virtues strike me as particularly important to scholarly work in the contemporary university. First are those virtues of the scholar commonly associated with a scientific-like rationalism, an "aping of the sciences" as Andrew Louth puts it:[8] intelligence, clarity, objectivity (understood as critical distance from one's object of study), and methodological doubt before all that is not clearly proven. The second group, at times at odds with the first, is composed of those virtues reflecting the critical "edge" of contemporary scholarship. We can describe them in terms of three dynamics familiar to scholars: agorism, circumscription, and unmasking. By *agorism*, I refer to the idea that the university in its best moments continues the spirit of the Greek *agora*, a place of conversation and public debate. But I also use the term more narrowly to refer to the type of adversarial debate that the academic community often judges as desirable in its task of understanding the world better. Deborah Tannen speaks of the "argument culture" of our society, which in the academic world expresses itself as a need "to position [one's] work in opposition to someone else's" and to "disprove others' arguments in order to be original, make a contribution and demonstrate intellectual ability."[9] *Circumscription* describes the inclination against comprehensive or universalist claims and comprehensive master narratives; it turns a postmodern disposition into a normative stance. Finally, *unmasking* points to what the academy often views as a virtuous suspicion: the belief that truth claims conceal subtle and pernicious advancements of self-interest (whether personal, group, social, or institutional) and unconscious desires of power. Nietzsche helped make us aware of the hidden strategies and assertions of power hidden within moral discourse, and the approach has been continued in the influential work of Jacques Derrida and Michel Foucault. Underlying each of these dynamics is the scholar practicing her trade with attitudes and dispositions that are deemed virtuous in the contemporary academy.

While my focus is on the virtues (i.e., inclinations and dispositions) of the scholar and not on the positions taken by them, it is also the case that these same virtuous dispositions incline the scholar toward particular substantive positions. For example, a rationalistic approach to ethics flows easily from a narrowly rationalist approach to scholarship. Peter Singer's utilitarianism, Alan Gewirth's "Principle of Generic Consistency," and John Rawls's neo-Kantianism presume not only that the moral life is a fundamentally rational enterprise but also that the endeavor to understand it is similarly rational. A commitment to methodological rationalism yields its desired fruit: a successful rationalistic ethics. The theoretical result justifies the scholarly virtue.

The issue here is not merely that of whether rightly ordered desires and affections are necessary for reason to achieve more sound judgments about concrete problems. There is a more fundamental moral question that requires a rightly ordered moral sense and affection: what is the nature of ethics itself? No theory of ethics is simply a deductive, rational pursuit, since in its justifications, every theory appeals, explicitly or implicitly, to our already existing ideas and intuitions about the moral life and about which ethical theory provides the "best account" of raw moral data (i.e., of the often inconsistent and chaotic manner in which moral claims are experienced by ordinary people).[10] The issue here is not whether intuitionism as an ethical system is valid or not. My point is, rather, that the ethical system that we find most persuasive will depend in part on whether the "answers" it generates on various moral issues fit well with our gut-level, moral intuitions about those issues. Once we are "in" an ethical system, its arguments will have their appeal to us; but first we have to accept that system, and doing so requires that it at least loosely fit with our preexisting moral views.[11] Thus, if our moral outlook and character have not been properly developed and are flawed, our choices about the nature of ethics might be similarly flawed. The soundness of our reasoning cannot always overcome bad starting points.

In regard to the second group discussed above, that is, the critical inclination of scholarship, one could argue that in no other place in the academy does its soundness prove itself than in the field of ethics. Critical doubt cast on past moral judgments, a belief that cultural and historical prejudices shape purported universal moral claims, and a suspicion of the ways conventional values hide attempts at control and power by the dominant group have been important to the valid insights of a wide array of contemporary thinkers, including, for example, most postmodern philosophers, liberation theologians, and feminist theorists. But while the field of ethics offers ample evidence of the value of these scholarly emphases, it is also uniquely able to indicate their limits. Relentlessly pursued, the biases driving the critical moment of scholarly work lead to nihilism, or, as Richard Rorty puts it, to a sense that

> there is nothing deep down inside us except what we have put there ourselves, no criterion that we have not created in the course of creating a practice, no standard of rationality that is not an appeal to such a criterion, no rigorous argumentation that is not obedience to our own conventions.[12]

Such a position goes against widely shared and, I think, valid moral intuitions (e.g., the belief that at least some moral requirements are not merely matters of social construction) and is decidedly at odds with traditional Catholic views. For Catholic ethicists at least, some traditional and conventional insights into what is moral and praiseworthy (e.g., respect for innocent life) have shown themselves to have enduring power, even in the face of the critical blows of Nietzschean unmasking and postmodern deconstruction.

These critique-oriented inclinations and rationalistic virtues (e.g., honesty, intelligence, and methodological doubt) do play a positive role in the aim of scholarly research. But they are not sufficient determinants of the character of the scholar—at least not for those sympathetic to the Aristotelian tradition (including Catholic ethicists). The Aristotelian tradition requires of moral authority something more than intellectual competency—that is, that he or she has undergone personal, moral transformations that have in turn engendered virtues such as prudence, justice, fortitude, and temperance. This approach to ethics requires conversion, not only performatively (doing the good) and epistemically (knowing the good), but also affectively (loving the good).

One way of getting at this need for something more than intellectual competency in ethics scholarship is to consider the role of our desires and affect. The Catholic tradition has long held that truly human desires serve as appropriate guides for human action.[13] Likewise, in the virtue-grounded, teleological approach of Aristotle, desires are not just distracting forces, "mere automatic pushes towards the world that can be directed only by brute suppression." They are, as Martha Nussbaum suggests, "responsive intentional elements, capable of flexible ethical development."[14] Desires are also key for our moral perception. They light up our moral landscape, helping to indicate worthwhile goals for intentional activity. To use the teleological language of Aristotle and Thomas, desires help incline us to our end, toward what is in keeping with a full human life. Our ends are not just intellectual ones; they have to do with what brings us emotional well-being, psychological peace, and deep satisfaction about a life lived well. If our affect is misdirected, so will our action be. The wrong goals are lit up, if you will, and thus deliberations about what is to be done will be similarly distorted.

Our desires and affections when properly functioning are not simply the docile sycophants of reason and intellect. Correlatively, we cannot make sound moral judgments and proper evaluations of circumstances merely through the process of academic research. However, our desires are just one level of our intentional response to the world in need of transformation. There is another, more comprehensive level: that of our moral perception and the values that form it. Our values reflect particular moral judgments that we make about our world and the events, actions, people and things within it. They shape our moral "vision" of the world—that is, how we perceive it morally. The moral space in which we make moral judgments is pervaded by and colored with moral values,[15] and we cannot do without such valuations and still "know" the world.[16] These moral values are not the results of conscious choice or scholarly discovery. Nor are they simply the work of either our desires and affection or our intellect but rather a complex interaction of both. The point for our discussion here is that values and moral goods are not qualities that we uncover only after we understand the world through other (rationalistic, critical) means. Moral insight is not a matter of deducing the moral implications of some factual or rationalistic understanding of the world or even of simply critiquing conventional views. It is "seeing a complex, concrete reality in a highly lucid and richly responsive way; it is taking in what is there, with imagination and feeling."[17] If we have painted the moral picture wrong, we cannot expect reason and critical work to come along and correct our errors. Our failure here is not simply one of critical reason but of vision. And thus any ethicist wishing to avoid such limitation must not only undertake conventional scholarly research but also undergo a change of heart—that is, a new moral perspective that touches the levels of affect and imagination. Something like a conversion to a different way of seeing the world would seem to be necessary before one can claim good moral judgment.

The virtues of reason and critical thought are not enough to guarantee sound development of moral knowledge. Scholarly work in ethics must include the difficult, and deeply free, choice on the scholar's part to be a different person and thus enter a different moral world because he or she now interprets the world differently. There is a "moral achievement" in the way we perceive the world.[18] And only with this achievement, through a conversion of heart that changes the way we approach our reality, can we do ethics well. Professional training and intellectual rigor alone cannot produce such a moral perspective, but little in the discipline directs the ethicist toward the moral achievement of looking at the world anew.

## THE ECCLESIAL CONTEXT

Much of this is not news to most ethicists; the only question might be why someone would see it as a particular concern of our generation. The issues are perennial. As noted, Aristotle believed only those experienced in a life of virtue knew what it meant to be virtuous, and thus only they were able to teach others.[19] Ethicists sympathetic to the Aristotelian tradition (including many Catholic moralists) believe, with some reason, that they can mitigate this problem through a type of vicarious virtue. That is, by attending to the acknowledged moral authorities of the past and present, ethicists can supplement the limitations of their own moral outlook. I return to this point later. In addition, I suspect that most ethicists can rightly hope that they have achieved in their lives a kind of basic goodness and thus can claim virtuous competency; they are, to borrow a phrase from papal documents, "men and women of good will." But there are good reasons to believe that the "misalignment problem"—the gap between the requirements of the scholarly life and those of moral reasoning—has increased over the last several decades. I have already addressed one problem contributing to this misalignment: the values and priorities of professional academia allow no methodological place for an interest in, and encouragement of, the moral character of ethicists themselves, which, at least for the approach to ethics advocated here, represents a significant weakness.[20] But in addition to academic pressures, three significant shifts in the institutional, ecclesial context in which Catholic moral theologians do ethics have affected the way they perform their task and have compounded the misalignment problem.

The first change is the shift away from the legalism associated with the confessional-driven ethics of the preconciliar period to personalist approaches that incorporate themes of Christian discipleship and spiritual growth. During the last several decades, much work has been done by Catholic scholars to recover the theological/Christological horizon of moral theology. This recovery is evident in a diverse array of projects: the renewal in studies of Scripture and its use for ethics, the work that has been done to restore the theological component of Thomas Aquinas's ethics, an increased awareness of the ways in which liturgical practices and reflection on Scripture tutor our desires, and the recovery of the doxological dimension of the Christian discipleship.[21] Collectively, these projects indicate a shift in Catholic understanding of moral theology from a legalistic and rationalistic science to a discipline much more centered on the meaning and implications of Christ's call to the Christian. Because the discipline now concerns itself with the full implications of that call, and not only what is within the legal bounds of "natural" ethics, Catholic moralists can no longer exclude considerations of what has traditionally been placed under the rubric of the holy life or Christian perfection.

The moral theology of the preconciliar era did not see "holiness of life" as part of its proper domain. The seminary textbooks at the time were clear: ethics was concerned with "natural" ethics, while the life of perfection belonged to the domain of ascetical or mystical theology.[22] Even virtue, a requirement for growth into Christian perfection and a central piece of Aquinas's ethical theory, was not a topic of great interest among moralists.[23] The call of Vatican II and the expansion of ethics beyond the confessional has transformed the discipline, and thus Richard McCormick, in describing how contemporary moral theology is distinctive from its earlier forms, could rightly speak of this present period of moral theology as an "age of holiness and witness."[24]

Yet, in spite of the large amount of work done in recovering the theological and Christological dimensions of the Christian moral life, more scholarly reflection is needed in regard to the role and function that the themes of holiness and saintly existence should have in Catholic moral thought. We can leave open the question of whether or to what degree the saintliness is normative for all Christians (or rather whether it simply represents an ideal to which all should strive and occasionally mimic), but it is no longer permissible for Catholic moral thought in this post–Vatican II era to keep it quarantined, separated from ethical reflection. As Norbert Rigali observed a generation ago, "if all Christians are called to perfection, moral theology as a science of the Christian life will have to turn itself explicitly into a science of the life of striving for perfection. It will have to say explicitly what perfection and a life of such striving are."[25] However, theorizing about such a life is not the work of scholarly reason alone. While I do not believe we have to go so far as to say that one has to be holy to know holy, some other skills and virtues besides those necessary for doctoral credentials are required of the Catholic moralist because of this new concern with holiness.

The second change compounds the problem of the first. What is required now more than ever are spiritual practices that nurture the ethicist's Christian vision. However, there is a marked diminishment within Catholicism of institutionalized forms of such practices. Some of these spiritual practices were widely available to the Catholic population in general (e.g., devotional readings, daily Eucharist, benedictions, first Fridays, regular feast days, Lenten fasting, and rosary recitations). Other practices were part of Catholic ethicists' lives because they themselves were often priests and even seminary professors educating seminarians for a life of pastoral ministry. In principle, these clerical ethicists participated in the liturgy of the hours, attended regular Eucharist, had annual retreats, were deeply rooted in a particular intellectual tradition, and shared in spiritual conversation. Their context offered them an interpretive horizon in which they were invited to understand themselves as being called to a special and higher holiness. The life of the church was their life; its documents, politics, and leaders shaped their hearts and intellects. While such institutionalized practices did not guarantee conversion and a life of holiness, they did offer important support.

Recent discussion has drawn attention to the importance of such moral formation. Much of the work relating liturgy and ethics, for example, has focused on the ways in which liturgy forms and shapes our affection. Similarly, recent studies in the ancient idea of *askesis*—exercises that were at once intellectual, moral, and spiritual—have reminded us of the ways in which classical, philosophical reflections on ethical matters were meant to be practices that shaped and transformed the individual. These practices were not strictly "ascetic" as we think of the term but were often more like critical reflections on life and the world as a means of self-cultivation and self-formation.[26] Ascetical practices developed in conjunction with these philosophical reflections to support the "development of particular virtues" and "strategies for the avoidance of vice."[27] This tradition challenges us today with its suggestion that moral wisdom involves more than learning principles, rules, and general theory and that apart from explicitly formative practices, we are in danger of being unduly influenced by, if not transformed in accord with, whatever formative or counterformative behaviors are encouraged by our consumerist culture. Growth in new spiritual practices within Catholicism, such as Bible studies and social activism, have not filled the *askesis* void left by the decline of pre–Vatican II devotions. And the lack of adequate formative practices promises to become more pressing because of the growing institutional marginalization of the younger generation of Catholics (and, one can presuppose, of some who will eventually become moral theologians).[28]

The third change relates to the kind of applied issues that the magisterium and Catholic ethicists address. The almost complete abandonment of scholarly reflection on specific, often personal, case studies paralleled (and was justified by) the change in the confessional needs of the church and a movement away from the confessional emphasis of preconciliar ethics. Issues of public policy, though always a concern of Catholic ethics, now occupy much of Catholic reflection on applied issues. A danger, however, accompanies this shift: it could skew the way Catholic moralists understand their profession and the role that a standard of holiness plays in it. Ethicists are affected by the issues they reflect on. They tutor ethicists into certain ways of understanding problems. Public policy issues, because they require widespread consensus in a pluralistic society, are often poor vehicles for exploring the radical implications of the call to discipleship for the individual Christian life. The practice of casuistry, with its focus on the ordinary dilemmas of everyday life, was done not only as a way of solving those dilemmas but also as a way of training the moral wisdom of the confessor—a kind of *askesis* for him.[29] Such *askesis* is needed today more than ever. Contemporary casuist reflections on daily life issues, with the expressed intention of exploring the implications of Christian discipleship, might serve to educate today's ethicist in a kind of moral reasoning appropriate to a discipline that concerns itself with matters of Christian holiness. Moreover, such reflections are part of the ecclesial responsibilities of Catholic ethicists; the church needs help in defining what it means to live holy lives, and it will not happen exclusively through studies of immigration, just war, or welfare reform, however clear and pressing the need for reflection on such issues is.

Consider, for example, the following case:

> John, a public hack driver, declares, in confessing sins, that he is in the habit of driving people to brothels. This he does at times on their simple request. At other times, in response to their demand if he knows of such places, he replies affirmatively, and drives them there. John argues that since such resorts are allowed to exist, it is not unlawful to drive his patrons to them, nor wrong to inform them of their existence and location; otherwise his business and income will suffer gravely, as others are prepared to do this work.[30]

The case appears in a 1925 article. It is one of those bewildering and complex cases that moralist confessors struggled with in an earlier generation. Such case studies no longer receive attention from ethicists (for reasons that have their merit: the cases were analyzed in rational, legalistic terms with an eye to the confessional). I would like to suggest, however, that such cases can still be fruitfully explored, not with the aim of "yes or no" determinations, but in light of present concerns with the Christian vocation (e.g., those concerning personalistic values, personal integrity, witness to Gospel ideals, personal vocation). For all the legalism and sin preoccupation at times of pre–Vatican II ethics, it tacitly recognized that in the small affairs of human existence a grand drama of goodness and evil was being played out. Ordinary existence is where our dialogue with God takes place, and, thus, ordinary existence must be a concern for Catholic moralists. Theoretical reflections on how quotidian acts can be lived as moments of discipleship should become part of the discipline of Christian ethics.

## SAINTLY VOYEURISM

One might think that with all my emphasis on the importance of saintliness for the vision of the ethicist that the straightforward solution would be simply to proclaim saints as the new moral authorities for our generation. However, saintliness is not a sufficient requisite for moral thought. The experience and wisdom of the saints do not provide norms that translate simply to the lives of other people; their experiences need further "disciplined reflection" as to how they might make normative claims on us.[31] In addition, their moral views, while on the surface edifying, become simplistic and unhelpful if propped up and made into universal norms. Most would presumably agree that Mother Teresa of Calcutta was a saint, but her saintliness does not guarantee that all her experiences should be paradigms for others or that her reflections be made normative. Her suggestion, for example, that the elderly are in nursing homes because of the insufficient love of children fails if we were to view it as an adequate and complete explanation of the actual situation of nursing home patients and their families in general.[32] Saintliness by itself does not guarantee moral wisdom.

And so the discipline faces a challenge, a perennial issue that has become more acute in this recent generation: there exist two forms of moral authority, that of the saint and that of the scholar, neither of which is by itself sufficient as a source of moral wisdom. The church of an earlier generation had an institutional location in which it tried to integrate these two moral authorities, even if not always successfully: the seminary professor, a scholar whose semimonastic existence was attuned to the liturgical rhythms of the Church and whose daily life exposed him to the symbols, images, and language of Christian discipleship.

A more promising antidote to the problems raised by postconciliar changes, other than simply transferring moral authority to the saint, can be found in a new type of casuistry—one we might call *discipleship casuistry*: ethical reflection on the ordinary acts of a holy existence to better understand the demands of Christian discipleship. I believe such a casuistry can be a supplement to existing scholarly work in ethics, not a replacement. Discipleship casuistry would analyze not only isolated cases but any situation or moral issue as it has been engaged by a saint. It would perform such explorations with an eye to discerning which action (or actions) is most consonant with a saintly life. These studies would also help in exploring the very meaning of saintliness itself, a particularly important topic for a church that has given new emphasis to the fact that all Catholics—religious, ordained, and lay—are called to holiness.

On first glance, such a practice might not appear promising. After all, the kind of mundane, ordinary cases that are the topic of casuist reflections are not likely to be experienced by many individuals, because they are so situationally specified and concrete. Little can be gained by reflecting on them, except if done by the few who might face such situations. Relatedly, to the degree that these cases are not concerns of public policy or are primarily personal matters, they seem to lie within that provenance of actions governed by what was called "counsels of perfection," free possibilities for Christian discipleship and not strict requirements of morality. However, one of the insights offered by the casuist tradition is that individual cases can help us develop our practical wisdom in a general way so that it becomes attuned to the goods and values of the Christian story, even if we never experience these particular cases ourselves. And thus, against the concern that these cases are often "private" issues, we can note that, even for those moral responses that are not be strictly demanded of the Christian, we can gain some clarity and insight into how such responses do embody important Christian values or sacrifice others.

Any moral reflection on the various kinds of decisions and concrete actions that make up a life of holiness is a kind of discipleship casuistry, but
here I want to explore one possible form of it: reflection on the lives of the
saints. Richard McCormick is right in suggesting that the meaning of Christian discipleship "is best gathered from the lives of the saints."[33] Elizabeth of
Hungary's disobedience of her husband's wishes in order to serve the poor,
Elizabeth Ann Seton's engagement with religious antagonism of her time,
and Ignatius of Loyola's apostolic choice to minister not only to the poor but
to the powerful represent choices that raise interesting ethical issues for
those wishing to better understand the saintly life. However, my suggestion
here is not, finally, that reflecting on saintly choices can help us determine
right choices for our time and situation. Rather, reflecting on saintly vignettes
and stories can do what the casuistry of a previous period did: train our
moral senses. Saintly vision cannot be presumed of the scholar, but a fruitful
substitutionary measure can be found in the practice of watching the saints
from a distance—that is, from our place of lukewarm virtuosity, a "saintly
voyeurism," if you will. The practice of studying the saints—historical, contemporary, and even fictional—to better understand Christian existence
could act as a type of Catholic *askesis* that tutors our moral vision.[34] The object of these reflections could take any number of forms: the specific acts of
canonized saints, the regular choices of a group of saints, a comparison and
contrast on the different choices made by popularly recognized holy men
and women in regard to a specific issue, and so forth. The reflection on
saintly existence is key; the goal is not answers to ethical dilemmas but new
insight into the nature of the life of discipleship. Casuist reflection on saintly
vignettes and critical examination of the moral goods and life possibilities
portrayed in saintly existence will not necessarily produce saintly character
in its practitioners, but we can hope that such reflection will attune them to
Christian goods and values and transform their ways of understanding the
world so that their worldviews better align with that of God's kingdom. I believe this formation of outlook can happen in five ways.

First, the saint confirms for the ethicist the ongoing viability of the Christian vision and the values it holds central and thus can in turn strengthen
ethicists' own commitment to them and their resolve in holding the Christian
community accountable to them. Lawrence Cunningham describes a saint as
a person "grasped by a religious vision" in such a way as to lead "others to
glimpse the value of that vision."[35] And thus the saint offers an "eloquent tes-
timony to the enduring value of certain Christian images or ideals."[36] Some
ideals of Christian discipleship are viewed, by Christians and non-Christians
alike, as naive and impractical. The saint, however, counters these charges
by living a life guided by such ideals and values, sometimes at great personal
cost, and thus concretely witnesses to the possibility of embracing God's
kingdom in the here and now. In a jaded and weary world, one that has

"grown unaccustomed to the expectation of holiness," the saints "constitute a kind of moral miracle."[37] Even the fictional saint, convincingly portrayed by the skillful artist, moves Christian ideals (and concerns over their plausibility) out of the realm of the abstract and into the realm of the "real" and the concrete; in so doing, these literary figures offer credible examples of possible embodiments of Christian sanctity. This strengthening of Christian commitment effected by the saint also occurs by way of counterwitness: against the utilitarian–calculus reasoning that dominates social policy discussion of issues such as welfare, immigration, and capital punishment, the saint witnesses to extravagant and, by some standards, wasteful, devotion to core Christian values (e.g., the sacredness of life, the possibility of conversion and redemption, the hope for reconciliation).[38]

Second, the saint underscores the theological dimension of the Christian life.[39] Christianity offers not only a "vision" of the world but a relationship with that which transcends it. The saints highlight aspects of that relationship that are critical for understanding the Christian moral life: surrender, obedience, participation in the paschal mystery, a source of hope that transcends our finite condition, a trust in the abiding power of love. Reflecting on the saint can help us "situate [our] moral reasoning in a decidedly theological sphere of inquiry, in a world of God's inexhaustible mystery, where human life . . . is invited into God's boundless goodness."[40] This theological context of moral theology cannot be reduced to a set of values that are then simply added into the Christian value mix (i.e., along with forgiveness, neighbor love, simplicity of life). As pointers to the divine mystery, theological markers such as surrender, obedience, and hope in the divine enter moral analysis as permanent destabilizers of human moral analysis.

Third, saints create new paradigms for how the Christian vision can be lived out in changing historical situations. They are "initiators and the creative models of the holiness which happens to be right for, and is the task of, their particular age."[41] What Christian peacefulness meant in St. Francis's time is not the same as what it means for us today. Aesthetics can offer an instructive parallel here. The capacity of quality art to elicit a positive response in the beholder endures across time. And yet each age produces forms of art that are particularly appropriate to that period. Recognizing this symmetry between aesthetics and ethics, Martha Nussbaum and Iris Murdoch, and in a different way, Hans Urs von Balthasar, have argued that living the moral life is analogous to the making of good art. The saints are the irruption of a lived moral artwork previously unseen and unfathomed but, once seen and understood, recognized as a form of discipleship that is right for this period. These moral art forms give us deep sensitivity to the ways in which values and goods can be furthered within the particularities of one's own cultural and historical situation.

Fourth, the narrative of the saintly life provides a context for examining how holiness appears in the finitude and even the brokenness of creaturely existence. The recent work done in narrative ethics has made us aware of the limitations of examining concrete acts apart from their narrative context. The moral qualities of concrete acts always take shape within the sedimented meaning provided by a life narrative. In addition, the in-depth scrutiny of human lives, made possible by the instruments of psychology and mass communication, have helped us recognize that even apart from the effect of sin, human life is always marked by the limitations of creaturely existence and the structural conditions of its social circumstance. When sanctity manifests itself, it does so within such conditioned, historical lives. Examining the concrete particulars of saintly lives can school the ethicist in the possibilities of discipleship within the limited and sometimes even broken forms of human existence.

Finally, the saints address us, challenge us to respond. The insights that the saints offer do not come to us as bits of information, something intellectually informative but otherwise indifferent to us. Their lives have an existential appeal. Indeed, to effect such an appeal is one aim of hagiography. As Edith Wyschogrod puts it, the lives of the saints are recounted in such a way that "the reader or hearer can experience their imperative power."[42] We can understand the source of this imperatival power in several different ways.

First, the stories of saintly lives present to us living options—that is, possibilities for our own lives. Good stories give satisfaction to us because they offer, as Nussbaum suggests, "patterns of possibility" that "turn up in human lives with such a persistence that they must be regarded as *our* possibilities."[43] This kind of existential satisfaction increases in the case of a story that resonates deeply with the religious commitments of the Christian. Because these stories present us with attractive options for our own lives, they stir in us a response that is at least affective and imaginative (i.e., as we come to imagine adapting these stories to fit our lives), if not behavioral.

Second, we can appeal to the classical Greek notion of *kalokagathia* (the convergence of the beautiful and the good, *kalon* and *agathon*): what is good is attractive to behold as it is valuable to embody. Iris Murdoch and Hans Urs von Balthasar have offered contemporary versions of this idea. Both underscore that what we perceive morally awakens in us a spontaneous response: love of the transcendent good as it radiates in the world. The moral life is not a matter of simply choosing by force of will what is rationally discovered as good, but it is rather first perceiving one's moral horizon well (i.e., truly, accurately, faithfully, honestly)—an act that is not just intellectual but also a matter of the heart and affect—and then allowing oneself to be moved (affectively and behaviorally) in accord with that perception. The narrative of the saints then focuses the light of the good in the world and magnifies its capacity to elicit our loving response to it.

Finally, we can develop the aforementioned aesthetic approach Christologically and suggest that the lives of the saints are sacramental signs, offering

us something like divine grace made visible. John Cardinal Newman wrote
that

> in the life of the saint, we have a microcosm, or the whole work of God. . . . The
> exhibition of a person, his thoughts, his words, his acts, his trials, his features,
> his beginnings, his growth, his end, have a charm to everyone; and where he is
> a saint they have a divine influence and persuasion, a power of exercising and
> eliciting the latent elements of grace in individual readers as no other reading
> can have.[44]

Contemporary sacramental theology and studies on symbols emphasize
that sacramental grace does not operate independently of human consciousness and intentionality without a visible object that manifests to human
perception the divine presence at work in us. In the context of liturgical
prayer, creaturely elements become symbols of the Christian story. Similarly,
the saint's life manifests the divine labor of Christ and the presence of God
in history and thus acts as a sacramental sign for the believing community.

These three approaches to understanding how the lives of saints can address us are not mutually exclusive, but each indicates a way in which the
lives of the saints do more than instruct human reason. They appeal to the
hearts and commitments of believers—including, one hopes, ethicists—and
draw forth a new response, acting as catalysts for their own conversion and
transformation.

## CONCLUSION

Christian moral theology is not simply a deductive or rationalistic science. It
requires that its practitioner have a well-formed heart that is attuned to the
Gospel and the values at its core. In an ideal world, Catholic moral theologians would be saints and scholars. However, Catholic ethicists now perform
their trade in a context that often does not sustain the kind of Gospel vision
associated with a saintly existence. The indifference of the academy toward
traditional virtues and the loss of preconciliar spiritual practices within
Catholicism leave Catholic moralists more susceptible than moralists of an
earlier generation to an almost exclusively secular and narrowly rationalistic
formation. I have argued that Catholic moral theology could benefit from a
"discipleship casuistry" in which ethicists reflect on the ordinary practices
and moral choices that reflect a deep commitment to the Gospels and a life
of holiness. One such form of a "discipleship casuistry" can be found in a
scholarly exploration of the lives of the saints. I do not suggest that such an
examination would be uniquely formative. Scriptural mediation, prayer, devotional practices, and liturgical participation are just some of the practices
that form the Christian into a disciple. But examining the lives of the saints,

ordinary people achieving great moral character, is one practice that also allows ethicists to practice their art—that is, scholarly reflection on human action—and thus represents a distinctive resource for moralists.

## NOTES

I am grateful to William Mattison, William Werpehowski, Cathy Kaveny, and an anonymous reviewer for their helpful comments and suggestions. A special thanks to James Keating for the work he has done in this area and his own comments on an earlier version of this chapter.

1. Throughout this chapter, I use the terms *Catholic ethicist, Catholic moralist,* and *moral theologian* interchangeably.

2. James Keating provides a very helpful list of the literature in this area in his "A Mystical Moral Theology," *New Blackfriars* 83 (2002): 276n1–4.

3. The "number of people categorized as 'professionals' by census bureaus throughout the developed world has been growing in a dramatic fashion. In the United States before World War II, for example, only one percent of all employed people were college-educated and classified by the Census Bureau as 'professional, technical, and kindred' workers. Today, the comparable group is twelve times as large." Steven Brint, *In an Age of Experts: The Changing Role of Professionals in Politics and Public Life* (Princeton, N.J.: Princeton University Press, 1994), 3.

4. Talcott Parsons, *Essays in Sociological Theory,* rev. ed. (Glencoe, Ill.: Free Press, 1954), 34.

5. See Burton J. Bledstein, *The Culture of Professionalism: The Middle Class and the Development of Higher Education in America* (New York: W. W. Norton, 1976).

6. Richard Posner, *Atlantic Monthly* (June 2002). Laurence Veysey finds three competing visions of higher education present in academia: career training, basic research, and liberal education. The pressures and needs of American business and society (i.e., the external culture) have put the last on the defensive, though it is also the one most innately resistant to a merely utilitarian and functional understanding of knowledge. Veysey, "Higher Education as Profession: Changes and Continuities," in *The Professions in American History,* ed. Nathan O. Hatch (Notre Dame, Ind.: University of Notre Dame Press, 1988), 15–32.

7. Michael J. Baxter and Frederick C. Bauerschmidt, "Catholics in the Academy," *Communio* 22 (Summer 1995): 288.

8. Andrew Louth, *Discerning the Mystery: An Essay on the Nature of Theology* (New York: Oxford University Press, 1983), 145, cited in James Keating and David M. McCarthy, "Moral Theology with the Saints," *Modern Theology* 19, no. 2 (April 2003): 208.

9. *Washington Post,* March 15, 1998, reprint available at www.georgetown. edu/tannen/argsake.html.

10. I am using *intuition* here to refer not to some innate human sense of basic moral goods but to those background values and moral beliefs that are shaped by a combination of unreflected experience, cultural conditioning, and explicit moral reflection. These values and beliefs often form an unacknowledged lens through which agents perceive their moral world.

11. The rationalist utilitarian Henry Sidgwick recognized this fact, to his dismay, over a century ago. In trying to decide which among the various forms of ethics—for example, intuitional ethics, egoism, utilitarianism—was most reasonable, he saw "in spite of [his] early aversion to Intuitional Ethics" that he had to make "a fundamental ethical intuition" and that without such an intuition, utilitarianism could not "be made coherent and harmonious." Sidgwick, *The Methods of Ethics*, 7th ed. (Indianapolis, Ind.: Hackett, 1981), xviii.

12. Richard Rorty, *Consequences of Pragmatism: Essays, 1972–1980* (Minneapolis: University of Minnesota Press, 1982), xlii.

13. Depending on which spiritual/theological school one follows, "true" may be distinguished from false by the fact that the desires are either deep, properly formed, or through grace reformed.

14. Martha Nussbaum, *The Fragility of Goodness: Luck and Ethics in Greek Tragedy and Philosophy* (Cambridge: Cambridge University Press, 1986), 307.

15. Iris Murdoch, *Metaphysics as a Guide to Morals* (New York : Allen Lane/ Penguin, 1993), 25.

16. "Value goes right down to the bottom of the cognitive situation." Murdoch, *Metaphysics as a Guide*, 384.

17. Martha C. Nussbaum, "'Finely Aware and Richly Responsible': Literature and the Moral Imagination," in *Anti-theory in Ethics and Moral Conservatism*, ed. Stanley G. Clarke and Evan Simpson (New York: State University of New York Press, 1989), 116.

18. Nussbaum, "'Finely Aware and Richly Responsible,'" 115.

19. *Nichomachean Ethics* 6.11.1143b11–14. For a helpful resource in Aristotle's ethics, see Amelie Oksenberg Rorty, ed., *Essays on Aristotle's Ethics* (Berkeley: University of California Press, 1980).

20. In keeping with the academic view of the professional ethicist, a recent *New York Times Magazine* article identified Daniel Callahan of the Hastings Center simply as "The Ethicist"; nothing else about his personal identity was necessary (*New York Times Magazine*, July 21, 1996, 24).

21. In regard to the use of Scripture in ethics, most Catholic works of late have tried to incorporate Scripture scholarship into their arguments. See, for example, Lisa Sowle Cahill's *Love Your Enemies: Discipleship, Pacifism, and Just War Theory* (Minneapolis, Minn.: Fortress, 1994). Discussions on recent interpretations of Thomas Aquinas can be found in *The Ethics of Aquinas*, ed. Stephen Pope (Washington, D.C.: Georgetown University Press, 2002). William Spohn explores the relationship between the emotions and morality in his "Passions and Principles," *Theological Studies* 52 (March 1991). For an important collection of essays dealing with the relationship between liturgy and ethics, see E. Byron Anderson and Bruce T. Morrill, eds., *Liturgy and the Moral Self: Humanity at Full Stretch before God* (Collegeville, Minn.: Liturgical Press, 1998). The doxological nature of Christian discipleship is developed in Frans Josef Van Beeck, *God Encountered: A Contemporary Catholic Systematic Theology* (San Francisco: Harper & Row, 1989).

22. "Ascetic Theology formulates rules for the more certain realization of Christian perfection. Mystical Theology enunciates the method of the ascent of the mind and will to God. . . . Since these two parts of Theology deal with perfection, it would seem better that they should not be formally included in any treatment of Moral Theology

as such." Henry Davis, *Moral and Pastoral Theology*, vol. 1 (New York: Sheed and Ward, 1943).

23. Charles E. Curran, *The Origins of Moral Theology in the United States: Three Different Approaches* (Washington, D.C.: Georgetown University Press, 1997), 300.

24. Richard McCormick, "Moral Theology 1940–1989: An Overview," republished in *The Historical Development of Fundamental Moral Theology in the United States*, vol. 11 of *Readings in Moral Theology*, ed. Charles E. Curran and Richard A. McCormick (New York: Paulist Press, 1999), 66.

25. Norbert Rigali, SJ, "Christian Ethics and Perfection," *Chicago Studies* 14 (1975): 238.

26. Maria Antonaccio notes that Pierre Hadot, whose important work *Philosophy as a Way of Life* has generated renewed interest in *askesis*, shows how "the term askesis was originally used by ancient philosophers exclusively to designate philosophical thought-exercises, 'inner activities of the thought and will' intended to cultivate certain habits of mind conducive to a life of wisdom." Antonaccio, "Contemporary Forms of *Askesis* and the Return of Spiritual Exercises," *Annual of the Society of Christian Ethics* 18 (1998): 70.

27. Vincent L. Wimbush and Richard Valantasis, eds., *Asceticism* (Oxford: Oxford University Press, 1995), xxix.

28. See James D. Davidson et al., "The Impact of Generations: Pre–Vatican II Catholics, Vatican II Catholics, and Post–Vatican II Catholics," in *The Search for the Common Ground*, (Huntington, Ind.: Our Sunday Visitor, 1997), 111–39, particularly 119–20, 137–39.

29. James Keenan notes that the early Jesuit general Jerome Nadal "recommended that Jesuit confessors study cases an hour daily." Keenan, "The Return of Casuistry," *Theological Studies* 57, no. 1 (1996): 127. Keenan cites John O'Malley's *The First Jesuits*.

30. John A. McHugh, "Cases of Conscience," in *Casuist*, vol. 15 (New York: Joseph F. Wagner, 1925), reprinted in *Readings in Moral Theology*, vol. 11, 115–19 (the case is presented on 115).

31. William Spohn, *Theological Studies* 58, no. 1 (1997): 113.

32. *Mother Teresa: In My Own Words*, ed. José Luis González-Balado (New York: Gramercy Books, 1996), 52

33. McCormick, "Moral Theology 1940–1989," 66–67.

34. Lawrence Cunningham examines examples of fictional saints, among them Graham Greene's whiskey priest (*The Power and the Glory*), Albert Camus' Dr. Rieux (*The Plague*), and Walker Percy's "firewatcher" priest (*Love in the Ruins*). Cunningham, *The Meaning of Saints* (San Francisco: Harper & Row, 1980), see in particular, 86–114.

35. Cunningham, *Meaning of Saints*, 65.

36. Cunningham, *Meaning of Saints*, 74.

37. John A. Coleman, SJ, "Conclusion: After Sainthood?" in *Saints and Virtues*, ed. John Stratton Hawley (Berkeley: University of California Press, 1987), 223.

38. A "society without saints tends to allow virtue to sink to the level of utilitarian value" (Coleman, "Conclusion: After Sainthood?" 221).

39. I was helped on this point by an essay by James Keating and David M. McCarthy, "Habits of Holiness: The Ordering of Moral-Mystical Living," *Communio* 28

(Winter 2001): 820–42. In keeping with their notion of a "moral-mystical living," I intend to emphasize here that Christian moral living cannot be viewed only as an alternate cultural ethics. Christian ethicists must take account of the theological nature of that life and the ways in which the divine mystery upsets neat patterns of moral analysis. The saints can help us do that.

40. Keating and McCarthy, "Moral Theology," 209.

41. Karl Rahner, "The Church of the Saints," in *Theological Investigations*, vol. 3 (New York: Seabury Press, 1974), 100, cited by Donna L. Orsuto, "The Saint as Moral Paradigm," *Spirituality and Morality: Integrating Prayer and Action*, ed. Dennis J. Billy, CSsR, and Donna L. Orsuto (New York: Paulist Press, 1996), 131.

42. Edith Wyschogrod, *Saints and Postmodernism: Revisioning Moral Philosophy* (Chicago: University of Chicago Press, 1990), 26.

43. Martha C. Nussbaum, *Love's Knowledge: Essays on Philosophy and Literature* (Oxford: Oxford University Press, 1990), 171.

44. John Cardinal Newman, *The Essential Newman*, ed. Vincent Ferrer Blehl, SJ (New York: Mentor Omega Books, 1963), 235–36, cited in Cunningham, *The Meaning of Saints*, 84.

# 2

## Finding a Place at the Heart of the Church: On the Vocation of a Lay Theologian

*Christopher P. Vogt*

"We become what we do."[1] There is no plainer statement of the idea that practices and habits are at the heart of the formation of character.[2] Although this statement glosses over some of the complexities of moral formation, it can serve as an important reality check. To be told that "we become what we do" breaks through a common tendency to think that who we are is more readily under our control than it really is. We cannot habitually long for the things our neighbors have without *becoming* covetous. Likewise, we cannot become generous without engaging regularly in charitable giving and similar acts of generosity. If the everyday routine of our lives does not match up to our ideals, it is only a matter of time before we will look into the mirror with disappointment. This is a very simple insight but one easily ignored or repressed.

It is valuable to remember the relationship between one's everyday habits and one's identity when considering how to pursue a vocation as a theologian. In recent years, there has been a significant amount of discussion regarding how to preserve and cultivate Catholic identity at Catholic colleges and universities.[3] These writings have often focused on the shape of the ideal Catholic college, at times to the neglect of how particular practices both embody and sculpt that vision.[4] This approach can make it easier to forget that we become what we do. Even if we draft the finest college mission statement and read widely on the nature of an academic vocation, we will remain largely unchanged and detached from these goals unless we develop practices that support them. We must ask precisely how, in the daily grind of pursuing a theological vocation, one goes about engaging in habits and practices that will lead one to become the sort of theologian that the church

45

needs and that one wants to become—a theologian whose intellectual and spiritual identity is deeply embedded in the life and faith of the Christian community.

There are many practices that could serve the purpose I have described; in this chapter, I focus on only one. I propose that preaching regularly in a parish community is a practice that bishops should invite lay theologians to embrace. There have been many calls from pastoral leaders in the church and from others for theologians to pursue their craft from the heart of the church—that is to say, from a vantage point that is rooted deeply in the liturgy and in scripture. My claim is that for a theologian to fulfill such a role she or he must actively engage in practices that solidify such a connection to liturgy and scripture. Preaching is one such practice that should be encouraged for the enrichment of both the theologian and the church.

In what follows I argue for the importance of the practice of preaching for lay theologians by turning first to an examination of what practices currently predominate in their professional lives (and thus are decisive in shaping their character and identity). I take up this issue by way of autobiographical, rather than sociological, reflection. Next, I explain why it is important for a theologian to have a deep connection to the community of faith, especially as that community comes together for worship and to hear the Word. In the third section, I explain why preaching is a practice particularly well suited for fostering precisely such a connection. Preaching would utilize skills and knowledge bases theologians already have but in ways that would benefit a specifically ecclesiastical audience and move the individual theologian toward ongoing growth. Finally, I take up the question of whether preaching by lay theologians is theologically justified and canonically permissible, answering that although this would be a novel practice, it would not violate the distinction between lay and ordained liturgical roles that is an important part of the Roman Catholic tradition.

## WHAT SORT OF PRACTICE IS MISSING?
## AN AUTOBIOGRAPHICAL ACCOUNT

Describing what he calls an ethics of mercy, Roger Burggraeve has written that if you desire to bring a person who is in some way disordered closer to God, you must meet that person "where she is." One does not begin with the ideal but with the real.[5] It is only after one has a sense of who one actually is and where one is in need of grace and growth that one can begin to think about practices that might move one toward the ideal of who one ought to become. It is for this reason that I begin with the question of my own existing personal situation with the intention of discerning where growth and development are needed.

Like many Catholic theologians today, I am a lay person. Furthermore, in contrast to many theologians of the generation or two before mine, I have never been ordained, nor have I lived as a member of a religious order.[6] This fact alone speaks volumes about my own particular identity as a theologian and that of many of my contemporaries.[7] Most significant, it means that I do not live with a professional identity inherently linked to ministry in the church. When I act in my role as a theologian, it is most often in an academic rather than an ecclesial context. These practices that I engage in my effort to become a successful, tenured moral theologian do not direct me toward the heart of the church—toward its narrative, toward its liturgical heart—but rather toward "the world." As I am conscious of the truth that we become what we do, let me sketch the practices that dominate how I spend my time and thereby influence my character and identity.

During the academic year, the majority of my days are spent interacting with students. Each semester, I work with about 120–150 undergraduates. The identity of these people and the questions that they bring to our theological conversations in the classroom shape my experience of teaching and my work as a theologian. For this reason, it is a significant fact that most of my students have no connection, or only a nominal connection, to the Roman Catholic community. In fact, a substantial minority are Jewish, Muslim, or Hindu. The kind of theology I pursue with them in the classroom is rarely the "faith seeking understanding" undertaken by informed Catholics seeking to make sense of their own tradition in today's complex world. Instead I find myself explaining the truth, logic, and application of the Catholic moral tradition to an audience who finds it foreign. This mode of teaching strikes me as a service I render *for* the church but rarely if ever as a vocation carried out *in* the church, much less at its heart (i.e., it is work carried out among people who are not themselves members of the church).[8] My experience of teaching is certainly in stark contrast to any practice that would be carried out in the midst of the faith community gathered at worship.

Teaching does not consume the whole of my time. Like many readers of this chapter, I learned very quickly that writing articles for peer-reviewed journals is the key to success in academic life today. For this reason, I devote as much time as possible to research and writing. When not writing with the aim of submitting my work to a journal, I am busy composing papers for presentation at the annual meetings of learned societies. I enjoy research and writing, and I recognize that theologians must engage in rigorous research and publication if we are to move the discipline forward and maintain our identity as scholars.[9] I also have a sense that my academic writing is in some way of service to the church. Careful scholarship can be an important means of integrating new insights from human experience and learning into the faith.[10] At the same time, this work is more properly addressed to the academy rather than the church.

This examination of the shape of my professional life points to a notice-able lack of any regular, sustained interaction with the church. I am deeply engaged in an encounter with "the world" in the considerable time I spend interacting with my students. I am deeply engaged with the academy in my writing.[11] But I find that there are no regularized, institutional, professional practices in place to develop my connection to what David Tracy has identi-fied as the third crucial public that theologians should engage: the church. There is no venue in which I regularly interact with the people of God as an audience or as a source for my work. There is no mechanism in place for me to be heard by local clergy or my local bishop, nor is there any ongoing prac-tice in place for me to hear the concerns, criticisms, or ideas of pastoral lead-ers. In the absence of such practices, I am becoming a professional academic but one with only loose, informal connections with the church.[12]

## THE IMPORTANCE OF FORGING AN ACTIVE
## CONNECTION WITH THE COMMUNITY AT WORSHIP

The disconnection I have experienced between my professional academic life and my life as a member of the believing, worshipping community of the church is a significant problem in the view of church leaders and theologians who have written recently on the vocation of the theologian. In these sources there is a strong emphasis on the importance of connecting a the-ologian's professional development with his or her ongoing spiritual identity as a member of the people of God. As Cardinal Ratzinger has written,

> The theologian, who is presumably a believer, is such only in and through the church. If this is not true, if the theologian does not live and breathe Christ through the church, his body, then I suggest we are not dealing with a theolo-gian at all. . . . The church is not, for theology, a demand extraneous or foreign to science, but rather the reason for its existence and the very condition for its possibility.[13]

Theological reflection is not engaged by a neutral observer in a context wholly separate from the church. Charles Curran has observed that to think otherwise would be to play into contemporary individualistic assumptions. For Catholics, the church does not exist as a voluntary association but rather as the chief instrument or sacrament of God's grace and love in the world. In Curran's words, "the church is the way in which God has chosen to come to us with God's saving love. We are saved by belonging to the people of God. Since this is the way Catholics believe God comes to us, we find God's sav-ing love in and through belonging to the people of God."[14]

Avery Dulles has written along similar lines in a book on method and the-ology. He describes contemporary theology as entering a "postcritical" stage in which the modern expectation that a scholar of religion must be detached and objective is now recognized as an inappropriate ideal for theology.[15] Theologians should approach their subject with a hermeneutic of trust rather than of suspicion. This trust and connection to the tradition are fully realized only when appropriate intellectual effort is joined to the practices of individual prayer and participation in the liturgy of the church. Dulles writes, "If theology is not to regress, it must retain its close bonds with prayer and worship."[16]

Theology may be able to proceed in an intellectually respectable sort of way without a connection to the lived belief and practices of the concrete community of the people of God and to its life of prayer and worship, but such a theology will likely cease to serve the needs of that community. Given the central importance of this connection, it is rather shocking that neither the church nor many departments of theology at Catholic colleges and universities have developed institutional programs and practices to nurture it.

One could conceivably say that forging and maintaining a concrete connection with the community of the church and to its life of prayer and worship is the responsibility of individual theologians, but this line of thinking seems suitable only for a time that has now passed. When individual theologians were mainly priests and women religious, it may have made sense to assume that those individuals would pursue such a connection to the church "on their own." The viability of this arrangement rested not so much on these individuals as it did upon the religious communities of which they were a part. These men and women were encouraged or required by their communities to live out a life of pastoral service in addition to a life of academic service. In this way, their professional and personal lives were oriented toward providing for a balance between a life of devotion to the academy and to the church that is envisioned by Ratzinger, Dulles, and Curran.

In contrast, the dynamics of life as a lay theologian (at least as I have experienced it) do not support that fusion as a matter of course. In fact, leaving such an important matter up to the initiative of individual lay theologians without offering them institutional support from the department or from the church means de facto that this dimension of their professional lives will remain underdeveloped. Therefore, practices must be developed to foster an ongoing sense of identity rooted in both the academy and the church.

It is not immediately clear whether universities or diocesan churches should be primarily responsible for supporting the development of practices that forge a meaningful connection between the academic and ecclesiastical identities of theologians. At least some academic departments of theology have expressed reluctance to accept responsibility for this role. Stephen Pope, former chair of the theology department at Boston College, made this point quite clear when he wrote, "The academic study of theology is not to be confused with monasticism. Though its prerequisite, effect, and complement, spiritual formation is not the proper focus of theological education."[17]

Pope states that the need to form theologians spiritually is "a need that ought to be met not by the theology department per se."[18]

One might legitimately ask how leaders of Catholic colleges and universities such as Boston College can say in one breath that the university is "where the church does its thinking" and then say in the next that the task of forming at least some of their faculty into scholars who draw their identity and inspiration from the life of the church is "not their responsibility per se." However, in fairness to Stephen Pope one must note that he is not refuting the importance of the connection under discussion in this chapter but rather questioning whether an academic department of theology is the most suitable organization to take on this responsibility. Indeed, his comments could be interpreted as suggesting merely that this is more properly the responsibility of the bishop.

I might be willing to concede that Stephen Pope is right to say that such support need not come from university departments of theology, although some way of recognizing the efforts of theologians in this regard seems in order (i.e., in terms of tenure considerations). It is for this reason that I am suggesting here that *the local bishop* should extend an invitation to the lay theologians of his diocese to preach on an ongoing basis. It is more properly the concern of bishops (rather than university presidents) to see to it that theologians serve not only the academy but the church and that they develop their craft in a way that is deeply embedded in the church and its life of faith.

It would therefore fall to the bishop to offer the resources (financial and otherwise) necessary to support lay theologians in their efforts to develop some competence for this ministry. Exactly what form the support for this initiative would take is beyond the scope of this chapter but would likely include some ongoing opportunities for spiritual formation and training in homiletics. Such a program of formation and development could serve as a valuable means of building regular points of contact between theologians and the pastoral leaders of the church. Simply issuing such an invitation to preach—expressing confidence and trust in a theologian's ability to share in the bishop's responsibility to spread the Gospel—would be a major step toward the goal of mutual trust and service envisioned in *Ex Corde Ecclesiae*.[19]

## PREACHING AS A PUBLIC PRACTICE LINKING LAY THEOLOGIANS TO THE HEART OF THE CHURCH

It could be argued that the devotional practices already available to all lay people should simply be utilized more thoroughly by lay theologians who wish to intensify connections between their professional work and their life of faith as Christians. One could ask whether it is not enough simply to seek out a spiritual director, engage more diligently in a life of private devotion, serve one's parish, and go to Mass more frequently. After all, is it not the vocation of every lay person to live out his or her professional life in the world in a way that expresses at once an identity deeply rooted in Christ and the church?[20] As Paul J. Wadell argues, the liturgy has as its purpose and aim the formation of the whole people of God into a community that is deeply formed by the Scriptures and whose identity is evidently marked by deep love for God or even friendship with the Divine.[21] Is it not enough to strive to be better *hearers* of the Word alongside one's brothers and sisters and to endeavor to allow ourselves to be changed ever more radically to be more like Christ by eating his body and drinking his blood?[22] In short, is it not right for lay theologians to be spiritually formed and to grow in communion to Christ and the church in exactly the same way as all other lay people?

It must first be made clear that I am not proposing a practice to replace the typical way in which lay people develop spiritually. It would be my expectation that lay theologians would continue to attempt to respond to the call to holiness in much the same way that all lay people are called to respond. What I am searching for here is an *additional* practice that would supplement the existing ways in which one seeks to build one's life of faith in ways that would simultaneously nourish the particular vocation of the Catholic theologian and benefit the community of the church. This practice would address the specific lack discussed here, namely, the disconnection many lay theologians experience professionally from the lived belief and practices of the people of God (especially their lives of prayer and worship). I propose that regular, ongoing preaching in one's parish should serve as just such a practice.

To support my assertion, let me begin with the question of why theologians should attempt to grow spiritually as all other lay people do *and* develop the ability to be effective preachers of the Word. Theologians are fundamentally teachers, charged with the task of giving a systematic account of the faith. A key part of this role of the theologian is to illuminate the meaning of the Scriptures. According to the "Instruction on the Ecclesial Vocation of the Theologian" issued by the Congregation for the Doctrine of the Faith, the theologian's "role is to pursue in a particular way an ever deeper understanding of the Word of God found in the inspired Scriptures and handed on by the living Tradition of the Church."[23] It is clear that theologians carry out this role of clarifying the meaning of the Word in communion with the magisterium and that it is primarily the role of the latter to preserve, explain, and spread the Word of God.[24] Theologians more typically draw upon culture and other areas of the arts and sciences to better illumine the mystery of faith, but by the congregation's own account, it is clear that it is the responsibility of theologians and the pastoral leaders of the church *together* to clarify the meaning of the Scriptures.[25] This explains why in seeking to connect lay theologians to the people of God and their lives of prayer and worship, we would choose a practice rooted in the Liturgy of the Word, but it does not yet answer why theologians should engage in an active practice such as preaching. For that we must reflect further upon how the vocation of the lay theologian is unique.

The work of a lay theologian is not a typical lay vocation. The laity characteristically bring the light of faith to the secular realm in which they work, thereby bearing witness to Christ and renewing the temporal order.[26] Lay theologians do this by bringing the light of faith to bear on all areas of knowledge (bearing witness to Christ and renewing the typically secular world of the academy). But the theologian—even the lay theologian—simultaneously has an ecclesiastical role to play in which she or he clarifies the meaning of scripture and tradition *for the church*. In the past, when theologians were predominantly clerics, they engaged in this role for the church as a matter of course. This is not the case for lay theologians. There is a need for a practice by which lay theologians can publicly exercise their vocation as leaders and as those called by the Spirit to clarify the faith within the church. Anyone who has studied a foreign language knows that there is an enormous difference between learning to understand a foreign tongue passively and learning to speak the language actively. Theologians, as those called to speak within the church on the nature of faith and the meaning of the Scriptures, should engage in practices that demand the active appropriation of that faith.

The practice of preaching commends itself as a logical expansion of the professional practices of the theologian because it is at once similar to what theologians already do as scholars and teachers, but different in significant ways. Preaching a homily is similar in many ways to teaching in the sense that it requires some of the same technical skills, such as clear communication, the ability to relate to and engage a large group of people, and so forth. At the same time, practicing the art of preaching develops different skills and sensibilities in the one who preaches because the unique character of the homily demands a different kind of focus, preparation, and connection with the material one is communicating. Stephen DeLeers has offered a summary of the qualities that characterize homiletic preaching.[27] A review of these qualities can be helpful for illuminating the ways in which preaching would serve as a practice that would complement the activities of teaching and research in which lay theologians typically engage.

The first characteristic quality of a homily is its personal nature. As DeLeers writes, "The homily is not a preaching of self, but it is a preaching by a self. The use of the first person singular suggests that a priest is speaking from his own faith and taking responsibility for what he is saying."[28] This description is in contrast to the typical style of academic writing where one may be personally connected to and invested in the tradition and material under study, but one's writing itself is clearly distinguishable from a testimonial. The personal qualities of a homily can also be distinguished from typical modes of engaging students in the classroom. Personally, I find it is not often that I can speak from the heart in class. As a teacher of moral theology, I always seek to get students to learn to think carefully about moral issues and to express their convictions about them. I have found that students are much more willing to engage in a genuine discussion about an issue if my own viewpoint remains unclear. My students are very pragmatic. They believe (wrongly) that their grades are determined by the extent to which they can mirror my opinions and convictions. As such, I must consistently try to avoid strongly expressing my own view of any matter. Thus, preaching would be a complement to the more impersonal forms of theological expression found in journals and in the classroom.

Effective preaching demands deep immersion in the liturgy. "The use of the first person plural in the homily echoes its use throughout the rest of the liturgy and accomplishes the same thing: a proclamation of our communal identity in Christ through baptism"[29] This combination of prayerful unity and shared identity is missing from the context in which theologians typically work.[30] In a teaching environment, one can never assume the faith of one's students because the public we serve as teachers is much wider than that of the church. In gatherings of theologians, one should anticipate some level of shared belief, but one cannot assume unity. When theologians come together at conferences or elsewhere, their mode of exchange is typically critical and argumentative (one would hope constructively so). Indeed, the purpose of such gatherings is to bring disagreements into relief and test the merits of competing points of view to determine whether one's thinking is sound and consistent with the tradition.

In contrast, a homily is not a moment for academic disputation. Instead, it would offer a lay theologian an opportunity to speak and to think about that which is not under a cloud of ambiguity. It would be an opportunity to move back from the edges where theologians usually work to move the tradition carefully forward and return to the heart of the faith. I think of the homilies of Karl Rahner and their great value for the people of God, and I wonder whether Rahner would have had occasion to write on those topics if he had not also been a preacher of the Word of God.[31]

The homily is to pertain to the liturgical readings for that day. A preacher must deal with what the liturgical calendar calls for on that particular occasion. How often do theologians begin with a selection from Scripture not of their own choosing and seek to understand that text in its original context, in terms of how it relates to the rest of the canon and in terms of how it remains meaningful for life and faith today? Even for theologians who draw liberally from scriptural sources in their work, preaching on a text would remain a distinct and helpful enterprise.

It is precisely the unchosen or given aspect of the Scripture upon which a homily is to be based that points to one way in which preparing to preach could help theologians become better hearers of the Word. In a lecture on preaching that he gave at the Confessing Church seminary in Finkenwalde, Dietrich Bonhoeffer said that a sermon must always begin in prayer over the biblical text and with the recognition that "the sermon is not a discourse in which I develop my thought; it is not my word but God's own word." Preparation of a sermon or homily should begin with meditation on the directive "Accept Thou this word."[32] Thus, preparing to preach is a time for a hermeneutics of trust rather than the hermeneutics of suspicion to which academics are far more accustomed.[33] It is a moment to allow a text not even of our own choosing to interrogate us with questions such as "What does this text say about me? Where am I in danger of being untrue to the wider significance of the text? What does it say about the church as a whole and my congregation in particular?"[34] The homily should be an occasion for the preacher and the congregation to reflect together on how these lectionary readings clarify what it means to have been incorporated into Christ's church—to be the people of Christ's church today.[35] This requires a distinctive and acquired habit of being a hearer of God's Word.[36]

Effective preaching must be actualizing. It can only ring true if there is congruence between the life of the preacher and the message preached.[37] A teacher can credibly explain the concept of the preferential option for the poor without the necessity of embracing such an option. A scholar can become an authority on virtue ethics without necessarily embracing a life of virtue. An effective preacher can do neither of these things. Therefore, to call a lay theologian to be a preacher is simultaneously to call him or her to a deeper life of holiness.

It is necessary for me to pause here and address directly an important underlying question: Is preaching a formative practice (i.e., is it a transformative experience that leads the preacher him- or herself to a deeper understanding of faith and a more profound devotion to Jesus Christ?), or is it better understood as a practice by which those more perfectly molded by the Holy Spirit shed the light of their wisdom and experience upon the Word for the betterment of others? This question is significant because some might object to the fact that I have proposed preaching as a practice that would lead theologians to deeper conversion and to a more conscious awareness of the importance of liturgy and the Word for their theological work and identity. They might ask whether we should not expect preachers to have accomplished that growth *before* they are invited to preach. Is it wise to call someone to the pulpit with the expectation the experience will make them grow?

First, let me be clear about the fact that I agree that some additional formation and training would be required for lay theologians who would preach (particularly for those who do not hold a master of divinity degree). As I have noted, preaching is an activity with its own integrity and distinctive qualities that set it apart from other practices theologians undertake. To preach well, lay theologians would have to go through a program of preparation in which they come to a deeper theological understanding of preaching and hone some of the skills necessary to do it well.[38] This period of preparation might also serve as a time of discernment during which the theologian (in consultation with others) might determine if preaching is a practice to which he or she is well suited.

At the same time, I believe that it is unhelpful to hold to an exceedingly exalted notion of what constitutes readiness for the task of preaching. Drawing an analogy with teaching is helpful here. One would not send someone into the classroom who has nothing to say or who has not been trained or who has no charisma for that art. But any teacher will tell you that even the most rigorous training and preparation do not render one entirely ready to teach. Teaching is a practice or an art that one truly learns only when one has begun to practice it. Becoming a good teacher is a process of growth. The same is true for preaching. We should ask that preachers receive adequate training, commit to sufficient preparation, and exhibit signs of conversion in their lives; but *perfection* should not be a prerequisite.

What I have said here about the need for lay theologians to embrace practices that will ground their identities more deeply in liturgy and Scripture remains true, but no one should be too easily dismissive of the level of spiritual development, depth of conversion, or degree of pastoral sensitivity that many lay theologians have already achieved. We are talking about people who have dedicated their lives to a theological vocation. We are talking about people who are already pastorally active, as when they speak to church groups or work with Catholic organizations (e.g., hospitals). Certainly, in most cases these men and women have moved far enough along on their pilgrim journey of faith to have a substantial basis upon which to draw for reflection on the Gospel. When I say that theologians will grow from the practice of preaching, one should not be misled into thinking that I see the pulpit as a magical locus of transformation. What I mean more properly is that in the *process* of becoming and remaining a good preacher (i.e., in the additional training that might be required and in the ongoing task of praying with the Scriptures and spending time preparing a homily) that theologians will grow and be shaped in the ways that I have described.

Let us now turn to a final quality of preaching that highlights the ways in which that practice complements other theological endeavors. Effective preaching is pastoral and therefore demands that one be in tune with the lives lived by the people of God and the culture in which both preacher and congregation live. A few years ago, Cardinal Francis George (then bishop of Yakima) wrote that theologians need to demonstrate that the intellectual content of faith is compatible with the popular expression of faith.[39] He complained that theologians never have the opportunity to hear from the faithful or to share their expertise beyond university settings.[40] Interestingly, preaching would offer just such an imperative and opportunity.

Specialists in pastoral theology tell us that one of the most important prerequisites for good preaching is a deep familiarity with one's congregation.[41] For theologians who perceive that they do not know the minds or lives of their fellow Christians well, receiving an invitation to preach would provide an added incentive and a new context for them to come to know the faith and concerns of the people of God more deeply. It would have the added benefit of making theologians a more visible presence in the church. If the goal is to put theologians more in touch with the sense of the people and their everyday faith, what better, more visible way to make a theologian present to that community than to invite him or her to preach on regular occasions in their parish? People would be more inclined to seek out a person who is familiar by face and who shares something of his or her personal faith regularly with the parish (recall the personal quality of homiletic preaching mentioned earlier). Cardinal George undoubtedly is more in touch with a sense of the people because they recognize him, understand his role of leadership in the community, and therefore communicate their concerns to him. For theologians similarly to avail themselves of the sense of the faithful as a theological source, it would be helpful for them to have a visible presence at the heart of the life of the church.

However, it may very well be the case that lay theologians already know firsthand the realities of life other parishioners face in a way that even the most pastorally sensitive priest can never match. Their unique vantage point, as attained by persons with substantial theological training who nevertheless live very much in the world, could enable them to break open the Word quite effectively. In this way, inviting lay theologians to preach would be to offer a unique gift to their parish community. Surveys of American Catholics have found that many lay people are not being nourished spiritually because the quality of preaching in their parishes is so poor.[42] Expanding the pool of preachers to include lay theologians could thus serve two pastoral needs simultaneously. It would provide an ongoing public practice that links lay theologians to the Word and the church's life of worship. It would also address the plea from many American Catholics for a higher caliber of Sunday preaching.

## IS THE PRACTICE CANONICALLY
## ACCEPTABLE AND THEOLOGICALLY JUSTIFIED?

At this moment in history, preaching is not a practice typically considered appropriate for lay people. However, it is not unheard of in the history of the church either.[43] For example, there was a surge in lay preaching toward the end of the twelfth century.[44] More recently, the German bishops requested and received a rescript from Rome to allow lay people to preach on a regular and ongoing basis (including at liturgy on Sunday) in their dioceses.[45] The bishops argued that the growing heterogeneity of the church in Germany presented itself as a pressing pastoral need that could best be addressed by diversifying the pool of people typically authorized to give a liturgical homily. The German bishops were not calling for a radical revision of the theology of priesthood but merely for a change in norms of practice in order to respond appropriately to the contemporary pastoral situation.

Similarly, I am not calling here for the creation of a new pseudopriestly office of theologian, nor am I advocating a revision of the theology of priesthood. That would be beyond my competence as a moral theologian. I am making a much more modest claim that our existing understanding of the nature of the vocation of theologian points to the legitimacy of expanding the modes of expression and leadership available to lay theologians in the church. I will leave it up to others more expert in the field of ecclesiology to decide whether the experiment I am suggesting here would point to the need to revise the present sharp distinction between lay ministry and priestly ministry more generally.[46]

Even if there is some agreement about what I have said regarding the likely benefits of preaching by lay theologians, both for the theologian and for the church, the current Code of Canon Law might stand as a major obstacle to the implementation of such a plan. Since the new Code of Canon Law was promulgated by John Paul II in 1983, the outright ban on lay preaching that had been in place since 1917 has been lifted.[47] The new code reflects changes in ecclesiology that emerged at the Second Vatican Council, where it was recognized that all of the baptized enjoy an equal level of dignity, a common call to perfection and share in the one priesthood of Christ.[48] In recognition of this movement in theology and the actual expanded role of the laity in the life of the church and the evangelization of the world, canon law now affirms the legitimacy of lay preaching in some contexts, particularly in catechetical situations.[49] Lay persons are also permitted now to conduct a Liturgy of the Word where there is a shortage of priests (with the approval of the local bishop).[50]

Although there has been a noticeable shift in recent years toward a more sympathetic view of lay preaching, the current code nevertheless explicitly prohibits lay people from preaching a homily. The main reason given for this restriction is that the homily is a part of the liturgy itself and therefore should be reserved for those who may preside at liturgy.[51] The restriction against lay people preaching a homily was stated with greater force in the Vatican's recent instruction on the collaboration of priests and the nonordained, where it was made clear that lay people not only are prohibited from giving a homily but are also restricted from speaking in a way that might be misconstrued by listeners as a homily.[52] A generous summary of the overall aim of this document would be that it seeks to sharpen the contrast between the lay apostolate (with a secular orientation to the world) and the role of the clergy.[53]

Even if one embraces this generous reading, the instruction does not bode well for those who would advocate regularized lay preaching of any sort. At the very least, it is clear that if such a practice were implemented, measures would have to be taken to ensure that the rightful distinction would be maintained between the role of the laity and the role of clergy within the church.

Despite the fact that canon law seems to impose an outright ban on lay people's preaching a homily, some still argue that there are ways of interpreting the law that would allow for some lay preaching (even of a homily) on an "extraordinary" basis. James Provost notes that in the absence of a priest, it is permissible for a lay person to conduct a Liturgy of the Word. Furthermore, he notes that there is the concept of "moral absence" in the tradition that holds that sometimes, for pastoral reasons or reasons of necessity, a priest may be regarded as "morally absent" even though he is physically present.[54] For example, if the presiding priest is wholly unprepared to preach, unknown to the community, and so forth, he may be considered morally absent. Provost argues for extending the concept of "moral absence" to include "grave pastoral reasons," such as the need for the community to hear from a variety of preachers, including lay preachers, so that right of the community to good preaching can be adequately fulfilled.[55] Provost overcomes the explicit prohibition against a lay person's preaching a homily by claiming that the term *homily* has taken on a legal definition such that it means simply the preaching by a priest or deacon in the context of the regular liturgy; if a lay person performs the same task of "offering a reflection," by definition it cannot be a homily, and therefore it can be permitted.[56]

Recent statements by the United States Conference of Catholic Bishops suggest that they are currently opposed to such a broad interpretation of canon 766. Complementary legislation passed by the conference states, "In providing for preaching by the lay faithful the diocesan bishop may never dispense from the norm which reserves the homily to the sacred ministers. Preaching by the lay faithful may not take place within the Celebration of the Eucharist at the moment reserved for the homily."[57] Nevertheless, Patrick Norris, another canonist, notes that it is the particular wording of the canons, rather than the theology underlying them, that would lead one to reject the permissibility of regularized lay preaching.[58] That is to say that an attempt to understand the canons in the context of history, a theology of ministry, and a rich ecclesiology might lead one to the conclusion that lay people should have the opportunity to preach at the Eucharist under certain circumstances even though such a practice might be prohibited under the current code (i.e., the code could be changed if the bishops saw fit).[59]

Sandra Schneiders has remarked that the existence of canonical exceptions to the rule that only ordained men may give a homily (as in the case of a dialogue homily or a homily at a liturgy oriented primarily toward children) indicates that there is no reason for the rule that pertains to "the very essence of preaching or of its relationship to the Eucharistic liturgy."[60] In other words, the rule against lay preaching is of a disciplinary nature, and it is legitimate to pose theological questions as to the appropriateness of that discipline.[61] Edward Schillebeeckx reaches a similar conclusion on the basis of a historical study of the origins of the prohibition of lay preaching. He writes, "In fact, the theological competence of the lay person to speak in the midst of a community of brothers and sisters with the substantial authority of the gospel was never discussed in the medieval disputes about the right to preach. Other questions and other interests were at stake."[62]

Given a lack of definitive theological closure on this issue, I would humbly suggest that it should be reconsidered whether the current discipline of an absolute prohibition on homiletic preaching by lay people is the best discipline by which to ensure the unity of the Liturgy of the Word and Eucharist and to preserve the theological distinction between ordained priesthood and the universal priesthood of the baptized. Patrick Norris has noted that deacons preach the Gospel and lay men and women read the Word on Sundays without threatening those goods or calling into question the presiding function of the priest over the entire liturgy.[63] Perhaps a similar delegation of the ministry of preaching would also be acceptable in the exceptional case of lay theologians, given the many potential benefits of such a practice.

For many years now, the magisterium and many theologians have agreed on the need to approach theology from a vantage point rooted deeply in Scripture and the liturgical life of the church. The practices that currently predominate in the everyday professional lives of lay theologians connect them with the world and the academy but rarely with the church, its narrative, and its worship. It is necessary for lay theologians to take up practices that will overcome this disconnection. Regular preaching would be a practice ideally suited for this purpose. It would be appropriate for theologians because their vocation demands that they serve the church as interpreters of the Word and because preaching would draw on their considerable training in a way that complements their pursuit of teaching and research and leads them to be more pastorally aware.

We become what we do. Stephen DeLeers describes what becomes of people who preach as follows:

> To preach is to grow in knowledge of the God of the Scriptures and the people whom we serve. To preach is to grow in appreciation of the Church in all that she is and believes, for a good preacher knows Scripture, liturgy, our doctrinal and moral tradition, and our practices. But above all, to preach is to grow in love of God and our neighbor.[64]

At a time when the church calls out for theologians who approach theology *ex corde ecclesiae*, it would seem wise to increase the number of those eligible to reap the fruits of a life of good preaching that DeLeers eloquently describes.

## NOTES

1. James F. Keenan, "There Are No Private Lives," *Josephinum Journal of Theology* 3, no. 2 (Summer/Fall 1996): 76–84.

2. William C. Spohn provides a very fine account of the importance of practices for the moral life and explains how they relate to narrative and community, both of which are also decisive for the formation of character. See Spohn, *Go and Do Likewise: Jesus and Ethics* (New York: Contiuum, 1999). Of course, the idea of the importance of practices and habits is also foundational in Aquinas's ethics. See St. Thomas Aquinas, *Treatise on the Virtues*, trans. John A. Oesterle (Notre Dame, Ind.: University of Notre Dame Press, 1984).

3. Some major recent monographs on this subject include Michael J. Buckley, *The Catholic University as Promise and Project: Reflections in a Jesuit Idiom* (Washington, D.C.: Georgetown University Press, 1998); Dennis O'Brien, *The Idea of a Catholic University* (Chicago: University of Chicago Press, 2002); Martin R. Tripole, ed., *Promise Renewed: Jesuit Higher Education for a New Millennium* (Chicago: Loyola University Press, 1999). For some historical perspective, see Alice Gallin, *Negotiating Identity: Catholic Higher Education since 1960* (Notre Dame, Ind.: University of Notre Dame Press, 2000), and Philip Gleason, *Contending with Modernity: Catholic Higher Education in the Twentieth Century* (New York: Oxford, 1995).

4. A notable exception is the recent volume edited by John Wilcox and Irene King, *Enhancing Religious Identity: Best Practices from Catholic Campuses* (Washington, D.C.: Georgetown University Press, 2000).

5. Roger Burggraeve, "Une Ethique de Miséricorde," *Lumen Vitae* 49 (1994): 281–96. For a work in English by the same author on a similar theme, see Roger Burggraeve, "Meaningful Living and Acting," *Louvain Studies* 13 (1988): 3–26 and 137–60.

6. For the purpose of identifying my generation, I should say that I was born in 1970.

7. Christopher Ruddy (who is a young theologian) notes that many young lay people who study theology today often lack the strong intellectual, spiritual, and pastoral formation that our colleagues of a generation or two before us take for granted. See Ruddy, "Young Theologians: Between the Rock and a Hard Place," *Commonweal* 127, no. 8 (April 21, 2000): 17–19.

8. Thus, my day-to-day experience as a Catholic theologian does not fit neatly with the idea expressed by many theologians that the Catholic college or university is a part of the church. For example, Joseph A. Komanchak suggests that the Catholic college or university is "in" or "part" or "instrument" of the church while retaining some institutional autonomy. While I can see his point that any institution "founded because of Jesus Christ and for his sake" exists to some extent *in* the church, I would note that the nature and experience of working "in" the church will vary considerably, depending on the demographic composition of one's students and one's de-

partment. See Joseph A. Komanchak, "Mission and Identity in Catholic Universities," in *Theological Education in the Catholic Tradition: Contemporary Challenges*, ed. P. W. Carey and E. C. Muller (New York: Crossroad, 1997), 34–48, esp. 38–42.

9. Stephen Pope, "A Response to Christopher Ruddy," *Commonweal* 127, no. 11 (June 2, 2000): 11–13. See also, William Shea, "The Future of Graduate Education in Theology," in Carey and Muller, *Theological Education*, 131–44. Shea argues forcefully that doctoral education in theology must maintain a research orientation, retaining the training of *scholars* as its primary objective.

10. Robert P. Imbelli, "Theologians and Bishops," in Carey and Muller, *Theological Education*, 131–44.

11. I would not concede that this work is irrelevant to the lives of ordinary believers nor that my sensibilities as a scholar are not informed by my own broader identity as a faithful Catholic. At the same time, a distinction must be maintained between an academic audience and a church audience. For more on this distinction, see David Tracy, *The Analogical Imagination: Christian Theology and the Culture of Pluralism* (New York: Crossroad, 1991), 3–31.

12. Many of my colleagues and I already engage church groups and Catholic organizations (e.g., Catholic health care organizations) by giving workshops and by serving on committees. However, this takes place generally on an ad hoc basis or as an informal arrangement. Furthermore, this type of service is different from the practice of preaching I propose in that it takes place apart from the context of liturgy.

13. Cited in Kevin Kelly, "The Role of the Moral Theologian in the Life of the Church," in *History and Conscience: Studies in Honour of Sean O'Riordian, CSsR*, ed. Raphael Gallagher and Brenden McConvey (Dublin: Gill and Macmillan, 1989), 8. The full reference to the original source of this quote is missing from Kelly's article, although an abbreviated reference of "Ratzinger 1986, 765–68" is noted. Ratzinger expresses a similar opinion elsewhere, calling a theology cut off from ecclesial life and worship "sterile." See Joseph Cardinal Ratzinger, *The Nature and Mission of Theology* (San Francisco: Ignatius Press, 1995), 116.

14. Charles Curran, "The Ecclesial Context of Moral Theology," in *Method and Catholic Moral Theology: The Ongoing Reconstruction*, ed. Todd Salzman (Omaha, Neb.: Creighton University Press, 1999), 127.

15. Avery Dulles, *The Craft of Theology: From Symbol to System* (New York: Crossroad, 1995), 9. For a concise treatment of Dulles's work in this book and how it relates to the cultivation of a healthy relationship between theologians and the magisterium, see Imbelli, "Theologians and Bishops," 131–44.

16. Dulles, *Craft of Theology*, 9.

17. Pope, "Response to Ruddy," 12.

18. Pope, "Response to Ruddy," 12.

19. U.S. Conference of Catholic Bishops, *Ex Corde Ecclesiae: An Application to the United States* (Washington: USCC, 2001), part 1, section 4.

20. John Paul II has recently reaffirmed the understanding of lay spirituality that was put forward at the Second Vatican Council. In *Christifideles Laici*, he speaks of the lay vocation as a "call to holiness" rooted in a devotion to Christ through the church that is begun in baptism and nurtured through the sacraments and the Eucharist. Shaped by this call to holiness, the laity are then called to go out into the world and go about their work in the secular sphere in a way that will "continue the

redemptive work of Jesus Christ, which by its very nature concerns the salvation of humanity, and also involves the renewal of the whole temporal order." John Paul II, *Christifideles Laici* (December 30, 1988), sec. 15. This is clearly the dynamic envisioned in the *Apostolicam Actuositatem* (Decree on the Apostolate of Lay People), which speaks of a lay spirituality as a "life of intimate union with Christ in the Church" maintained by regular participation in the sacraments and the liturgy. This spirituality is paired with a vision of lay work as permeating the whole range of temporal affairs with the presence of Christ. See *Apostolicam Actuositatem*, in *Vatican Council II: The Conciliar and Post-conciliar Documents*, new rev. ed., ed. Austin Flannery (Collegeville, Minn.: Liturgical Press, 1992), secs. 4–5.

21. Paul J. Wadell, *Becoming Friends: Worship, Justice, and the Practice of Christian Friendship* (Grand Rapids, Mich.: Brazos Press, 2002), 15–37.

22. Wadell uses this image of the effect of the Eucharist, or "spiritual food." In contrast to the way in which the food that we eat ordinarily becomes a part of us, in eating the Eucharist we are changed to be more like Christ. The image is originally from Aquinas and his interpretation of Augustine's *Confessions*. See Thomas Aquinas, *Summa Theologiae* (New York: McGraw-Hill, 1963–1969), 3.73.3.

23. Congregation for the Doctrine of the Faith, "Instruction on the Ecclesial Vocation of the Theologian" (May 24, 1990), sec. 6.

24. Congregation for the Doctrine of the Faith, "Instruction," sec. 14.

25. This view also finds support in the documents of the Second Vatican Council— see *Dei Verbum* (Dogmatic Constitution on Divine Revelation), sec. 10. Robert Imbelli explains well the way in which bishops and theologians are both "bound to a common hearing and submission to the Word of God as it is conveyed in the sacred Scriptures, in tradition and in the *sensus fidei* of the whole redeemed people." Thus, neither theologians nor bishops are above the Word of God, but both seek to be worthy interpreters of Scripture and tradition. Imbelli, "Bishops and Theologians," 230. See also, Walter Brueggemann, *Interpretation and Obedience* (Minneapolis, Minn.: Fortress Press, 1991).

26. *Apostolicam Actuositatem*, sec. 7.

27. Stephen Vincent DeLeers, "The Place of Preaching in the Ministry and Life of Priests," in *The Theology of Priesthood*, ed. D. J. Goergen and A. Garrido (Collegeville, Minn.: Liturgical Press, 2000): 87–103.

28. DeLeers, "Place of Preaching," 100.

29. DeLeers, "Place of Preaching," 100

30. Both teaching and writing might be experienced subjectively by theologians as a form of prayer, but my point is that its presentation takes place typically in a formal academic context where those gathered do not necessarily share any faith commitments or necessarily perceive their common enterprise as prayerful. For a recent piece that examines writing as an expression of spirituality, see Stephanie Paulsell, "Writing as a Spiritual Discipline," in *The Scope of Our Art*, ed. L. G. Jones and S. Paulsell (Grand Rapids, Mich.: Eerdmans, 2002), 17–31.

31. Karl Rahner, *The Great Church Year: The Best of Karl Rahner's Homilies, Sermons, and Meditations* (New York: Crossroad, 1995).

32. Dietrich Bonhoeffer, *Worldly Preaching: Lectures on Homiletics*, ed. and trans. with critical commentary by Clyde E. Fant (New York: Crossroad, 1991), 119.

33. Mary Catherine Hilkert provides a helpful contrasting position by highlighting the dangers of an uncritical hermeneutics of trust. She calls for a hermeneutics of suspicion vis-à-vis biblical passages that have served as "texts of terror" for women, gays, Jews, and others. See Hilkert, *Naming Grace: Preaching and the Sacramental Imagination* (New York: Contiuum, 1997), 71–88. Hilkert's use of the term *texts of terror* refers to Phyllis Trible's work in this area. See Trible, *Texts of Terror* (Philadelphia: Fortress Press, 1984).

34. Bonhoeffer, *Worldly Preaching*, 120.

35. Gerard S. Sloyan, *Worshipful Preaching* (Philadelphia: Fortress Press, 1984), 39.

36. My description of how theologians should be hearers of the Word would not be universally accepted. For example, a liberationist approach to Scripture and preaching would likely place more emphasis on experience as the starting point or hermeneutical key for understanding the Scriptures (although the liberationist method involves an interplay between narrative and experience). See James H. Harris, *Preaching Liberation* (Minneapolis, Minn.: Fortress Press, 1995). Similarly, many feminist approaches to Scripture would place more emphasis on the authority of women's experience. See Elisabeth Schussler Fiorenza, *Bread Not Stone: The Challenge of Feminist Biblical Interpretation* (Boston: Beacon Press, 1984).

37. DeLeers, "Place of Preaching," 101–2. Edward Schillebeeckx makes the same point, noting that the authority to preach traditionally arose not from juridical authority but rather from the authority that emerges from the preacher's own "evangelical lifestyle." See Schillebeeckx, "The Right of Every Christian to Speak in the Light of Evangelical Experience 'in the Midst of Brothers and Sisters,'" in *Preaching and the Non-ordained*, ed. N. Foley (Collegeville, Minn.: Liturgical Press, 1983): 36–37.

38. I believe that an extensive description of what such preparation would entail is unnecessary and perhaps even presumptuous here. Such details could be worked out in due time if the concept of lay theologians preaching should come to be embraced by ecclesiastical authorities.

39. Francis E. George, "Bishops and Theologians," in Carey and Muller, *Theological Education*, 216. Archbishop Oscar Lipscomb expresses a similar sentiment in an essay in the same volume. See Lipscomb, "Faith: Normative for Bishops and Theologians," 237–42.

40. George, "Bishops and Theologians," 217.

41. Henderson, "Liturgical Preaching," 218. DeLeers, "Place of Preaching," 101.

42. Willard F. Jabusch, "Pappa Don't Preach," *Commonweal* 130, no. 6 (March 28, 2003): 31. See also, Arthur Jones, "Entrusting God's Word to the Entire Church," *National Catholic Reporter* 38, no. 5 (November 23, 2001): 12–13.

43. Mary Catherine Hilkert maintains that lay people including women preached in New Testament times. She cites 1 Corinthians 11:3–6 as one piece of evidence (the passage speaks of "a woman who prays or prophesies" publicly, admonishing such women for doing so with their heads uncovered). See Hilkert, *Naming Grace*, 147–49. For a more detailed treatment of New Testament evidence that women preached, see Elisabeth Schüssler Fiorenza, *In Memory of Her: A Feminist Reconstruction of Christian Origins* (New York: Crossroad, 1994), esp. 226–36; and Hilkert, "Women Preaching the Gospel," *Theology Digest* 33 (1986): 65–91. On the question of preaching by both women and lay men, see Sandra Schneiders, "New Testament

Foundations for Preaching by the Non-ordained," in Foley, *Preaching and the Non-ordained*, 60–90.

44. Yves Congar, *Lay People in the Church: A Study for a Theology of Laity*, rev. ed., trans. Donald Attwater (Westminster, Md.: Newman Press, 1965), 298–302. For a thorough discussion of the rise of lay preaching during this period and the controversies concerning it, see William Skudlarek, "Assertion without Knowledge? The Lay Preaching Controversy of the High Middle Ages," (Ph.D. diss., Princeton University, 1979). For a more concise treatment, see Schillebeeckx, "Right of Every Christian," 11–47.

45. William Skudlarek, "Lay Preaching and the Liturgy," *Worship* 58 (1984): 501.

46. For a recent discussion of the state of this distinction, see Jack Risley, "The Minister: Lay and Ordained," in *The Theology of Priesthood*, ed. Donald J. Goergen and Ann Garrido (Collegeville, Minn.: Liturgical Press, 2000), 119–37. In the same volume, see also, Benedict M. Ashley, "The Priesthood of Christ, the Baptized and the Ordained," 139–64.

47. James H. Provost, "Lay Preaching and Canon Law in a Time of Transition," in Foley, *Preaching and the Non-ordained*, 135.

48. *Lumen Gentium*, secs. 32 and 10. See also, *Christifideles Laici*, sec. 14, where it was more recently affirmed that the lay faithful have a share in the threefold mission of Christ as priest, prophet, and king.

49. Provost, "Lay Preaching," 138–41.

50. Provost, "Lay Preaching," 141. See also, Patrick F. Norris, "Lay Preaching and Canon Law: Who May Give a Homily?" *Studia Canonica* 24 (1990): 447. It is canon 766 that specifically permits lay persons "to preach in a church or oratory if it is necessary in certain circumstances or if it is useful in particular cases according to the prescriptions of the conference of bishops and with due regard for c. 767, sec. 1" (the canon that restricts the preaching of a homily to ordained members of the community.

51. Norris, "Lay Preaching," 447 (see canon 767). See also, Henderson, "Liturgical Preaching," 218–19.

52. John Paul II, *Instruction on Certain Questions Regarding the Collaboration of the Non-ordained Faithful in the Sacred Ministry of Priest* (August 15, 1997), art. 3, secs. 1–2. The freedom to allow lay testimonials "on special occasions" is explicitly permitted so long as "these testimonies or explanations may not be such so as to assume a character which could be confused with the homily" (sec. 2).

53. Those employing a hermeneutics of suspicion might interpret the instruction as an attempt to eliminate lay aspirations to speak authoritatively or exercise power within the church or even to see themselves as ministers in any sense on par with ordained ministers. The instruction's insistence that it is "unlawful for the non-ordained faithful to assume titles such as pastor, chaplain, coordinator, moderator or other such similar titles" (art. 1, sec. 3), despite the fact that lay people may in fact be acting in those roles, is particularly telling.

54. Provost, "Lay Preaching," 146 and 150.

55. Provost, "Lay Preaching," 150. William Skudlarek disagrees with Provost's assessment of the flexibility of the current Code of Canon Law but agrees with his assessment of the gravity of the need for better preachers who have a variety of lived experiences. He writes, "Ultimately, the real issue, I believe, is not whether or not lay

people should be able to preach in the liturgical assembly, but whether or not the church will maintain its policy of ordaining only unmarried men to the ministry of word and sacrament." See Skudlarek, "Lay Preaching," 595.

56. Provost, "Lay Preaching," 148.

57. United States Conference of Catholic Bishops, "Canon 766—Lay Preaching," released December 13, 2001, at www.usccb.org/norms/766.htm.

58. Norris, "Lay Preaching," 454. For Norris's exact criticisms of Provost's thinking, see 450–51.

59. Norris, "Lay Preaching," 453.

60. Schneiders, "New Testament Foundations," 61.

61. Schneiders, "New Testament Foundations," 61.

62. Schillebeeckx, "Right of Every Christian," 33. The "other questions and interests" to which Schillebeeckx refers are primarily issues about jurisdiction and authority. With the rise of the Dominican and Franciscan orders, which existed as trans-diocesan entities with a mission of preaching, the question arose as to the basis of the authority to preach. Was it possible for the pope to grant such authority over and against the wishes of local bishops? Was the right to preach based on priestly ordination as such? Schillebeeckx describes the resulting decisions on these and related matters as pertaining to the specific intraecclesial disputes of the time (between Rome and local bishops, diocesan priests and the preaching orders, etc.).

63. Norris, "Lay Preaching," 451. Mary Catherine Hilkert argues that one of the strongest reasons supporting the expansion of the pool of those eligible to preach is theological. She writes that the imaging of Jesus and the Word in a new person can release new aspects of the Gospel that were previously hidden. See Hilkert, *Naming Grace*, 164.

64. DeLeers, "Place of Preaching," 102.

# 3

# Transparent Mediation: The Vocation of the Theologian as Disciple

*Margaret R. Pfeil*

When the Congregation for the Doctrine of the Faith released the "Instruction on the Ecclesial Vocation of the Theologian" in 1990, Cardinal Ratzinger vigorously resisted the notion that the theological vocation pivoted on the juridical issue of consenting to or dissenting from magisterial teaching. "The panorama is much wider and much more beautiful than that. . . . A theologian would have to be somewhat stupid if he didn't see new terrain to be explored."[1]

Venturing forth into new theological territory requires the intelligence and spiritual vision of a true Christian disciple. Like the way of Jesus, the path of those who choose to follow him leads to the cross, and the light of the cross beckons the believer forward. Only eyes grown accustomed to spiritual darkness can perceive this luminous quality of the cross.

Times of ecclesial impasse afford theologians an extraordinary opportunity to see anew the meaning of their vocation reflected in the panorama unfolding before them, at once beautiful and dreadful. Precisely in the darkness of the church's institutional brokenness, the theologian's vocational journey comes into sharper focus. In conversation with the work of Constance FitzGerald, I consider points of correlation between John of the Cross's account of the spiritual dark night and a particular experience of ecclesial impasse that reveals one possible meaning of the theological vocation as a call to transparent mediation of God's love.

## AN EXPERIENCE OF ECCLESIAL IMPASSE

On Easter Monday 2001, an American cardinal invited more than ninety
Catholic theologians of his archdiocese to discuss the implementation of *Ex
corde ecclesiae*. He began the day by extending a warm welcome, noting
that it was the first time that he had met with theologians of his archdiocese
in more than sixteen years as the local ordinary. He assured them that he val-
ued their insights into the *sensus fidelium*, and he looked forward to cultivating a relationship with them.

As the day's events unfolded, though, these worthy aims receded steadily
from any hope of fulfillment. The encounter was carefully structured to foster a starkly different kind of relationship. The theologians had submitted
questions in advance, to which the cardinal gave prepared responses. The
format included small-group discussion, but the points relayed in the subsequent plenary session did not meet with any substantive response.

In his prepared remarks, the cardinal repeatedly invoked canon law as his
principal point of departure in addressing the theologians' largely pastoral
concerns. One example was particularly striking. Alluding to the website
mandata.org, the theologians asked if the cardinal would take measures to
protect their reputations in the face of public attempts to discredit or coerce
them.[2] He responded by citing canon 220 and did not elaborate further, apparently presuming that such legal assurance should suffice.

Those well versed in ecclesiastical law remembered canon 220: "No one is
permitted to damage unlawfully the good reputation which another person
enjoys nor to violate the right of another person to protect his or her own privacy." But, the letter of this law did little to allay the concern expressed. The
theologians were seeking some indication that the cardinal would defend
the integrity of their conscientious discernment regarding the *mandatum* by
precluding coercive efforts within the church to intimidate them. Since
canon 220 would be invoked principally in the event that one's reputation
had already been assailed, such legal recourse would be of little solace or
practical value.

The central issue, from the theologians' perspective, was not legal but
moral. They were expecting charity rather than juridicism from the cardinal.
Charity, after all, constitutes the heart of canon law. "That love which Christ
enjoined upon His disciples, and for which the Christian community strives,
is another way of describing the ultimate purpose of the Church's law," James
Coriden writes.[3] When the law falls short of protecting essential communal
values, such as the primacy of conscience and one's good reputation, Christian charity remains as the church's fundamental ethical guide for action.

The theologians who gathered that Easter Monday experienced cognitive
dissonance. The "Instruction on the Ecclesial Vocation of the Theologian"
had affirmed the hope that they might enter into "trustful dialogue with the

pastors in the spirit of truth and charity," especially in the face of theological difficulties.[4] Yet, after having voiced a desire for a broadly based relationship with them, the cardinal seemed to abandon this language and vision in practice, choosing instead to communicate in constrained legal terms. The fact that the rubrics of the day's events did not permit the theologians to further explain their concerns in dialogical fashion underscored the narrow scope of the encounter. If a relationship between this local ordinary and theologians was being forged, it was to be strictly juridical.

## AN ECCLESIAL DARK NIGHT

The reduction of the relationship between bishops and theologians to legal formalities reveals a profound spiritual impasse in the life of the church. As Constance FitzGerald describes, this kind of crisis point means

> that there is no way out of, no way around, no rational escape from, what imprisons one, no possibilities in the situation. In a true impasse, every normal manner of acting is brought to a standstill, and ironically, impasse is experienced not only in the problem itself but also in any solution rationally attempted. Every logical solution remains unsatisfying, at the very least. The whole life situation suffers a depletion, has the word *limits* written upon it. . . . Any movement out, any next step, is canceled, and the most dangerous temptation is to give up, to quit, to surrender to cynicism and despair, in the face of the disappointment, disenchantment, hopelessness, and loss of meaning that encompass one.[5]

These limit situations prove spiritually liminal, laden with the promise of new modes of relationality. Drawing on John of the Cross's image of the dark night, FitzGerald has shown that a moment of impasse presents an opportunity to be transformed through the purifying truth of humble surrender and to gain clarity of insight in the process. The dynamics of the spiritual dark night apply to interpersonal and societal impasses, and they also find resonance in ecclesial moments of liminality.

According to John of the Cross, there are three signs by which one may discern whether he or she is experiencing the purifying passage in prayer from meditation to contemplation, and by correlation, this dark night experience illuminates the theologians' Easter Monday impasse. First, one enters a profound dryness or emptiness that cannot be satisfied or alleviated through one's usual spiritual practices and discursive forms of meditation.[6] This marks the beginning of the purgation of the dark night. Deprived of sensory satisfaction, the person will be driven deeper and inward to find God.

Second, the person remains strong and focused spiritually, striving continually to turn to God in spite of an utter emptiness that pervades his or her experiences, both interior and exterior.[7] It is precisely in this utter desiccation that one can find a way forward to new life if one "knows how to remain quiet."[8] This stage constitutes the transformative crucible of the dark night experience. FitzGerald emphasizes that "right in this situation of unassuaged emptiness and apparent deadness of desire, in the very area of life in which one is most involved and therefore most vulnerable, desire is being purified, transformed, and carried into deeper, more integrated passion."[9] Finally, still unable to advance through the usual methods of discursive meditation, the person totally surrenders in loving, peaceful awareness of God, an experience of radical openness to God's gracious action.[10]

As perceived through the Easter Monday encounter, the crux of the dark night experience seemed to be located in the dissonance between the language and expectation of the fullness of relationship, on the one hand, and the narrow juridical perspective that governed the day's events, on the other hand. The latter precipitated a profound emptiness that became acutely apparent precisely in the awareness of a genuine desire to cultivate a meaningful relationship between the local ordinary and the theologians in service of the church. This spiritual chasm between the desired end and the lived reality, coupled with the relentless but apparently futile effort to break through the impasse, coincides with the first and second signs of the purifying dark night experience.

For John of the Cross, God's love draws the believer into the dark night precisely to strip away all that would keep the person from falling more deeply in love with God. One of the most painful aspects of the Easter Monday impasse grew from the subordination of charity to juridicism throughout the meeting. Love's felt absence revealed and reinforced a distinct lack of trust on the part of both the cardinal and the theologians. Each side seemed braced for the worst from the other. At one point, the cardinal even commended the theologians on their decorum, as if he had expected them to grow contentious.

Perhaps sensing the reality of impasse, the cardinal had anticipated some outward manifestation of it. As FitzGerald observes, the dark night experience of emptiness can reveal one's shadow side: "Is it any wonder we witness the effects of impasse among us—anger, confusion, violence—since real impasse or dark night highlights destructive tendencies? Frustrated desire fights back."[11] At such moments of crisis, the chasm between the desired end and the lived reality may lead one to turn away from the risk of love's freedom in order to rest in the familiar, enslaving grip of interior attachments of ego. In this particular impasse, both the local ordinary and the theologians faced the real temptation to resort to violence in word and spirit precisely to defend aspects of their vocational identities that they perceived to be threatened.

Violent actions tend to elicit violent responses, René Girard has noted.[12] Unfortunately, it is not difficult to find examples of such mimetic violence at work in the life of the church. In the case at hand, neither the local ordinary nor the theologians took the courageous steps necessary to break the powerful vortex of mutual distrust. Left unchecked, it fed on itself through the course of the day. No wonder, then, that the cardinal sought some modicum of consolation in the theologians' civility.

The palpable suspicion between a representative of the hierarchical magisterium and theologians at a meeting convened ostensibly to forge a closer relationship between the two parties ran directly counter to the particular calling of all concerned to serve the mission of the church. The grip of impasse found them at some remove from the hopeful vision put forth by the National Conference of Catholic Bishops: "Bishops and theologians involved in ongoing collaboration are likely to grow in respect and trust for one another and thus to assist and support their respective service to the Gospel."[13] Rather than bearing witness to the truth and charity of the Gospel, the local church's shepherd and theologians verged on giving scandal.

But the Easter Monday encounter did not end there, for there is some evidence of correspondence with John of the Cross's third sign of the spiritual dark night, the promise of new life born of impasse. "Darkness is the place where egoism dies and true unselfish love for the 'other' is set free," FitzGerald writes. "Moreover, it is the birthplace of a vision and a hope that cannot be imagined this side of darkness."[14]

From the spiritual darkness of that Easter Monday emerges the beginning of a new vision, if not the full panorama, of the theologian's vocation as a disciple drawn by God's love to surrender attachments of ego. Precisely in broken, violent ecclesial relationships, theologians with eyes grown accustomed to the darkness of the cross can discern the movement of God's love freeing humans from the slavery of selfishness so that they might mediate that love transparently.

## TRANSPARENT MEDIATION:
## THE VOCATION OF THE THEOLOGIAN AS DISCIPLE

Near the end of his life, Karl Rahner was asked what he found lacking in his theological and priestly work. He responded, "I'd like to have had more love and more courage in my life, especially with respect to those who have authority in the Church. But I'd also like to have shown a deeper understanding of the contemporary person and his or her way of thinking."[15]

Rahner's wisdom of hindsight offers a glimpse into the theologian's way forward into new terrain. Called in baptism to a life of discipleship as a member of the People of God, the theologian responds in a particular way by offering herself or himself as a conduit. As the U.S. bishops have indicated, the theologian "seeks to mediate, through the discipline of scholarship, between a living faith and the culture it is called to transform (*Gaudium et spes* 44, 62)."[16]

This theological mediating function unfolds in the contexts of both society and the church. Within society, as *Gaudium et spes* 62 emphasizes, theologians play an essential role as scholar-believers in mediating understandings of faith in ways intelligible within their particular cultural circumstances.[17] Using the tools of their academic discipline, theologians are called to convey the church's living tradition in a manner that will bear fruit in a given time and place. "When we study the traditions and the cumulative wisdom of the past," Monika Hellwig writes, "it is with a view to evaluating how that past serves the needs of the present. That is Catholic fidelity, and that is the heart of the enterprise."[18]

In exercising this interpretive function within society, the theologian's departure point as a member of the People of God is always located within the church itself. Intraecclesially, theology entails a twofold process of mediation between the magisterium and the People of God.[19] First, as Paul VI noted when he addressed theologians immediately following Vatican II, theology serves as a bridge between the faith of the church and the magisterium. "It earnestly seeks to discover how the Christian community might translate its faith into practice, and it tries to grasp the truths, opinions, questions, and tendencies which the Holy Spirit stirs up in the People of God." Second, theology brings the scholarly tools of critical interpretation to bear in rendering doctrine intelligible to the church.[20]

The task of serving society and the church as a scholar-believer takes root in each theologian's journey with God. Like other expressions of Christian vocation, theological discipleship entails an intimate personal response to the experience of God's love in accordance with one's particular charisms, the multiplicity of gifts freely given by the Holy Spirit for service to the church (1 Corinthians 12).[21] These may accent and coincide with natural abilities, but they are distinguished precisely as charisms by their essential direction toward the common good of the ecclesial community.[22] Since their purpose is to serve the church, there is nothing accidental about the gifts of the Spirit. As Avery Dulles has rightly noted, "It would be a mistake to imagine that charisms are always given in an unconvenanted and unpredictable way, without regard for a person's status and official responsibilities."[23]

Taking shape around these gifts of the Spirit, the theological calling is intensely personal but always ecclesially oriented. Faith draws each disciple to nurture his or her gifts not as private possessions but rather as instruments of God's love for God's people. Jesus's witness invites the theologian as disciple to mediate transparently God's love through the Spirit's gifts. To the extent that inordinate attachments of ego interfere with the free expression of charisms, the theologian's service to the church will suffer. To paraphrase Monika Hellwig, the best theologian is the forgotten one: "It must finally be said that the theologian is most successful and most acceptable when no longer visible, because the ideas have been assimilated so that they are no longer credited to a particular person. It may be a hard saying, but our destiny is to surrender what is intellectually our own, and to die and disappear."[24] Jesus asks nothing less of his followers than that they take up the cross and renounce all that would interfere with the radical freedom to say yes to the Reign of God.[25]

The Christian tradition bears abundant witness to the truth of total surrender as a constitutive dimension of discipleship. In his account of the journey toward wholeness in God, John of the Cross regarded complete renunciation of attachments as essential.[26] The path of Jesus's followers leads to the cross by way of love's freedom. When the disciple "is brought to nothing, the highest degree of humility, the spiritual union between his soul and God will be effected. . . . The journey, then, does not consist in recreations, experiences, and spiritual feelings, but in the living, sensory and spiritual, exterior and interior death of the cross."[27]

Transparent mediation of God's love constitutes the essence of the theologian's vocation as disciple because it is the way of Jesus. On the journey to God, John of the Cross writes, one "makes progress only through imitation of Christ Who is the Way, the Truth, and the Life. No one goes to the Father but through Him, as He states himself in St. John [John 14:6]. Elsewhere He says: *I am the door, if any man enter by Me he shall be saved* [John 10:9]."[28]

A radical liminality marks the theological call, and it comes into sharper focus precisely in the limit situation of ecclesial impasse. The theologian as disciple at once enters through the door that is Jesus Christ while also opening a way forward for others on the journey with and to God.[29] A beautiful image from Seamus Heaney comes to mind here: "All these things entered you / As if they were both the door and what came through it. / They marked the spot, marked time and held it open."[30] As a portal marking God's time, the theologian as disciple holds open a passageway toward new terrain for other followers of Jesus.

But, departing from John of the Cross's description of the disciple's imitation of Christ, the theologian performs this service as another *follower* of Jesus, not as an imitator. The disciple does not mimic the one being followed but must rather adapt to the particular circumstances encountered along his or her own journey and in accord with his or her own discrete gifts and calling. "By 'following' Christ," Walter Ong writes, "a person participates in the life of Jesus not simply by reduplicating the historical life of Christ, as the term 'imitation' would suggest, but by entering into his or her own life so as to make it an extension of Christ's life."[31]

One's ongoing response to Jesus's invitation to discipleship takes shape within a particular ecclesial context. Moments of spiritual impasse within the church impel the disciple to discern anew what it means to follow Jesus. As an experience of ecclesial impasse, the Easter Monday encounter yields a transformative understanding of the theologian's vocation: The theologian as disciple is called to transparent mediation of God's love both in society and within the church in accordance with his or her particular charisms, leading the way forward into new terrain.

The illumination of this meaning of theological vocation in the midst of that Easter Monday's darkness reveals fresh ground on which theologians might nurture authentic relationships with their local ordinaries. In naming and surrendering all the personal and ecclesial attachments that would keep them from mediating God's love transparently, theologians will remain true to their vocation. They will be free to witness to the proper ordering of ecclesial life according to Christian charity. They will be free to mediate God's love for God's people in service of the church's mission.

## NOTES

1. Cardinal Joseph Ratzinger, press conference given in Rome, June 26, 1990, reprinted in *Origins* 20 (July 5, 1990): 120.

2. Even before the U.S. bishops voted on implementation of the *mandatum*, Fr. John Stryjewski, a priest from the Mobile, Alabama, diocese, developed the website, mandata.org, to publicly track whether theologians teaching at Catholic institutions of higher education had been granted a *mandatum*.

3. James A. Coriden, Thomas J. Green, and Donald E. Heintschel, eds., *The Code of Canon Law: A Text and Commentary* (New York: Paulist Press, 1985).

4. Congregation for the Doctrine of the Faith, "Instruction on the Ecclesial Vocation of the Theologian," *Origins* 20 (July 5, 1990): 125.

5. Constance FitzGerald, "Impasse and Dark Night," in *Women's Spirituality: Resources for Christian Development*, 2nd ed., ed. Joann Wolski Conn (New York: Paulist Press, 1996), 411.

6. St. John of the Cross, *Ascent of Mt. Carmel* 13.2 and *The Dark Night* 1.9.2 in *The Collected Works of St. John of the Cross*, trans. Kieran Kavanaugh, OCD, and Otilio Rodriguez, OCD (Garden City, N.Y.: Doubleday, 1964). All subsequent references to these texts will be taken from this volume. See also, FitzGerald, "Impasse and Dark Night," 416–17.

7. St. John of the Cross, *Ascent of Mt. Carmel*, 13, 3; *Dark Night*, 1, 9, 3.

8. St. John of the Cross, *Dark Night*, 1, 9, 6.

9. FitzGerald, "Impasse and Dark Night," 419.

10. St. John of the Cross, *Ascent of Mt. Carmel*, 13, 4; *The Dark Night*, 1, 9, 8–9.

11. FitzGerald, "Impasse and Dark Night," 423–24 (cf. St. John of the Cross, *Dark Night*, 1, 14).

12. René Girard, *Violence and the Sacred*, trans. Patrick Gregory (Baltimore: Johns Hopkins University Press, 1977), 81. See also, "Mimesis and Violence," in *The Girard Reader*, ed. James G. Williams (New York: Crossroad, 1996), 9–19. For insight into the

interrelationship of ego, possession, and violence, see Dorothy Soelle, *The Silent Cry: Mysticism and Resistance*, trans. Barbara Rumscheidt and Martin Rumscheidt (Minneapolis, Minn.: Fortress Press, 2001).

13. National Conference of Catholic Bishops, "Doctrinal Responsibilities: Approaches to Promoting Cooperation and Resolving Misunderstandings between Bishops and Theologians," *Origins* 19 (June 29, 1989): 103.

14. FitzGerald, "Impasse and Dark Night," 418.

15. Karl Rahner, "The High Point of an Eighty-Year-Old Theologian's Life" (interview with the editors of *Vida Nueva*, Madrid, March 1984), trans. Roland J. Teske, SJ, in *Faith in a Wintry Season: Conversations and Interviews with Karl Rahner in the Last Years of His Life*, ed. Paul Imhof and Hubert Biallowons (New York: Crossroad, 1990), 39.

16. National Conference of Catholic Bishops, "Doctrinal Responsibilities," 101.

17. *Gaudium et spes*, in *Catholic Social Thought*, ed. Thomas Shannon and David O'Brien (Maryknoll, N.Y.: Orbis Books, 1992), para. 62. See also, *Ad gentes* in *Vatican Council II*, vol. 1, rev. ed., ed. Austin Flannery, OP (Collegeville, Ind.: Liturgical Press, 1992,), para. 22.

18. Monika K. Hellwig, *The Role of the Theologian in Today's Church* (Kansas City, Mo.: Sheed & Ward, 1987), 36. This text was given as the presidential address at the 1987 Annual Convention of the Catholic Theological Society of America.

19. International Theological Commission, *Theses on the Relationship between the Ecclesiastical Magisterium and Theology* (Washington, D.C.: USCC, 1977), thesis 5, no. 2.

20. Paul VI, "Theology: A Bridge between Faith and Authority" (address to the International Congress on the Theology of Vatican II, October 1, 1966) *The Pope Speaks* 11 (1966): 351–52.

21. Compare Hans Küng, "The Charismatic Structure of the Church," in *The Church and Ecumenism*, Concilium 4 (New York: Paulist Press, 1965), 51.

22. Margaret M. Mitchell, "'Be Zealous for the Greater *Charismata*': Pauline Advice for the Church in the Twenty-first Century," in *Retrieving Charisms for the Twenty-first Century*, ed. Doris Donnelly (Collegeville, Minn.: Liturgical Press, 1999), 22; John C. Haughey, SJ, "Charisms: An Ecclesiological Exploration," in Donnelly, *Retrieving Charisms*, 2. See also, Avery Dulles, SJ, "The Charism of the New Evangelizer," in Donnelly, *Retrieving Charisms*, 36; and Rene Laurentin, "Charisms: Terminological Precision," trans. Theo Weston, in *Charisms in the Church*, Concilium 109, ed. Christian Duquoc and Casiano Floristan (New York: Seabury Press, 1978), 7–8.

23. Dulles, "Charism," 34–35.

24. Hellwig, *Role of the Theologian*, 42–43.

25. See, for example, Mark 8:34–38, Matt. 16:24–26, and Luke 9:23–26.

26. John M. Lozano, CMF, "John of the Cross: A Radical Reinterpretation of Discipleship," in *John of the Cross: Conferences and Essays by Members of the Institute of Carmelite Studies and Others*, Carmelite Studies 6, ed. Steven Payne, OCD (Washington, D.C.: ICS Publications, 1992), 123–140, at 127 and 138.

27. St. John of the Cross, *Ascent of Mt. Carmel*, 2, 7, 11.

28. St. John of the Cross, *Ascent of Mt. Carmel*, 2, 7, 8.

29. As Enda McDonagh puts it, "In specifically Christian terms the best expression of the end of all theologising is the making of disciples" (*The Making of Disciples: Tasks of Moral Theology* [Wilmington, Del.: Michael Glazier, 1982], 2).

30. Seamus Heaney, "Markings," in *Opened Ground: Selected Poems, 1966–1996* (New York: Farrar, Straus and Giroux, 1998), 312–13.

31. Walter Ong, "Mimesis and the Following of Christ (1994)," in *Faith and Contexts*, vol. 4, ed. Thomas J. Farrell and Paul A. Soukup (Atlanta, Ga.: Scholars Press, 1992), 178.

# 4

## Dare We Hope Our Students Believe? Patristic Rhetoric in the Contemporary Classroom

*William C. Mattison III*

What is the relationship between our teaching and our students' faith? The question at hand concerns the extent to which our students' beliefs in fundamental propositions about God, humanity, and so forth, should or does serve as a goal of a Catholic professor of theology teaching at a Catholic university. Given the nature of the theologian's subject matter, one would not be surprised if engagement with the material in a theology class were to prompt some sort of change of heart in the student. However, this is far from saying such change is the goal, or a goal, of the teacher. In fact, one might immediately object that the goal of a teacher can never be an increase of faith in the heart of the student, since (at least for Christians) faith is traditionally regarded as a gift from God. This is certainly true. I will not enter my classroom next term and consider it my primary goal to convert or renew the faith commitments of the students in each of my classes. However, I would indeed be thrilled should the study involved in my course enkindle a student's faith. Should, then, this "hope" shape how I teach?

Too often the only two possibilities envisioned for a teacher's attention to students' faith lives are either proselytizing manipulation of their freedom or radical disengagement from students' beliefs in theological material in order not to do violence to their freedom in assenting to or rejecting foundational theological affirmations. Is it possible for the Catholic theology professor to engage her students at the level of faith without doing so in a manipulative or violent fashion? In fairness it must be recognized that for the Catholic professor, presumably an engagement at the level of faith entails at least some hope that one's students assent to the Catholic faith. One sees why the path of radical disengagement from students' faith commitments is alluring, given the religious diversity present in even the most predominantly Catholic of American universities.

One thesis of this article is that a strategy of nonengagement with students' faith commitments while studying theological material is not only impossible but undesirable. The first section explains what exactly is meant by engaging students "at the level of faith." The second section argues why the professor of theology should not prescind from engaging students at this level. However, since such engagement is necessarily directive, there is understandable hesitation to engage students at this level. Thus the third section delineates what constitutes manipulative engagement of students' faiths. We are then left with the question of how a theologian can engage students at the level of faith in a manner that is not manipulative.

In response to the situation delineated in the first three sections, the fourth section of this chapter presents a vision of "Christian rhetoric," relying primarily on the work of St. Augustine and St. Gregory Nazianzen. It may seem odd to suggest that the use of rhetoric can help a teacher engage students in a nonmanipulative fashion. Yet as will be seen here, an understanding of the proper occasion for rhetorical discourse reveals that rhetoric is most appropriate for such an engagement. Further, Augustine and Gregory transformed the pagan rhetoric of their day so that it was not only the most effective but, more importantly, the most truthful vehicle for teaching about God and God's relationship to humanity. Their work is of great help in addressing the dilemma posed by the first three sections of this chapter.

Finally, the fifth section presents a (relatively) contemporary example of "Christian rhetoric." Over the past several years, I have assigned C. S. Lewis's *Mere Christianity* over a dozen times to undergraduate students in three different courses.[1] In style and content, Lewis's book exemplifies the sort of Christian rhetoric that is portrayed in the previous section of this piece. It is hoped that a concrete example of Christian rhetoric will further illuminate the argument in the fourth section and provide a particular text with which to extend or criticize the claims of this chapter about the proper stance of the Catholic theologian in the classroom.

## ENGAGING STUDENTS "AT THE LEVEL OF FAITH"

What is meant by the claim here that the Catholic theology professor ought to "engage students at the level of their faith"? St. Thomas Aquinas claims that faith is a stable disposition to certain acts of belief. So to best understand faith, one must understand what is involved in an act of belief. According to Thomas, "to believe" is "to think with assent."[2] Here Thomas defines "to think" as the "movement of the mind while yet deliberating, and not yet perfected by the clear sight of truth."[3] Yet even in the absence of "perfection by clear sight," such thinking occurs "with assent" or with the firm cleaving that marks demonstrable knowledge, or *scientia*. Thomas distinguishes *scientia* from other sorts of knowledge.[4] Among these latter forms of thought, Thomas distinguishes doubt, suspicion, opinion, and belief, depending on one's level of assent:

> Some acts of the intellect have unformed thought devoid of a firm assent, whether they incline one to neither side as in doubt; or incline one to one side rather than the other, but on account of some slight motive, as in one who suspects; or incline one to one side yet with fear of the other, as in one who opines. But this act to believe cleaves firmly to one side, in which respect belief has something in common with *scientia*; yet its knowledge does not attain the perfection of clear sight, wherein it agrees with doubt, suspicion, and opinion.[5]

Thus, belief does cleave firmly despite the absence of "clear sight." Whence this cleaving that so resembles *scientia*? Unlike *scientia*, where the demonstrability of the material at hand suffices to move the intellect, in instances of belief "the intellect of the believer is determined to one object not by reason, but by the will, wherefore assent is taken here for an act of the intellect as determined to one object by the will."[6] Faith is not purely an intellectual activity, although it is primarily this.[7] It also involves the will. Belief is "willful assent."[8] One believes a proposition about God, salvation, and so forth, not only as true (the object of the intellect) but also as good (the object of the will), which leads one to cling to the belief despite the lack of "perfection of clear sight."

What does this imply for one's teaching? The Catholic theologian invites students to think about an incomprehensible God and related questions that are not fully demonstrable or, in other words, that do not involve the "perfection of clear sight." Intellectual inquiry on its own, without involvement of the will, will not suffice to generate assent. Engaging students at the level of faith means challenging them not only to intellectually engage the material at hand but also to engage it with their wills in acts of belief (or disbelief). Students of theology should indeed ratiocinate about different sides of an argument, demonstrating an understanding of both sides and an awareness of the complexity of the issue at hand. These abilities are crucial and form an important goal in higher education. Yet the theology professor's "material" is such that intellectual inquiry alone does not suffice. It is only properly presented as eliciting (or repelling) the belief of the student. This belief involves both the intellect and the will of the student. Intellectually, the university theologian must rigorously challenge students to better understand the stakes, problems, and nuances of theology. Yet if theology is taught as an intellectual pursuit that does not demand some volitional response on the part of inquirer, the teacher actually fails to do justice to the type of knowledge that is the object of theology.

Teachers and students too frequently lament the stale character of introductory theology classes. It is suggested here that this reflects an inchoate awareness that material is often presented without attention to the assent of faith. Students seek not simply an intellectual grasp of relevant concepts or historical critical methods but a "hot" knowledge, which not only is grasped but also moves and influences. They recognize, even if they are unable to articulate it, that an encounter with the subject matter of theology should move them with conviction and not simply lead to greater understanding. Engaging students at the level of faith means challenging them to intellectually explore questions whose answers are not achievable by one's intellect alone but require also an act of belief.[9] It just so happens that theology is full of such questions, from the Arian controversy, to the resurrection of the body, to whether or not there is meaning in life.

## DISENGAGED THEOLOGY—MORE
## PREVALENT THAN YOU MIGHT THINK

What is one to do when exploring a question that is not fully demonstrable by one's reason? Or better, when one's intellect is "unformed," leaving one "devoid of full assent," from where comes that assent? Traditionally, this question has been answered by some sort of authority. The nature of authority is far beyond the scope of this chapter, but it should be noted that though authority is presented here as a source of truth claims not fully accessible to one's reason, one should not assume that authority is therefore unreasonable or antireasonable or based solely on power. We appeal to authorities all the time, as when out of town and asking a local resident for directions, when consulting a doctor, or when seeking the advice of a friend. Authority can be based on experience, knowledge, or even friendship. Of course, authority can also be powerfully manipulative, and it is not difficult to find historical examples of coercive religious authority.[10] Fear of such coercion frequently drives people to do "disengaged theology."

I call here *disengaged theology* the study of God and God's relation to humanity in a manner that aims to obviate the involvement of willful assent, particularly given the influence of potentially manipulative authority on such assent. There are several manners in which theology may be disengaged from the assent of belief and protected from the will's "susceptibility" to authority. What they have in common is the attempt to circumscribe acts of belief and the role of the will in the study of foundational human questions.

One version of disengaged theology brackets the importance of willful assent in academic study of religion by employing more epistemologically grounded disciplines. Such study can be of great service for better understanding religion. There are innumerable scholars today who study religion through the lenses of sociology, psychology, economics, and so forth. What they have in common is the use of an intellectual discipline based on a scientific methodology to better understand religion.[11] The results of such inquiries are not based on acts of intellect and will but rather simply the intellect.[12] While the fruits of such study are enormously helpful, one must recognize what those fruits are and are not. The central questions of theology cannot be definitively answered with such scientific disciplines alone. Given that we lack the perfection of clear sight, intellectual inquiry alone cannot engender assent to answers to questions such as "Is Jesus Christ the Son of God?" or "Is there life after death?" This does not preclude the importance of rigorous intellectual discourse concerning such questions; in fact, it further necessitates it. But it is to say that the study of religion that fails to recognize the necessary role of the will in answering such questions fails to adequately grasp the nature of theological questions.

This depiction of disengaged theology is a sort of caricature of what some theologians derisively connote by the label "religious studies." This derision is unfortunate, as professors of religious studies who do not reduce all theological inquiry to scientific methodology or who subversively seek to eliminate the inevitable presence of belief (or disbelief) in questions of theology do make important contributions to the study of religious belief and religious communities. Yet the skepticism of theologians is warranted to the extent that religious studies scholars do dismiss the importance of belief for their topics of study.

This brief description of an attempt to obviate the role of will and faith in theological inquiry is perhaps the most obvious example of disengaged theology. But there is a more subtle version of disengaged theology, one that is more prevalent in Catholic universities today. While Catholic professors of theology generally do not reject the importance of faith in people's lives, they frequently fail to engage their students' faith convictions while doing theology, even though this is a necessary component of asking and answering questions about God and God's relationship to humanity. Their thinking is that questions of faith are best addressed outside the academic environment. The benefit of this approach is its recognition of the importance of rigorous intellectual inquiry regarding questions of faith. Too often students are not practiced in examining such questions in an intellectually thorough manner. Yet such inquiry only becomes more than an "academic" (in the pejorative sense of the word) exercise, only does justice to the nature of the material at hand, if presented as enabling students to better answer foundational theological propositions that require an act of faith involving both intellect and will.

Consider these common goals of contemporary theology courses:

1. We will teach the students how to read theological texts.
2. We will teach the students how to make theological arguments, with reference to available sources such as Scripture, tradition, reason, and experience.

3. We will raise the level of theological discourse among our students, so they are able to discuss the questions of theology with greater acumen.
4. In recognition of the religious identity of our institution, we will examine the foundational texts, history, and claims of, say, the Catholic faith. (So at Notre Dame, a student's introduction to theology course surveys Old Testament, New Testament, and Early Church texts.)[13]

I would argue that all of these are most worthy goals, to which I will aspire in my own classroom. However, note that each of these may be achieved in a manner that enables the professor *not* to engage the student at the level of faith, an engagement seemingly demanded by the subject matter. One could meet the aforementioned objectives in the same manner in which one could list the articles of the Treaty of Westphalia or debate the pros and cons of different literary theories. Yet the questions of theology demand a response at the level of conviction and not merely an intellectual understanding. Is Jesus Christ God and man, sent to give eternal life to those who believe? Is there life after death? Is self-giving love not simply an effective ethical norm but an actual participation in God's Triune communion, and an imitation of divine self-giving love most clearly manifest in the Incarnation? Such questions demand intellectual apprehension *and* acts of belief or disbelief.

Of course theological study does require knowledge of names, dates, arguments, and counterarguments, as well as analytic discussion of, say, the nature of prophecy and so on. Yet all of these are intimately tied to one's faith commitments. To what fundamental responses to questions about God does one assent? If theology professors prescind from asking this question and yet proceed to explore intellectual issues raised by possible answers to this question, they implicitly teach that the intellectual enterprise is divorced from one's beliefs. Such an approach enables one to teach the names, dates, and formulae of Chalcedon without providing the students an opportunity to engage the core Christian claim that God became a human being in Jesus Christ so that people might have eternal life. It is clearly the case that the nature of the classroom environment, the requirements of assessment, and even a theologically grounded respect for student freedom and development all necessitate formal educational objectives at a less-engaged level. Again, the aforementioned goals are worthy. However, what distinguishes an engaged from a disengaged theology class is the former's attention to the students' beliefs, rather than simply a recognition that religious phenomena are worthy of serious study or that, out of respect for the faith identity of an institution, a certain *corpus* of texts or historical events warrants specific study. To not engage the students beyond this latter plane is not only a failure to present students with core life questions in a manner that indicates their significance; it is also an injustice to the material at hand.

What both of the said versions of disengaged theology have in common is a failure to engage students at the level of conviction. They also share epistemological assumptions that drive this failure to engage students' faith. Both share a willingness to examine only those questions regarding that which we are able to attain a high degree of epistemological certainty. As noted, one way to understand the modern project of Enlightenment, with its investment in the notion of "pure reason," is an attempt to obviate the role of authority by instead establishing a more epistemologically reliable foundation of pure reason from which to judge basic human questions concerning God and the moral life. Yet the attempt to adjudicate basic theological questions on the grounds of pure reason mistakenly assumes that we have "clear sight" regarding these questions such that intellectual apprehension alone—without the need of the will—can engender a firm cleaving to one proposition over another.

The second version of disengaged theology does not reject the importance of faith in students' lives. However, by embarking on the intellectual inquiry in a manner that fails to explicitly relate that study to questions that require belief or disbelief, this type of disengaged theology mistakenly dichotomizes faith and reason, will and intellect, such that the intellectual exercise never informs or is informed by the students' faith. The underlying assumption here seems to be that since epistemological certainty is not available concerning questions of faith, academic theology is best off bracketing such questions and examining facets of theology that lend themselves to demonstration. Again, consider Chalcedon. We can study the political events leading up to this council. We can survey the various arguments leveled in the Christological debates. We can even explore how different sides in the debate worshipped differently, reflecting and engendering doctrinal differences. But this entire exercise is rather uninteresting unless students are taught to see how these lessons all concern the question—quite relevant in their lives no matter what their response—of whether or not they believe Christ was the Son of God and a human person sent to redeem humanity. Perhaps the failure to engage students at the level of faith is driven by a respect for student freedom and a refusal to coerce/manipulate students on questions where more epistemological certainty is unavailable. While seemingly admirable, this either denies the need for belief in such questions (first version) or strips faith of the intellectual resources that make it something more than a blind leap (second version). In sum, both versions are driven by the lack of available epistemological certainty to *not* engage students at the level of faith. We will see through the work of Augustine and Gregory that recognition of this lack of available clear sight need not lead one to disengaged theology.

## ENGAGED THEOLOGY THAT DOES VIOLENCE

Before suggesting how one might avoid the pitfalls of a disengaged theology that fails to engage students at the level of their belief despite the demand for such engagement by the nature of the subject matter at hand, it would be helpful to recall another excess against which disengaged theology rightly reacts, albeit in overcompensation. Some words that describe this other extreme are *ideological, proselytizing,* and *manipulating.* The previous section demonstrates the necessity of both the intellect and the will for grasping the subject matter of theology. Yet when one stops to imagine how the theology professor might engage students at the level of belief, the difficulties of maintaining an appropriate balance between respecting student freedom and yet doing justice to the subject matter become evident. On college campuses there is no dearth of professors who either drive students away with their ideological style that fails to recognize any truth in other positions or who neglect the students' own readiness for assenting to certain foundational claims about reality. Note that such ideological professors are found among conservative, liberal, radical, and deconstructionist thinkers. Note also that these folks may not be wrong in all of their ideas. Rather, their error is either an assumption that questions that are matters of belief require no willful assent or impatience in awaiting that volitional movement in the student. This approach tends to drive away many students and inspire a cultic following among a smaller coterie of students starved to witness a college professor willing to make a truth claim. The error here is not the refreshing willingness to make such a truth claim in matters requiring belief. It is the failure to humbly recognize both the difficulty of the change of heart required for belief and the grains of truth in positions that draw others away from the truth claim at hand. Hence the term *violence* is repeatedly used here to describe this other extreme. These professors do engage students at the level of belief, but they manipulate where persuasion is called for. They also do violence to proponents of rival truth claims by failing to charitably interpret possible good reasons that draw people to those other claims.

Once again we see that error in engaging students at the level of belief is related to an epistemological error. On the one hand, those who teach a disengaged theology fail to reach the students at the level of faith because they find no justifiable epistemological grounds for adjudicating questions at this level. There is a paralyzing irresolution to challenge students in an arena concerning which we are not certain of the truth. Since at the level of faith, one believes and does not know with certainty, we are understandably hesitant to engage this arena as opposed to arenas wherein more certainty exists, such as the map of the solar system or the dynamics of plate tectonics. It is this fear of uncertainty that even prompts some to explicitly or implicitly assert the unimportance of this level. On the other hand, ideological professors are quite willing to engage students at this level, but they fail by assuming an obvious certainty to answers to questions that entail acts of belief. This renders them impatient with students whose hearts are not yet similarly moved (rather than grateful at the movement of their own hearts) and facilely dismissive of others who cling in belief to counterpositions. Ironically, both errors entail a failure to appropriately recognize questions that involve faith and to discuss them accordingly. How might this be done? The following section suggests one avenue: a selective retrieval of Christian rhetoric.

## CHRISTIAN RHETORIC AND ENGAGED THEOLOGY

This section argues that there exists a viable alternative to either a disengaged theology that insipidly refrains from engaging students' beliefs or a violent theology that manipulates students and facilely dismisses proponents of other truth claims. Christian rhetoric is adduced as an appropriate form of discourse when engaging students at the level of belief, where the questions are of tremendous import and yet no epistemologically foundational certainty is available to adjudicate possible answers. Once one recognizes that disengaged theology is neither possible (since one always influences students' beliefs in matters of theology—if only toward the position that acts of faith are either unneeded or unrelated to intellectual theological study), nor desirable (since it does injustice to the nature of theological material of study, which requires belief or disbelief) and that students' beliefs must be engaged in a manner respectful of their freedom and development, one is left in a dilemma. How do we as teachers use our influence in a manner that is not violent and manipulative and yet does justice to the nature of the subject matter at hand? Teaching theology always involves persuading students.[14] Rhetoric is the art of persuading well. Therefore, our question has essentially become one of the nature of Christian rhetoric. How can the professor of Catholic theology influence and persuade students in a manner that is Christlike?

Unfortunately, the term *rhetoric* connotes manipulation in its crudest form. David Cunningham notes several contemporary senses of the term. They include "flowery or ornamental language," "intentionally deceptive language," and "stylistics and delivery."[15] Such an understanding of rhetoric implies it is at best a form of speech without regard to content and at worst communication whose deceptive purpose is veiled by ornamental language.[16] There is no shortage of historical examples of this debased form of rhetoric. Christine Sutherland describes the rhetoric of the "Second Sophistic" in Augustine and Gregory's time as "concerned almost exclusively with style" of speech rather than the content of message. "And for such rhetoric [Augustine] had nothing but contempt."[17] However, Saints Augustine and Gregory, while dismissive of rhetoric concerned with style to the neglect of content, simultaneously posit a Christian vision of rhetoric.

Yet why attempt to salvage rhetoric at all? Why not take an approach described by Sutherland as an opposite extreme to the Second Sophistic: the Platonic approach, which so relied upon the inherent attractiveness of truthful discourse that no attention at all was given to rhetorical effectiveness?[18] Many early Christians were dismissive of any role for rhetorical "style" in speaking about God, particularly given Paul's recognition of his own rhetorical inadequacies (1 Corinthians 2:4, 2 Corinthians 11:6) and the exhortation of Christ Himself not to premeditate on what to say when one is delivered up, for it is the Spirit who will guide (Mark 13:11). Some assume that Christian rhetors such as Augustine and Gregory employ rhetoric simply as one neutral weapon in an arsenal that can be used in service of virtue or vice. Augustine seems to indicate this himself:

> Rhetoric, after all, being the art of persuading people to accept something, whether it is true or false, would anyone dare to maintain that truth should stand there without any weapons in the hands of its defenders against falsehood; that those speakers, that is to say, who are trying to convince their hearers of what is untrue, should know how to get them on their side . . . while those who are defending the truth should not? . . . Could anyone be so silly as to suppose such a thing? So since facilities are available for learning to speak well, which is of greatest value in leading people either along straight or along crooked ways, why should good men not study to acquire the art, so that it may fight for truth, if bad men can prostitute it to the winning of their vain and misguided cases in the service of iniquity and error?[19]

Is rhetoric simply a "neutral" tool, which may be employed in the service of God or those "in error?" Notwithstanding the said quotation, this is simply not the case. It is easily demonstrated in the cases of Gregory and Augustine by examining how their Christian faith transformed their practice of rhetoric. There is an extensive literature on patristic (particularly Augustine's) appropriation or transformation of pagan culture.[20] While that larger debate is not engaged here, the following discussion of five distinctive marks of Christian rhetoric will reveal how the art practiced by Augustine and Gregory is far from neutral *as they practice it*. When put in the service of teaching Christianity, rhetoric is transformed to rightly be called "Christian rhetoric." Augustine famously recognized the value in "despoiling the Egyptians," in that pagan achievements (philosophical, rhetorical, etc.) should be usurped and placed in service of the Christian God.[21] Yet it is best to imagine these spoils as melted down, re-formed, and regilded in their service to God. So transformed, the practice of rhetoric enables the Christian rhetor to imitate her heavenly Father (Matt. 5:48), who sent His only Son, the Word (John 1), into the world that people might believe and have eternal life (John 3:16).[22] Thus, one reason to salvage rhetoric is that practicing Christian rhetoric is a form of imaging God's very self. Another reason concerns the proper occasion for the use of rhetoric, which is notably similar to the classroom encounter that is the topic of this chapter.

The primary task of this section is to articulate five distinctive marks of Christian rhetoric as practiced by Augustine and Gregory. Yet before examining the five marks of their transformed Christian rhetoric, it would be helpful to situate the role of this inquiry in the question that drives this article. Why is Christian rhetoric helpful in engaging students at the level of faith? To answer this question, we must take a brief look at the nature of, and proper occasion for, rhetorical discourse. In his extensive work on rhetoric in antiquity, George Kennedy helpfully identifies the nature and circumstances of rhetorical discourse, primarily through an exploration of Aristotle's work on rhetoric.[23] Aristotle divides the methods, or tools, of intellectual activity into two areas: analytics and dialectics.[24] Analytical reasoning proceeds from an agreed-on set of first principles and reaches conclusions that are necessary and certain yet tautological. Analytical argument is a "closed system." Dialectic argument, however, begins with "common opinion." While such a starting point can be wrong, and would thus claim less certainty, "its ambiguity makes it able to achieve genuinely new (non-tautological) insights."[25] The former is employed in physics, metaphysics, and logic, while the latter is used in ethics and politics.

Where does rhetoric fit into this schema? Aristotle calls rhetoric a "counterpart" to dialectic.[26] David Cunningham offers a more colloquial translation: the two are opposite sides of the same coin.[27] Both proceed from common opinion regarding the issue at hand, bereft of the certainty of analytic argument. They differ in that rhetoric deals with practical matters while dialectic is reserved for more speculative, or theoretical, examinations. For this piece, it suffices to contrast the demonstrable certainty of analytic knowledge with lack of demonstrability in the case of rhetorical discourse. The point here is that the very use of rhetorical discourse is itself recognition of both the lack of demonstrability surrounding the subject at hand and the practical importance of the question at hand since rhetorical discourse aims to persuade the hearer to adopt a position despite the enduring lack of clear sight. If rhetoric is the proper tool of discourse for considering important practical questions in which there is a lack of self-evident demonstrability, then it is the perfect tool for theological study in the classroom, where the material at hand requires a student's response in belief or disbelief even without the "perfection of clear sight." Gregory and Augustine illuminate the present discussion by demonstrating that the best way not to do violence to students in treating questions of ultimate significance, which demand of the hearer some act of belief, is neither to neglect them nor to discuss them in a disinterested way but rather to debate them in an intellectually responsible, just, and charitable manner. Their visions of Christian rhetoric, of which five "marks" are considered here, suggest some details of how to do just that.

## Humility

Recognized or not, humility is inherent to rhetorical discourse for the reasons mentioned here. The very use of rhetoric is an admission that the subject matter eludes analytic certainty. Of course, we know that it is often those who are most uncertain who are also most dogmatic and assertive in their communication. Thus they often enlist the tools of rhetoric for their cause. But their discourse belies them. Were their message fully demonstrable, they would have little use for rhetoric. A sense of humility is most evident in all spiritual masters who endeavor to speak of their God with fear and trembling. The introduction to Teresa of Avila's *Interior Castle* is a fine example.[28] Perhaps the finest is Gregory's *Theological Orations*.[29] This five-oration treatise probes the mysteries of the triune God, focusing primarily upon the Son and Spirit. Amazingly, before embarking on such discussion, Gregory spends an entire oration apophatically wondering at the ultimate ineffibility of our God. Gregory claims that the proud (in the sinful sense) rhetor cannot possibly speak truthfully about God, since she cannot know her subject at all if she remains proud. Knowledge of God dispels conceited pride, and so any theological discourse that does not begin with recognition of God's incomprehensibility is "knowledge falsely so-called" (1 Timothy 6:20).

Note that Gregory's emphasis on humility is not simply recognition of the incomprehensibility of God but also an epistemological claim regarding a moral quality that must be present in one who speaks truthfully about God. In other words, one who does not possess such humility cannot know, and thus cannot speak truthfully about, the God who far exceeds all human understanding. How does this translate into the Catholic theologian's classroom? There must be, it seems, an honest recognition that the questions under discussion do not avail themselves of the certainty of clear sight; thus, belief, regardless of the direction of that belief, is required in one's engagement with the material. Failure to do so indicates a misunderstanding of the nature of the material at hand. Note that this does not mean one cannot speak intelligibly about, and debate, theological questions. And certainty it is not to imply that there is no Truth. Gregory responds to this objection himself:

> Do not take our frankness [regarding the limits of human knowledge of God] as ground for atheistic caviling and exalt yourselves over against us for acknowledging our ignorance.[30]

Gregory thus recognizes from the beginning of the *Theological Orations* that he is in the odd position, reminiscent of the classroom situation described in this chapter, of attempting to speak persuasively on a topic concerning which he cannot have complete and certain understanding.[31] Yet rather than emphasizing solely our inability to have full knowledge of God's nature, he employs a method of argument appropriate to the task of persuading people of something that cannot be proven analytically. Gregory's use of rhetoric does not imply God's nature is completely inaccessible; it merely confirms that God's nature is not circumscribable by human analytic reasoning and that faith "gives fullness to reasoning."[32]

## God as Primary Mover of Hearts

A second and related mark of Christian rhetoric is the relativization of the rhetor.[33] The Christian theologian passes on a message handed down to him. He did not construct the message at hand, and the words are not meant to point people toward himself but toward God. This realization leads Augustine to make some practical suggestions to the Christian rhetor that would have been ludicrous to the pagan rhetor. He claims that one may borrow another's speeches if they are particularly well done and effective.[34] He exhorts Christian rhetors to trust the Lord's claim that the Spirit will put words into their mouths.[35] He even encourages them to carry on in their work even if they feel their words are ineffective or they do not delight in their task, since God may be working on a hearer through them even if they are not aware of it.[36] Finally, the Christian rhetor must pray.[37] All of these exhortations make it clear that God is the primary agent when engaging the faith of a hearer. God is also the final goal of the rhetor's engagement with his audience. If the Christian rhetor speaks not to garner acclaim and personal gain but rather to point the audience toward God Who Is Truth, then the use of others' work, the exhortation to prayer, and the recognition that God may move the hearer at times in spite of the rhetor all make complete sense to the Christian rhetor though they be absurd to the pagan rhetor.

Lest one think this implies that the teacher's work is unimportant or her teaching methods irrelevant, Augustine warns in the prologue to *Teaching Christianity* that though God is the primary agent in moving people to believe, one should not underestimate the importance of the teacher who serves as God's instrument. Despite his recognition of miraculous events (such as St. Anthony's understanding and learning how to read Scripture after only one hearing—despite the fact that he could not read!), Augustine points to a slew of scriptural greats (such as Paul and Moses) who relied on the instruction of others, knowing "of course, that from whatever soul good advice had issued, it was to be attributed not to that person, but to the one who is truth itself, the unchanging, unchangeable God."[38] The Christian rhetor is relativized in serving as an instrument of God, but she is simultaneously dignified by taking part in that most beautiful encounter between a student and God.[39]

## Wisdom and Eloquence

At this point one may wonder what the Christian rhetor, and for our purposes the Catholic theologian, has substantively to say given the first two marks. Is there no concern for the content of the theology professor's words? This may be one of the areas in which Augustine and Gregory most radically transform pagan rhetoric. Even Cicero, who was more concerned with actually teaching his audience than rhetors of the Second Sophistic, claims that the three goals of rhetoric are to teach, to delight, and to sway—and that, of these, teaching is least important to Cicero. Most essential is influencing the hearer in a manner desired by the rhetor.[40] Augustine turns this on its head and claims that proclaiming the gospel is the primary responsibility of the Christian rhetor.[41] Truthfulness of the message is primary, despite the recognized importance of style. His work on rhetoric is full of exemplary narratives that one might use to present the Christian message.[42] James Murphy argues that Augustine charts a middle course between the "Sophistic and Platonic heresies" regarding the Christian use of rhetoric. While the Sophists attended to the persuasiveness of their discourse with practically no attention to content, Platonists emphasized the persuasive power of truthful content to the near total neglect of the style of discourse.[43] For his part, Augustine embraces "wisdom with eloquence" as the ideal descriptor of the Christian rhetor's discourse.[44]

What does this mark add to our discussion of engaging students' belief? There can be no doubt that Augustine would decry theological discourse that does not boldly proclaim the content of Christian faith, including propositions that most obviously require faith, such as the Incarnation or the Trinity. There is no substitution for the teacher's presenting true wisdom. However, he is also most aware that assent to such propositions requires more than simply hearing them pronounced. There must be wisdom but also eloquence. The Christian rhetor humbly yet boldly proclaims truths held in faith and presents them in a manner that is most fitting for the audience.[45] The requirement of eloquence is not a ruse to keep hearers' attention, nor does it take such precedence that the content of Christian teaching is governed by its accessibility to the audience. Rather, the attention to eloquence is an acknowledgement that in teaching matters of faith persuasion is necessary so that the audience not only understands the matter at hand but is also moved to respond in belief.

### Importance of Love

The fourth mark of Christian rhetoric unites the form and content of theological discourse in a manner similar to Augustine's "wisdom with eloquence." Since the purpose of Christian rhetoric is to point the hearer toward God, Who is revealed in the Scriptures, which are themselves understood through the hermeneutic of love of God and love of neighbor,[46] the entire rhetorical enterprise is centered on love.[47] Love is both the content of the Christian rhetor's message and the principle that guides the rhetor's own engagement with the audience.[48] The Christian rhetor seeks ultimately to enkindle love of God and undertakes the rhetorical enterprise out of love for the hearer. Thus the Catholic professor of theology engages the faith of her students in the hope of increasing their love of God. That hope shapes one's teaching such that students are themselves engaged out of love.[49] Augustine is in line with pagan rhetors in attending to the emotions and circumstances of his audience. Yet Augustine claims that the Christian rhetor seeks to better know his hearers not to more easily manipulate them but to better understand how they may be best served in the proclamation of the Gospel.[50] For Augustine, love of the hearer is necessitated by the content of the Christian message. At the same time, that love is one of the reasons why the Christian message is persuasive to the hearer. He appeals to First John in noting that God loved us first, sending His Son to lay down His life for us as sinners. Making the hearer aware of that "greatest love" is most persuasive in moving the person to love God.[51] Similarly, love for the student is both required due to the Catholic theologian's material and most persuasive in engaging the student's faith regarding that material.

### Ethos of the Rhetor

The fifth and final mark of Christian rhetoric concerns the *ethos*, or manner of living, of the rhetor. Pagan manuals of rhetoric list *ethos* as one of the three primary means of persuasion at the disposal of the rhetor.[52] Aristotle's treatment of this topic is illustrative. He claims that the character of the rhetor *as expressed during his discourse* is crucial in establishing the trustworthiness of the speaker and hence his persuasiveness.[53] In other words, *ethos* is important for the speaker's authority, or credibility, concerning the matter at hand. Clearly Aristotle's limiting the scope of *ethos* to the speaker's character *as manifest in the speech* indicates that one may "put on airs," so to speak, to win the audience while orating. Augustine and Gregory, however, expand the importance of *ethos* to the individual and communal life of the Christian rhetor. Augustine claims that the rhetor must be formed in the Spirit to know the truth.[54] He even claims that the speaker's life carries more persuasive weight than her discourse.[55]

Yet *ethos* is important to Augustine and Gregory for more than simply rhetorical effectiveness. They also suggest that good character is related to one's ability to speak truthfully about God. For instance, Gregory lambasts the error of his Eunomian opponents by pointing out their unchristian practices. In doing so he indicates that their questionable *ethos* indicts their ability to speak truthfully about the theological matter at hand. Note this intertwining of rhetorical effectiveness and epistemology. It is seen again when Gregory asserts the truthfulness of his own theological position and proceeds to test it by examining his community's practices.

> Do we commend hospitality? Do we admire brotherly love, wifely affection, virginity, feeding the poor, signing the psalms, nightlong vigils, penitence? Do we

mortify the body with fasting? Do we through prayer take up our abode with God?[56]

These questions may seem irrelevant to us today. What have they to do with whether or not the position Gregory articulates is true or not? For Gregory, questions of *ethos* are important beyond the evasion of charges of hypocrisy. He is not simply saying that his community consists of upstanding folks, whether they are right or wrong theologically. His claim is that the manner in which one leads one's life is relevant for the very truthfulness of one's theological discourse.[57] For Gregory, not only do actions speak louder than words, but the *ethos* of the Christian rhetor also has epistemological significance for the disputed matter under discussion.[58]

## CHRISTIAN RHETORIC IN *MERE CHRISTIANITY*

As this chapter was read by several friends and peer reviewers, one suggestion they continually made was to provide a real-life example of this vision of Christian rhetoric. It being easier to wax on in theory than practice, I initially resisted. But I soon recognized that their suggestion was actually a necessity. Part of the initial resistance was the difficulty of presenting a teaching style in a chapter. I realized that I could bypass this problem by pointing to such an example in the written word and that I had the perfect example right in front of me. I have assigned C. S. Lewis's *Mere Christianity* to over a dozen classes over the past few years with great success. Students repeatedly tell me on anonymous evaluations that it was a highlight of the course. A main reason for that glowing evaluation is Lewis's style of writing. That style epitomizes many features of Christian rhetoric that this chapter seeks to identify and promote.

C. S. Lewis's book is a classic example of apologetic theology. In other words, it presents the content of Christian teaching in language accessible to those (whether Christian or not) who have not been formed in that teaching. This raises the question of the relationship between apologetics and Christian rhetoric as presented here. I actually suspect that apologetics *is* Christian rhetoric. Whether it be St. Justin Martyr or C. S. Lewis, apologists do not present the Christian life simply to make it more comprehensible to the audience but rather for members of the audience to change their minds. I also suspect that what differentiates me (as a professor of theology at a Catholic university) from an apologist is that while I agree with Christian apologists such as Justin and Lewis and thus assign them with the hope that students are persuaded by them, I do present alternative positions. I also assign papers and exams that evaluate students' comprehension of the questions at hand and the stakes involved, without any formal assessment of their beliefs. Thus while I employ the art of Christian rhetoric in the classroom, my role as professor in an American university is not simply that of apologist. Yet the larger question of the relationship between apologetics and Christian rhetoric is beyond the scope of this chapter. For now let us consider how *Mere Christianity* exemplifies Christian rhetoric.

Lewis certainly engages his reader at the level of faith. Lewis presents the virtue of faith as a necessary complement to human reason (139). He acknowledges that we may reason extensively about Christian faith; his own book is an example. But he also knows that reasoning alone is not enough. People must grasp on to what they think is true about God, even when that is difficult to hold. This virtue of "holding on" he calls faith. His entire book, whatever the particular topic at hand, is an exercise in placing the reader in position to make such an act of faith. For a perfect example, consider the following passage, which concludes Lewis's discussion of God's response to human sin with the Incarnation:

> I am trying to prevent anyone from saying the really foolish thing that people often say about Him: 'I'm ready to accept Jesus as a great moral teacher, but I don't accept His claim to be God.' That is one thing we must not say. A man who was merely a man and said the sort of things Jesus said would not be a great moral teacher. He would either be a lunatic—on a level with the man who says he is a poached egg—or else he would be the Devil of Hell. *You must make your choice.* Either this man was, and is, the Son of God: or else a madman or something worse. You can shut Him up for a fool, you can spit on Him and kill him as a demon; or you can fall at his feet and call Him Lord and God. But let us not come away with any patronizing nonsense about His being a great human teacher. He has not left that open to us. He did not intend to. (52, emphasis added)[59]

Here we see the sort of "wisdom with eloquence" that is further discussed in the following. But note for now that Lewis makes it quite clear that the reader must respond to Jesus with some sort of choice, some act of belief. He recognizes other possibilities, but his own position is also clear. There is no attempt to eliminate the need for the reader to commit herself in a manner that is not simply settled by neat intellectual discourse. Lewis writes some of the most eloquently straightforward prose I have encountered about Christology. Yet at the end, he makes it perfectly clear: "You must make your choice."

Moving on to consider the five marks presented in the previous section, Lewis exemplifies the sort of humility described here. First of all, he recognizes that the "mere Christianity" he presents is not the only option for his reader. In fact, he spends two chapters situating Christian belief among other belief commitments, acknowledging at each turn what is at stake in believing one or the other (35–46). Second, he recognizes that his reader must make a belief commitment for or against Christianity and, furthermore, that this commitment is tremendously practically important (155, 161). Third and most dramatic, Lewis recognizes he cannot fully convince the reader of his own position. In the midst of explaining the dynamics of God's grace in assisting human action, Lewis takes on (in just three pages!) difficult questions, such as the relationship between faith and works and the relationship between God's grace and human action. After a wonderfully lucid foray into this question, he concludes with the humble "At any rate that is as far as I can go" (149, cf. 145). Lewis's entire project exemplifies the proper occasion for Christian rhetoric. We have at hand questions that are practically—and ultimately—important. Yet they address matters that are not fully demonstrable. There are other available options, and commitment to any one requires an act of belief. Knowing this, Lewis employs the proper mode of discourse for such an occasion—Christian rhetoric. His mode of discourse is itself an expression of humility, a humility that Lewis further reinforces by recognitions that he cannot fully demonstrate to the reader his own position.

Skipping ahead to "wisdom with eloquence," one should not assume from the last paragraph that Lewis's humility prevents him from taking a stand. Far from it. Lewis makes quite clear his own belief in Christianity, and his goal of persuading the reader to such belief—even while acknowledging other options, the need for a commitment, and his inability to make his own position fully demonstrable with the perfection of clear sight. He knows that the lack of such clear sight must not prevent one from tackling the "big questions"; after all, refusing to do theology "will not mean that you have no ideas about God. It will mean you have a lot of wrong ones—bad, muddled, out-of-date ideas" (155, cf. 161). So even in this introductory book—and against the advice of his friends (153)—Lewis boldly takes on some of the most complex topics in theology. He explores the triune nature of the Christian God (153–65), the need for (and even efficaciousness of) the Incarnation (47–59), and the dynamics of God's grace (141–50, 187–217). He refuses the temptation to allow "accessibility to the intellect" dictate how he presents the Christian faith. Though such an approach might obviate the need for a commitment at the level of will (belief), it would do violence to the nature of the material at hand. Lewis claims that reality is not simple, and thus neither is the content of the Christian faith. Any attempt to make it such transforms it into a creation of humanity. He claims that his reader deserves more (153, cf. 41). He recognizes that presenting Christianity in an accessible and persuasive manner (eloquence) must not contradict the truth of Christian teaching. The Christian rhetor is wise as well as eloquent.

Yet eloquent she is. Consider two examples of wisdom with eloquence in Lewis. As noted, Lewis rails strongly against a Christology that considers Christ to be primarily a great moral teacher. As a professor of theology, I myself can attest that this view is quite prevalent. Lewis refuses to rest in this more easily accessible Christology. He describes the fallen state of human nature that necessitated the Incarnation. He explains the two natures of

Christ in the context of that salvific mission. He even briefly examines atonement theory during this discussion. He is certainly not presenting a "watered down" Christology that is demonstrable to the intellect alone! Nonetheless, he presents each of these ideas with imagery that is simple and persuasive. He speaks of civil wars, toy soldiers, and vitamins to explain these difficult Christological concepts. Thus his presentation is accessible and persuasive (eloquence) even while the content he offers is rich and complex (wisdom). Lewis does the same with his discussion of the Trinity. He refuses not only to ignore the Trinity but also to discuss it in a manner that is more accessible but less wise. For instance, rather than simply refer to the three persons as three different ways we humans apprehend one God,[60] Lewis explains how God's very own being is itself "three–personal" (160–65). Lewis's wisdom with eloquence provides his reader the chance to believe in a robust presentation of Christian teaching. He equips that reader with the intellectual resources to make that act of belief more than a blind leap.

The last three marks of Christian rhetoric are also present in Lewis's *Mere Christianity*. He quite willingly relativizes his own role as rhetor in recognition that God is the primary mover of hearts. This is particularly evident when he begins a few more difficult discussions by admonishing the reader to simply skip ahead if she finds what he says incomprehensible. For instance, before describing the human surrender to God's grace in faith, Lewis states, "If this chapter means nothing to you, if it seems to be trying to answer questions you never asked, drop it at once. Do not bother about it at all" (144, cf. 59, 166). Lewis is clearly more concerned with his readers' overall relationship with God than their recognition of his persuasiveness. His acknowledgement that his reader may simply not be ready for a certain subject is combined with a firm acknowledgement that God does indeed move people with grace. Thus God is both the goal of the Christian rhetor's engagement with the audience and the primary agent for moving the hearer to that goal. Lewis's concern for the developmental stage of the reader also indicates the love that must mark Christian rhetoric. Lewis proclaims the love of God that is the central message of Christianity and, while doing so, exhibits that same love in the concern for his reader that drives both his writing of this book and his acknowledgement of different readers' stages of faith.[61] Finally, *ethos* is the most difficult mark of Christian rhetoric to ascertain in Lewis's book. Occasionally there are references to Lewis's own life, and these are persuasive in the humility Lewis demonstrates (cf. 144, 35). But absent periodic student references to the biographical movie about Lewis called *Shadowlands*, we know too little in our class about Lewis's life to be able to speak about how the authority of his book is substantiated or not by the way Lewis lived his life.[62] Nevertheless, the strength of the other four marks makes Lewis's *Mere Christianity* an excellent example of the Christian rhetoric delineated in this chapter on the basis of the thought of Saints Gregory and Augustine.

## CONCLUSION

Christian rhetoric, as delineated by Saints Gregory and Augustine and exemplified by C. S. Lewis, is an invaluable method of intellectual discourse for someone teaching theology in a Catholic university today. These three Christian rhetors employed their art not simply for its effectiveness in persuading people to adopt one position. They also recognized that the particular occasion of teaching about matters of faith calls for the use of rhetoric. After all, the subject is one of immense practical importance and yet does not avail itself to the sorts of analytic certainty possible in other fields of inquiry. For this reason, their work is most fitting for the Catholic theology class today. In such a situation, one must simultaneously not do violence to students by coercively addressing matters of faith but yet still engage the students at the level of faith demanded by the subject matter at hand. Rhetoric is properly employed on precisely such an occasion.

Gregory and Augustine's transformation of pagan rhetoric also informs some of the epistemological observations made here regarding inadequate ways of engaging students at the level of faith. It was noted that disengaged theology attempts to obviate the role of willful assent by attending only to those questions that are amenable to more certain explanation. The assumption is that it is at worst necessarily subversive and at best too epistemologically uncertain to engage students regarding matters of faith. Christian rhetoric as practiced by Gregory and Augustine humbly recognizes the limitations particular to its subject matter and yet proceeds boldly due to the importance of the matter at hand. C. S. Lewis's *Mere Christianity* proceeds precisely in the same manner. All three recognize that there is no way to proceed in theology with an epistemological guarantee.

Augustine and Gregory further suggest, in a way we were unable to gauge in Lewis, how a proper use of rhetoric can actually serve as a test of theological content. For instance, both insist on the humility of the rhetor. If this quality is not present, the rhetor reveals not only the presence of a vice but also a condition that is inherently incompatible with a truthful knowledge of God. The theologian tainted by pride actually speaks less truthfully.[63] Further, both patristic saints insist on the epistemological relevance of the *ethos* of the rhetor. It is not merely the case that the rhetor must be credible. Living Christian charity is an indicator of how truthful a grasp a teacher has over her "material." Augustine is also particularly explicit on the extent to which love should serve as both the content and method of the Christian rhetor's discourse. These "tests" are far from infallible and will disappoint the one seeking some new, epistemologically secure foundation on which to base theological discourse. There is no escaping the need for assent of the will. Yet they help guide the Christian rhetor, or the Catholic professor of theology in the classroom, in her task of guiding students in theological inquiry.

# NOTES

Thank you to Bill Collinge and Paul Martens, both of whom were kind enough to read earlier versions of this chapter and offer suggestions.

1. C. S. Lewis, *Mere Christianity* (San Francisco: HarperSanFrancisco, 2001). *Mere Christianity* was first published in 1952 as a collection of three previously published works: *The Case for Christianity*, or *Broadcast Talks* (1942), *Christian Behavior* (1943), and *Beyond Personality* (1944). Citations to this work in the fifth section of this chapter are given parenthetically.

2. St. Thomas Aquinas, *Summa Theologica* [*sic*], trans. English Dominicans (New York: Benziger, 1948), 2-2.2.1.

3. St. Thomas Aquinas, 2-2.2.1.

4. For an outstanding discussion of faith and *scientia* in Aquinas, see John Jenkins, CSC, *Knowledge and Faith in Aquinas* (New York: Cambridge University Press, 1997).

5. St. Thomas Aquinas, 2-2.2.1.

6. St. Thomas Aquinas, 2-2.2.1. See also, St. Thomas Aquinas, 2-2.2.2: "To believe is an act of the intellect, in so far as the *will* moves it to assent" (emphasis added).

7. Thomas insists that faith is first and foremost an act of the intellect, since its object is essentially truth (rather than goodness). It is equally important to insist on the intellectual nature of faith today since faith is too frequently divorced from intellectual life in higher education, rendering theology purely intellectual and faith simply a matter of one's (read: nonintellectual) "spirituality."

8. The notion that certain types of knowledge require "willful assent" neither begins nor ends with Thomas. As noted in the following, Aristotle is just one ancient thinker with a sophisticated understanding of this sort of knowledge. For a more contemporary example, see the work of Chaïm Perelmen, who uses the term *adherence* as well as *assent*. Perelmen, *The New Rhetoric* (Notre Dame, Ind.: University of Notre Dame Press, 1969), 4. There, Perelman explicitly rejects the identification of "self-evident" with "reasonable," resulting in the need for attention to persuasion and convincing (26ff.). For Perelman's application of his new rhetoric to other disciplines, see his *The New Rhetoric and the Humanities* (Holland: D. Reidel Publishing, 1979).

9. One must be careful here. Affirming that the intellect alone cannot answer such questions as "Do I believe that Jesus Christ is the Son of God?" does not mean that this question cannot be discussed in an intellectually thorough manner. Yet, given that the matter under discussion cannot be demonstrated by the intellect alone, assent involves an act of the will as well as an act of the intellect.

10. For an excellent study on authority and religious belief, see Jeffrey Stout's *The Flight from Authority: Religion, Morality, and the Quest for Autonomy* (Notre Dame, Ind.: University of Notre Dame Press, 1981).

11. There are notorious problems in articulating some general concept of "religion." For a recent piece that raises this question in the context of the formation of theologians, see Stanley Hauerwas, "Between Christian Ethics and Religious Ethics: How Should Graduate Students Be Trained?" *Journal of Religious Ethics* 31, no. 3 (2003): 399–412.

12. Ever since the work of Thomas Kuhn, we are rightly skeptical of scientific claims to be cleansed of adulterating influences beyond the data gathered. This caveat is granted here. The role for the will in acts of faith, as articulated here relying

on Aquinas, is far more substantial than even the role of nonscientific factors recognized by Kuhn.

13. All of these goals were explicitly articulated in different fora for teacher formation, which I attended at Notre Dame.

14. As noted, this is the case even if one is simply convincing students that faith is not necessary for, or separable from, theology. For a recognition of the persuasive nature of teaching, see John Bennett and Elizabeth Dreyer, "Spiritualities of—Not at—the University" (unpublished manuscript), 7. They rely primarily on Parker Palmer's work, but a similar recognition of the "directedness" of hospitality is seen in Jacques Derrida's *Acts of Religion* (New York: Routledge, 2002), 358ff.

15. See David Cunningham's "Theology as Rhetoric," *Theological Studies* 52 (1991): 416.

16. For the delicate relationship between rhetorical argumentation and violence, see Perelman's *New Rhetoric*, 54ff.

17. See Christine Sutherland's "Love as Rhetorical Principle: The Relationship between Content and Style in Saint Augustine," in *Grace, Politics, and Desire: Essays on Augustine*, ed. H. A. Meynall (Alberta, Canada: University of Calgary Press, 1990), 139–154, at 142. Augustine's disdain is easily seen in scattered derogatory comments about debased rhetoric in *Confessions*—for example, 2.3, 5.6, 6.6.

18. See Sutherland, "Love as Rhetorical Principle," 143–44. Here she relies on James Murphy's *Rhetoric in the Middle Ages* (Berkeley: University of California Press, 1974). For the purposes of this chapter, it is not necessary to further explore whether this is an accurate portrayal of Plato.

19. See the translation of St. Augustine's *De doctrina christiana* by Edmund Hill, OP, *Teaching Christianity* (New York: New City Press, 1996), 4.3 (citations here are given by book and section number, with the latter being the second and usually larger of the two section numbers provided in this translation.) For a recognition of this passage in the context of an article (like this one) arguing for a substantively transformed Augustinian Christian rhetoric, see David Tracy, "Charity, Obscurity, Clarity: Augustine's Search for a True Rhetoric," in *Morphologies of Faith*, ed. Mary Gerhart and Anthony C. Yu (Georgia: Scholars Press, 1990), 123–43, at 141.

20. The classic text on this question is Henri-Irénée Marrou's *Saint Augustin et la fin de la culture antique* (Paris: Boccard, 1949), esp. 505–40. See also, Peter Brown's *Augustine of Hippo* (Berkeley: University of California Press, 1967), 263ff. Further sources regarding the relationship between Augustinian and Ciceronian rhetoric are listed in the following.

21. See St. Augustine *Teaching Christianity* 2.61–63. The scriptural reference is Exodus 12:35–36, where the Israelites "despoil" the Egyptians. See also, Tracy, "Charity, Obscurity, and Clarity," 139.

22. See also, John Cavadini's "The Sweetness of the Word: Salvation and Rhetoric in Augustine's *De Doctrina*," in *"De Doctrina Christiana": A Classic of Western Culture*, ed. Duane W. H. Arnold and Pamela Bright (Notre Dame, Ind.: University of Notre Dame Press, 1995), 164–81, at 166. Here, Cavadini refers to the Word made flesh as God's eloquence. See also, St. Augustine *Teaching Christianity* 1.11 where Augustine cites 1 Corinthians 1:21 in noting that God comes to humanity in the folly of preaching.

23. Aristotle's work is referenced here due to its clarity on the nature and role of rhetoric. The degree to which Gregory and/or Augustine shared this vision of rheto-

ric is beyond the scope of this chapter. Yet, two things may be said. First, the basic sketch of rhetoric offered here accurately applies to Augustine's and Gregory's views of rhetoric. Second, Gregory spent ten years studying rhetoric in Athens. The rhetoric taught there included the more stylistic approach of Hermogenes and the more "philosophical rhetoric" of Plato and Aristotle. Gregory apparently excelled in these studies, as he was asked to remain in Athens to teach rhetoric. For Gregory's training in Aristotelian rhetoric, see Frederick W. Norris, "Gregory the Theologian," *Pro Ecclesia* 2, no. 4 (1993): 474–75. See also, George Kennedy, *Greek Rhetoric under Pagan Emperors* (Princeton, N.J.: Princeton University Press, 1983), 215ff. Kennedy devotes some attention to the way that Gregory's Christian use of rhetoric transforms that art (234ff.) For more on this topic, see Rosemary Radford Ruether's *Gregory of Nazianzus: Rhetor and Philosopher* (Oxford: Oxford University Press, 1969), 156–67; and Frederick Norris, "Of Thorns and Roses: The Logic of Belief in Gregory Nazianzen," *Church History* 53 (1984): 455–64.

24. Aristotle identifies four arenas of intellectual activity: theoretical sciences (such as mathematics and physics), practical sciences (such as politics and ethics), productive arts (including medicine and crafts), and methods or tools (such as logic and dialectic). Rhetoric is one of the methods and tools. For more on these categories of intellectual activity, see David Cunningham, "Theology as Rhetoric," 408–9, 414–17, as well as his *Faithful Persuasion* (Notre Dame, Ind.: University of Notre Dame Press, 1991), 16–18

25. Cunningham, "Theology as Rhetoric," 408.

26. Aristotle, *On Rhetoric* 1354a. See Richard McKeon, ed., *The Basic Works of Aristotle* (New York: Random House, 1941), 1325.

27. Cunningham, "Theology as Rhetoric," 414.

28. See St. Teresa of Avila, *The Interior Castle*, trans. Kieran Kavanaugh and Otilio Rodriguez (New York: Paulist Press, 1979).

29. Gregory of Nazianzen, *Faith Gives Fullness to Reasoning: The Five Theological Orations of Gregory Nazianzen*, trans. Lionel Wickham and Frederick Norris (New York: Brill, 1991), cited hereafter as *Theological Orations*. See the second oration in this collection, also called oration 28. Since the "five theological orations" are actually orations 27–31 in Gregory's larger corpus, citations here reflect that more common numbering.

30. Gregory, *Theological Orations* 28.5.

31. This is not to say that there are no resources in the Christian tradition for understanding theology as a "science." The classic example is St. Thomas Aquinas's discussion of theology as a science in the *Summa Theologiae* 1.1.2. He claimed that theological discourse can proceed from agreed-upon first principles in the manner of a "science," and he calls these principles the "articles of faith." However, he also acknowledges that these principles are accepted by authority of revelation, an assent that is not a matter of clear sight (2-2.1.5) and that is infused in a person by God (2-2.6.1). So not only does assent to such articles require belief, but such "seeing" is not complete in this life (1.12.11) and even in the next does not involve complete comprehension of God in a manner "capable of scientific demonstration" (1.12.7).

32. Frederick Norris uses this phrase as a title to his translation of Gregory's theological orations. He gets this phrase from *Theological Orations* 29.21.

33. I use this term in favor of Augustine's *use* since the latter has the negative connotation associated with instrumentalization.

34. St. Augustine, *Teaching Christianity* 4.62.

35. See St. Augustine, *Teaching Christianity* 4.15.33. He cites Matt. 10:20.

36. See C. L. Cornish's translation of Augustine's *De catechizandis rudibus*, "Of the Catechizing of the Unlearned," in *Seventeen Short Treatises of Saint Augustine* (Oxford: J. H. Parker, 1847), 187–242 (see secs. 20–22).

37. St. Augustine, *Teaching Christianity* 4.32ff.63.

38. St. Augustine, *Teaching Christianity*, prologue 7.

39. Several scholars have argued that *Teaching Christianity* (in particular book 4) is far more than simply a handbook in rhetorical technique. It is the story of how divine and human agency intermingle in conversion of the heart. In his "Sweetness of the Word," John Cavadini calls book 4 an exploration of teaching as more than a presentation of knowledge. It is an invitation to conversion. J. Patout Burns describes book 4 as a description of the mysterious process by which God moves us to conversion. See Burns's "Delighting the Spirit: Augustine's Practice of Figurative Interpretation," in *"De Doctrina Christiana": A Classic of Western Culture*, ed. Duane W. H. Arnold and Pamela Bright (Notre Dame, Ind.: University of Notre Dame Press, 1995), 191.

40. For more on the relationship between content of message and rhetorical style, see Sutherland, "Love as Rhetorical Principle," 140ff. There is an extensive literature on the extent to which Augustine adopts, subverts, and/or transforms Ciceronian rhetoric. Some think Augustine adopts a Ciceronian rhetoric rather than that of the Second Sophistic, while others recognize Augustine's attention to content but question to what degree his rhetoric is properly Ciceronian or whether it so transforms Cicero's rhetoric that the latter's vision influences only certain terminology. For a helpful overview of this debate, mapping out the work of several twentieth-century scholars, see Ernest Fortin, "Augustine and the Problem of Christian Rhetoric," *Augustinian Studies* 5 (1974): 85–100.

41. See St. Augustine, *Teaching Christianity* 4.24–30 for Augustine's use and transformation of Cicero's three functions of rhetorical discourse: to teach, to delight, and to sway.

42. Augustine does not simply speak technically about proclaiming the Christian message using rhetoric. His works on the subject always include some form of a narrative of the Christian story that ought to be presented to the audience. In "Of the Catechizing of the Unlearned," he offers longer and shorter versions of this story. See also, *Teaching Christianity* 1.11–19.

43. Murphy, *Rhetoric in the Middle Ages*, 60.

44. Augustine explicitly uses this phrase in *Teaching Christianity* 4.7, 4.8, 4.9–10, 4.21, 4.56, 4.61.

45. St. Augustine, "Of the Catechizing of the Unlearned," 18–19.

46. St. Augustine, *Teaching Christianity* 1.39.

47. St. Augustine, "Of the Catechizing of the Unlearned," 7–8.

48. See Tracy, "Charity, Obscurity, and Clarity," 135.

49. St. Augustine, "Of the Catechizing of the Unlearned," 6, 23.

50. St. Augustine, *Teaching Christianity* 4.6.

51. St. Augustine, "Of the Catechizing of the Unlearned," 7–8, citing 1 John 4:10.

52. For discussion of these three *pisteis*, see Aristotle's *On Rhetoric* 1356a.1329.

53. Aristotle *On Rhetoric* 1356a.1329. Aristotle actually states that the persuasion of *ethos* "should be achieved by what the speaker says, and not by what people think of his character before he begins to speak."

54. St. Augustine, *Teaching Christianity* 2.9–10.

55. St. Augustine, *Teaching Christianity* 4.59.

56. Gregory, *Theological Orations* 27.7.

57. See a similar claim by Augustine in *Teaching Christianity* 1.9–10, where he speaks of the purification needed to *know* the Divine.

58. These words may seem chilling to an academic today. Does how we live really impact the truthfulness of our thinking? This question is answered affirmatively by Augustine, Gregory, this chapter's author, and several other authors in this volume (see, for example, Christopher Steck, SJ, and Margaret R. Pfeil). Ought this lead to invasive examination of theologians' personal lives or tests of lifestyle to gauge theological acumen? Of course not. How to balance these two claims is the task of another paper.

59. Robert Barron takes a similar approach in his *The Strangest Way: Walking the Christian Path* (New York: Orbis, 2003): "God died in order that we might be his friends. Whatever you think of that last statement; whether you deem it true, false, or nonsensical, the one thing it is not is bland; the one thing that it is not saying is what everyone else is saying" (11).

60. This modern form of Sabellianism, which places the Triune nature of God in our apprehension of God rather than in God's own being, can be a powerfully attractive way to teach something as challenging as the Trinity.

61. See 145 for a comment typical of Lewis—that is, wise and eloquent (and brief!)—on the relationship of love of God and neighbor.

62. In *Shadowlands* Lewis falls in love with a woman who later suffers and dies of cancer. This movie, and the books it is based on (including *Surprised by Joy* and *A Grief Observed*), do indicate that Lewis's experience of the joy and anguish of this relationship both tried Lewis's faith and brought it to a depth previously unknown. Those who know these other works can see that Lewis's *ethos* did seem to reflect what he taught about Christianity.

63. Lewis does address the incompatibility of pride and truthful discourse about God while examining the sin of pride (124–25).

# 5

# Promoting Social Change: Theoretical and Empirical Arguments for Using Traditional Community-Based Learning When Teaching Catholic Social Thought

*William P. Bolan*

All educators know the challenge of capturing their students' attention. Anyone who has ever turned from a blackboard to face unengaged faces recognizes that apathy is always knocking at the door. No matter what the subject, personally involving students is essential to learning. However, captivating students is not easy or even an end unto itself. Educators must further decide how to cultivate students' interests and must make choices about their roles as people with interests and beliefs of their own. Just how far should a professor's commitments enter the classroom? Should a teacher be satisfied with illustrating the importance of relevant issues? Should any views be presented as normative? Should a professor go so far as to encourage students' committed involvement with exclusive opinions and positions?

Both the debate on motivating students and how to develop that motivation come to a head in the "new" pedagogy of community-based learning, also commonly known as "service learning" or "experiential education."[1] By integrating traditional academics with hands-on experience, community-based learning (CBL) has enjoyed an impressive run as a way to attract and retain students in courses, prompting more than one educator to use it for this reason without further questioning.[2] The prospect of quickly energizing students is admittedly attractive. But, of course, provoking student interest is not the ultimate goal of educators. What kind of learning does CBL actually promote? Is it simply a powerful instrument for making alternative viewpoints come alive? Does it readily lead to substantive value decisions? Does it promote practical involvement with issues (i.e., beyond the course's site placement)? At a more minimal level, is it even effective at improving test scores? These questions are particularly acute for moral theologians teaching in the modern Catholic university. At a time when CBL is increasingly the pedagogy of choice in courses that deal with questions of values—especially social values—teachers must judge which of the outcomes are actually promoted by CBL. Moreover, they must discern which outcomes are optimal for their students. Deciding whether and how to use CBL touches on key issues concerning the role of the moral theologian as teacher.

In an attempt to look beyond CBL's mere popularity, this chapter considers the particular appropriateness of CBL for courses that deal with Catholic social teaching. Not only do such courses raise all of the questions mentioned here, but it is especially in such courses that CBL is being used with greater frequency in Catholic universities. Specifically, this chapter offers an analysis of arguments for the theoretical compatibility and the practical effectiveness of CBL in such courses. Are the pedagogical methodology and, moreover, the "goals" of Catholic social teaching truly compatible with those of CBL? Further, is CBL empirically effective in achieving these goals? Depending on the form of CBL considered, the answer may vary. Whereas some, more recent understandings and applications of CBL seem to conflict with the goals and aims of Catholic social teaching, a "traditional" approach and use of CBL affirms the goals and pedagogy inherent in Catholic social teaching quite markedly.

This research issues a challenge to Catholic educators to understand and implement the full potential of traditional CBL. Instead of seizing on CBL as a way to merely "spice up" course material, this chapter calls on Catholic educators to restore and reaffirm CBL in its original focus on questioning social values and helping students to see themselves as agents of social change. This, it is maintained here, is the proper goal of the Catholic theologian teaching social ethics. If practiced effectively, CBL helps students understand the implications of social justice in a more than academic way. Likewise, by virtue of its steadfast focus on embodying the gospel, Catholic social teaching helps prevent CBL from pretending to be a "value-neutral" pedagogy.

After first considering the theoretical and practical roots of the early CBL movement, this chapter considers how CBL's original goals and practices have been attenuated in its recent instantiations (first section). Calling on Catholic educators to reject this recent development, it then examines how the pedagogy inherent in Catholic social teaching resonates with the "traditional," that is, socially engaged, practice of CBL instead. That is to say, it argues that Catholic moral theologians are most true to Catholic social teaching when they practice the form of CBL that makes students confront judgments of value and facilitates the social commitments that follow them (second section). Moreover, it is argued here that the more substantive, or morally "thick," social values found in Catholic social teaching offer a way to bolster CBL's focus on social change without threatening its commitment to open inquiry. In this way, Catholic social teaching provides a means to both consciously and appropriately lead CBL to the goals for which it was originally conceived (third section). After concluding that "no holds barred" CBL and Catholic social teaching are sufficiently compatible to be endorsed by Catholic educators, this chapter then demonstrates why traditional CBL should be so attractive to Catholic educators not simply as a movement that shares kindred goals but also as a pedagogy that has been empirically proven to achieve these goals. Here Janet Eyler and Dwight Giles's singular study on the effects of CBL on over fifteen hundred students is considered. CBL is examined as a pedagogy that not only improves and enhances students' learning of raw data and concepts but moreover promotes transformational changes in their views and engagement with societal problems (fourth section). Finally, the chapter considers what concrete practical steps distinguish a course that simply has an off-site component from one that actively promotes social change. That is to say, it examines what practices used in some CBL classes have the statistically greatest correlation to changing and empowering students' social outlooks (fifth section). With this outline in mind, first consider the differences between traditional CBL and some of its more popular manifestations.

## THE THEORY AND AIMS OF
## MODERN COMMUNITY-BASED LEARNING

CBL is so universally referred to as a single pedagogy that it is easy to be unaware of the multiple ends for which it is and has been practiced. This fact is bolstered by the fact that CBL is commonly taken to be a "new" pedagogy— that is, few suspect it could have had much time to differentiate itself and take places among different schools of educational thought. Thus, the choice for moral theologians appears to be a simple one: should CBL be used or not? The reality, however, is that modern CBL has roots going back over seventy years. Knowledge of which historical strand of CBL is being considered is the first step in discerning its possible appropriateness for a course on Catholic social teaching.

The theoretical roots of modern "service learning" or "community-based learning" are generally traced to John Dewey.[3] Dewey's principles of education maintain that "learning occurs through a cycle of action and reflection, not simply through being able to recount what has been learned through reading and lecture."[4] Education, then, must necessarily have an experiential element. D. A. Kolb extended this idea with an articulation of four stages of student reflection, widely referenced by community-based learning practitioners:[5] concrete experience, reflective observation, abstract conceptualization, and active experimentation.[6] Each stage provides the material for the next one. Thus, in experiential education, students work in the community, think about what they have experienced, attempt to structure and critically correlate that experience with other research and analysis, and then construct and implement a plan of action.[7] These stages are part of a dynamic cycle that always begins anew since the results of "active experimentation" itself forms a concrete experience.

The idea of correlating traditional academic learning with experience-based judgments was taken up by the pioneers of the CBL movement in the 1960s, particularly in their attempts to address social, economic, and political problems.[8] Adopting the general principles of Dewey, they held that that experience was a necessary—and logically prior—component in any learning and problem solving. Furthermore, these pioneers were generally unified in their assessment that social injustice characterized the society in which they lived. Community-based learning, then, was viewed as a way for students to more accurately analyze social problems and to find more effective and far-reaching solutions to them. Among other things, it was a necessary instrument for students to effect social change.[9]

With the rapid expansion of CBL, however, many wonder if the theoretical roots and social aims of the movement have been forgotten. As Stanton, Giles, and Cruz put it, "Has this pedagogy been adapted to survive and expand in the mainstream?"[10] Questions of this type can be put to both the educational theory and social aims of CBL. As for educational theory, many ask if CBL is now merely a tool to illustrate and apply predetermined analyses and solutions.[11] Is modern CBL really utilized to empower students to think reflectively and form their own critical judgments and plans of action? Are students' experiences considered an original and legitimate source of learning? Are they actively correlated with the discussions and determinations of the classroom? Or is CBL merely used to spice up traditional texts, analyses, and conclusions? Many believe that the latter practice has become the dominant one.[12]

In the area of social aims, CBL has likewise been threatened with a loss of its original focus. For many, community-based learning now represents a relatively "value-neutral" pedagogical tool.[13] This is, some think, in part a function of its successes and rapid proliferation. CBL is often seen as a "new" educational phenomenon with no conceptual or historical roots.[14] As a result, CBL is increasingly understood as it is commonly presented—as an effective way to get students interested and involved in courses by offering them a hands-on "application" of what is learned in the classroom. Little if any reference is made to empowering students to use their experiences as a starting point for original learning, critical reflection, and social change.[15]

While some believe this recent phenomenon is the result of underinformed practitioners, others also name fear on the part of those who understand that social change is a conscious goal of traditional CBL. Janet Eyler and Dwight Giles observe that "some educators shy away from activities where students take a political stand, wary of being accused of using students to advance their own personal agendas."[16] Sometimes objections to CBL stem from a wariness of introducing politics into the classroom. As an example of possible reaction, Eyler and Giles note that they "were asked not to include [in a summary report on CBL courses] even the mildest and most abstract criticisms of politicians made by the students."[17] Specific fear of funding cuts on the part of educators, and general opposition to any pedagogical process that issues in making political choices and threatening the status quo, has led, in some corners, to a self-imposed limiting of CBL. The more safe option, it is seen, is to try to effect the pedagogical advantages of community-based learning—for example, the increased interest and involvement that on-site experience brings—without assuming the political disadvantages involved in following up with deeper analysis of societal institutions and making decisions about the current social structure.

However, this safe approach to CBL itself entails a value judgment about the state of society and the students' ability to effect change. As Kahne and Westheimer note, "It is important to acknowledge that the choice of service-learning activities—like the choice of any curricular activity—has political dimensions."[18] Among other things, how a social phenomenon is studied implies something about possible solutions. Drawing on actual classroom examples, Kahne and Westheimer distinguish between two general strands of community-based learning and examine each of these trends' outcomes in moral, political, and intellectual areas. One strand they label "charity," the other "change." In the "charity" model, they observe, students are pressed to see the need for greater concern and "giving" to social problems on an individual basis and for increased civic participation—for example becoming more aware of issues and voting. The intellectual focus is on making the studied problems "more real" to students. In the change model, however, while students are of course not made averse to altruistic urges, they are asked to extend these concerns to an active care for those they work with—that is, a commitment to not seeing them as "other." Likewise, while increased civic participation is not foregone, students are asked to further consider whether and what institutional changes are necessary to address certain problems. The intellectual outcome of this approach is, optimally, a transformation of the way students consider social problems.

## MODERN CATHOLIC SOCIAL TEACHING'S RESONANCE WITH COMMUNITY-BASED LEARNING

Is it, however, the Catholic moral theologian's job to transform students' social outlooks? I argue next that modern Catholic social teaching resonates with the "change" model of CBL, both in terms of social aims and educational theory. In addition to criticizing the justice of the current social order, Catholic social teaching offers a way to frame students' analyses and social actions in a way that integrally values and incorporates the insights that they develop through community work. In this way, Catholic social teaching promotes a change in students' social outlooks without forcing transformation on them. If true to the social encyclicals, the teacher of Catholic social teaching need not worry that he is "imposing" his views.

Key documents in Catholic social teaching affirm that today, more is needed than mere altruism and increased civic participation to address the world's problems. Using Kahne and Westheimer's terms, Catholic social teaching offers support for traditional CBL at the level of desired "moral" and "political" outcomes. First, at the moral level, modern Catholic social teaching has stressed the need to develop a virtue of solidarity that is more than an attitude of altruism. In the encyclical *Sollicitudo Rei Socialis*, John Paul II specifies that this solidarity "is not a feeling of vague compassion or shallow distress at the misfortunes of so many people, both near and far. On the contrary, it is a firm and persevering determination to commit oneself to the common good; that is to say to the good of all and of each individual, because we are all really responsible for all."[19] This determination is felt and enacted at a personal level. "Solidarity," he continues, "helps us to see the 'other' . . . as our 'neighbor,' a 'helper' to be made a sharer, on a par with ourselves, in the banquet of life to which all are equally invited by God."[20]

Second, at the "political" level, the commitment to solidarity calls for social change that is more than an increase in civic participation. "An effective political will is needed," John Paul II writes, to overcome the "misguided mechanisms" of the contemporary world and to "replace them with new ones which will be more just and in conformity with the common good of humanity."[21] The problem of poverty perhaps forms a paradigm for the tradition's approach to social change. "The motivating concern for the poor," John Paul writes, "must be translated at all levels into concrete actions, until it decisively attains a series of reforms."[22] This transformational kind of social change is both the logical and actual desire of both traditional community-based learning and modern Catholic social teaching.

At the level of educational theory, Todd David Whitmore has pointed out that modern Catholic social teaching has implications for pedagogy.[23] In particular, the form of practical reasoning embodied in Catholic social teaching affirms the general pedagogy of CBL. Whitmore writes that "experiential learning . . . follows from the insights from the tradition of practical reasoning"[24] found in modern Catholic social teaching. The emphasis is on building upward from experience and not downward from fixed notions about social issues. The pedagogy of community-based learning is particularly appropriate for courses that incorporate Catholic social teaching because, like practical reasoning, it insists on attention to the varying specifics of individual social problems. It does not assume, Whitmore notes, that answers to these problems are self-evident and deductible from any theoretical first principles. As *Gaudium et spes* states, we are charged with "scrutinizing the signs of the times and . . . interpreting them in light of the gospel."[25] Moreover, the tradition's principle of subsidiarity insists that the most competent persons to understand and frame answers to social problems are presumed to be those most involved with them. Although the services of more "removed" institutions (such as the state) may sometimes be necessary to assist in actions that cannot be performed at the local level, this necessity is not generally determined and ordered by any higher principles and authorities acting "above" practical reasoning and the immediate community. The presumption is that such services should originate precisely from the conclusions and invitation of those with more immediate experience of the issues involved.[26]

## CHALLENGES AND ADVANTAGES OF INTRODUCING THE VALUES OF CATHOLIC SOCIAL TEACHING IN COMMUNITY-BASED LEARNING

The previous section helps to illustrate that there is not a fundamental disagreement between Catholic social teaching and CBL on maintaining academic freedom while advancing values. Admittedly, Catholic social teaching offers a manner of ready-made political, economic, and social critiques that the pedagogy of CBL does not. This does not, however, point to a fundamental incompatibility between Catholic social teaching and CBL. While recognizing that Catholic social teaching offers a more morally "thick" account of social values and analyses, I maintain that it does this while staying faithful to the spirit of open and free-ranging inquiry that is the hallmark of traditional CBL. Moreover, I hold that discussing the principles and values of Catholic social teaching (helpfully) avoids the pitfall of pretending that there exists a "value-free" way of education—that is, the type of CBL discussed in the first section. The moral theologian, then, may advance a specific moral framework while honoring and even buttressing the traditional practice of CBL. She achieves this precisely by being faithful to Catholic social teaching.

Modern Catholic social teaching gravitates around several guiding themes and principles, such as the dignity of the human person, the promotion of human rights, and the preferential option for the poor. While committed to these concepts, however, and to consequently putting forth analyses of the contemporary world (criticizing, for example, the increasing gap between the poor and the rich, the North–South gap, and the excesses of capitalism), the tradition has been increasingly careful not to suggest that these principles and analyses are set or sufficient or to overly specify what they should mean concretely—for example, in the form of policy decisions.[27] As Whitmore points out, the Catholic tradition itself has come to recognize that its social doctrine by necessity develops.[28] While affirming that the church's social doctrine remains in relationship to its past, John Paul II states that it is "ever new."[29] The reason is that "it is subject to the necessary and opportune adaptations suggested by the changes in historical conditions and by the unceasing flow of the events which are the setting of the life of people and society."[30] Moreover, the Catholic social tradition does not claim that its principles and analyses are definitive or adequate for the contemporary problems to which it addresses itself.[31] Evoking the principle of subsidiarity discussed here, Paul VI notes that final judgments about social questions fall more properly in the hands of the men and women—and, one might add as a subset, students—who confront their social realities more directly. *Octogesima Adveniens* states,

> There is . . . a wide diversity among situations in which Christians—willingly and unwillingly—find themselves according to regions, socio-political systems, or cultures. In the face of such widely varying situations it is difficult for us to utter a unified message and to put forward a solution which has universal validity. Such is not our ambition, nor is it our mission. It is up to Christian communities to analyze with objectivity the situation which is proper to their own country, to shed on it the light of the Gospel's unalterable words and to draw principles of reflection, norms of judgment, and directives for action from the social teaching of the Church.[32]

The tradition itself invites men and women to engage their social situation hand in hand with—and not led by—the Catholic social tradition in order to discover evermore adequate analyses and solutions. Calling men and women to "reflect on the complex realities of human existence," it requires them to themselves "interpret these realities, determining their conformity with or divergence from the lines of the Gospel teaching on man and his vocation."[33] Its self-expressed aim is to "guide" human behavior, not dictate it.[34]

This open and nondeterminative invitation to reflect on and interpret the complex realities of human existence is precisely the end aimed at by traditional community-based practicioners. Community-based learning allows students to question both the nature of their own preconceptions and also the adequacy of concepts and analyses that have been constructed to meet social problems—including those of Catholic social teaching. So-called middle axioms provide substantive and important guidelines for social policy, but they themselves are not immune from debate. Only the most fundamental principles—for example, that every woman or man has a fundamental dignity and worth—are treated as immutable axioms of social analysis in Catholic social thought. Furthermore, there is nothing in Catholic thought that prevents a teacher's exploring the nature and utility of such principles with her students.[35] (Indeed, the question of the definition, scope, and general application of concepts such as human dignity has been the subject of substantial evolution in the history of modern Catholic social teaching.)

However, at the same time as it embraces the place of experience and promotes intellectual inquiry, there is no question that Catholic social teaching holds to normative social values and the need for change. In this way it avoids the trap of claiming that the most that social policy and planning can do is to maximize the values currently assumed and inherent in the contemporary social order. By questioning the adequacy of the current social order, Catholic social teaching points to the possibility of alternatives and the fact that modern social institutions and modern culture are not "givens" that proceed from immutable laws of society. Furthermore (at least if discussed with any depth), Catholic social teaching prevents students from believing that an infinite array of different social viewpoints can be readily accommodated in the same society. Unlike "value-neutral" CBL, courses on Catholic social teaching force students to see that social questions often involve choices among irreconcilable policies and values. Whether in agreement with Catholic social teaching or not, students must confront the fact that even "not taking sides" involves a value choice.

The benefit of a CBL course that treats Catholic social teaching, then, is twofold. On the one hand, students are invited to correlate their own and their societies' social sensibilities with the moral principles and social analyses expressed in Catholic social teaching. The necessity of making value decisions is clear. A course on Catholic social teaching that aims to promote the call to be "responsible builders of society"[36] states that the church's beliefs about Jesus's teaching and the nature of the human person have social consequences and, furthermore, necessitate a choice. It further gives guidelines—in the form of its principles and social analyses—for informing the nature of that choice. In other words, the less morally "thick" approach that threatens to attenuate CBL is not present in a Catholic social teaching course that is faithful to the social encyclicals. In the Catholic university, at least, this faithfulness can prevent CBL from becoming just another tool to "compare and contrast" without committment.

On the other hand, students are given tools to test even the most basic principles of the church's social doctrine—which of course is of paramount importance if they are ever to weigh them seriously and perhaps critically appropriate them.[37] By working in the concrete setting of community problems, students are empowered as experts. The possible analyses and solutions to social problems are no longer received exclusively through "secondary sources." In dialogue with the tradition and each other, the experience gained through CBL allows students to more informedly and concretely scrutinize their own, each other's, and the church's stance toward the people and problems they engage. Moreover, as we have seen, the Catholic social tradition itself empowers students to consider more adequate analyses and solutions to social problems. The proper "outcome" of a community-based learning/Catholic social teaching course is not predetermined.

## THE EFFECTIVENESS OF COMMUNITY-BASED LEARNING

I have argued, then, that traditional CBL and Catholic social teaching both share the goal of social change. Also, both CBL and Catholic social teaching espouse a "hands-on," nondeductive approach to social problems. Furthermore, Catholic social teaching is especially honest in denying that there exists a "value-free" way of education and social decision making. This general compatibility makes CBL an attractive pedagogy to moral theologians who teach Catholic social teaching. But the question remains of whether CBL is actually effective in encouraging students to think creatively about social problems and in promoting social engagement. Is it a trend in the worst sense of the word? If it is indeed effective, which practices are the most effective? In this section I consider some of the general results of the first large-scale study of the impact of CBL upon students' learning processes.[38] The last unit examines which specific CBL techniques are the most successful in achieving the goals of traditional CBL and Catholic social teaching.

In addition to the more political objections mentioned here, community-based learning has previously faced the criticism that it is not worthwhile as a pedagogy. Gray, Ondaatje, and Zakaras report the common objection that community-based learning "waters down the curriculum, further weakening the quality of higher education, and that the time students spend volunteering in community agencies as part of a course might be better spent [elsewhere]."[39] In essence, critics wonder whether community-based learning has any real impact on "what students learn."[40] As the most comprehensive study of the pedagogy demonstrates, however, CBL is an effective tool not only in promoting student engagement but moreover in transforming students' perspectives of social problems. While the latter result is not overly great, it is consistent and demonstrably greater than in courses that do not incorporate community-based learning.[41]

In 1999, Janet Eyler and Dwight Giles conducted the first in-depth study to assess the impact of community-based learning on a large number of students.[42] This study remains the most serious and scientifically valid study of CBL to date. Surveys were administered to over eleven hundred students both before and after they took courses that incorporated community-based learning. Surveys were also administered to four hundred students who were not enrolled in community-based learning classes, as a control. In the area of student engagement, students reported a marked improvement in multiple areas of traditional interest to educators. A majority of students, 58 percent, reported that they had learned more in courses that incorporated CBL than those that did not (24 percent reported that they had learned the same as in traditional courses); 55 percent of students indicated that they worked harder in community-based learning courses than traditional courses.[43] Moreover, students reported that "the learning that results from their service-learning experiences is richer and more applicable to real-world contexts than material they learn in traditional classes."[44]

Such results give the lie to those who claim that community-based learning is not an effective pedagogical tool. Of even greater interest to the promoter of social justice, however, is the effect that community-based learning has on what Eyler and Giles call "transformational learning."[45] Such learning occurs when students attempt not just to expand their "knowledge base" about a persistent social problem but to scrutinize the presuppositions that underlie that base. (As an example they contrast the student who learns about the more immediate causes of homelessness [e.g., deinstitutionalization] versus one who begins to question the policy decisions that may indirectly or directly contribute to these causes.[46]) While Eyler and Giles recognize that such learning may not issue in the reversal of a student's "fundamental assumptions about society"—what they call "perspective transformation"[47]—their study shows that community-based learning promotes a climate that allows such perspective transformation to take place. Fully one-third of CBL students claimed that they gain a "new perspective" on social problems through community-based learning.[48] Furthermore, Eyler and Giles's study shows that community-based learning has a demonstrable impact on students' views of the institutional nature of societal problems and their necessary solutions. This reported impact included students' ability to see the systemic nature of social problems, their perception of the need for greater social justice, and their opinion that "the most important community service is to change public policy."[49] Finally, students reported an increased personal commitment to community involvement and political change. Students in CBL courses indicated a greater dedication to affecting the political structure than students in traditional courses.[50] In this vein, 75 percent of students participating in CBL courses said that they would continue to work in their community during their next semester.[51]

## PRACTICES OF CBL THAT WORK

As alluded to earlier, all CBL courses are not equally effective in attaining the results just described. Simply sending students to an off-campus site does not guarantee a transformation of their social outlooks. Besides deciding whether to use CBL, the Catholic educator needs to know which CBL practices are most effective in achieving the goals of traditional CBL and Catholic social teaching. Accordingly, this section considers Eyler and Giles's findings on the correlations between sought-after goals and certain practices of CBL.

First, it should be noted that there are positive effects of most kinds of courses that incorporate placements that deal with social issues (e.g., in social service or community development organizations), regardless of how they are structured. As a start, within reasonable limits one can expect that CBL will act to promote the sense that those suffering from social injustices are real people, that the "other" is really a "neighbor."[52] To this end, community-based learning has proven to have a dramatic effect on the way that students view the clients and employees of the community-based organizations with which they work. Eyler and Giles report that the majority of students in CBL courses "showed reductions in stereotyping, greater appreciation for diverse cultures, increased tolerance, and the sense that the people they met through community service were 'just like me.'"[53] This is often true even for short-term placements.[54] Even if nothing else is achieved through a course, this is a first and vital step toward building social consciousness.

Another effect not statistically tied to specific practices of CBL is the pedagogy's ability to make students aware of the reality and extent of social problems. As large numbers of students in higher education are privileged and unexposed to the realities of social problems, this is not a negligible result.[55] Direct exposure to social problems can have an impact on students regardless of its duration.[56] CBL of many forms allows students to engage the realities of social problems in a manner that is personal and immediate. Students are not told that certain social problems are real and that they have a duty to do something about them. Rather, they are left to experience this.[57] The mere fact of being "on-site" makes the recognition and analysis of social problems both more possible and more real.

However, beyond allowing students to become personally aware of the "real" dimension of social problems, Catholic social teaching courses also seek to promote awareness of the systemic nature of social problems and a commitment to structural change. It is in these areas that Eyler and Giles show that certain CBL courses are more effective than others. First and foremost, courses that incorporate frequent critical reflection on students' CBL experiences are more likely to issue in systemic analyses and student commitment than those that do not.[59] These reflections may take many forms, including written essays and journals, as well as class discussion and presentations. If the reflections are written, their study indicates, this work is most effective when it is more than a consideration of personal experiences. Instead, the work should critically relate the students' experiences with the subject matter of the class. Furthermore, written reflections optimally attempt to incorporate "action planning,"—that is, efforts to structure solutions to social problems.[60] The same points hold for discussion and reflection. Discussion should not, Eyler and Giles caution, be a simple exchange of various students' stories. The most effective student dialogues are those that attempt to mutually correlate students' experiences with social analysis and the further attempt to discover social solutions.[61] When all forms of student reflection are frequently and critically related back to the subject of the course, CBL courses have an even greater transformative effect on students' perspectives and social commitment.[62]

Eyler and Giles also report that greater student impact requires quality student placements of significant duration.[63] Students should receive adequate training, have on-site supervision, and get substantive feedback from both the work-site staff and their teacher.[64] In addition to these factors, a second study shows that a minimum of twenty placement hours (overall) is necessary for deeper student impact.[65] Eyler and Giles also specify that quality placements should include "varied tasks, important responsibilities, interesting work, and challenge."[66] Furthermore, there should be a close connection between the subject matter of the course and the work done in the community organization.[67] Such qualities allow students to have more meaningful interactions with clients and employees of the organizations at which they work, to observe social problems firsthand, and to think reflectively on their experiences. Most important, Eyler and Giles observe, the quality of "challenge" seems to be the greatest indicator of placement success. If a student is simply serving meals in a soup kitchen (i.e., and not further interacting with that kitchen's guests in any way), his or her social analysis is not liable to proceed terribly far. However, more significant interaction is more likely to engage and challenge students' opinions and spur them on to critical reflection.[68]

Finally, the possibility for students to continue CBL experiences beyond a given course seems crucial in promoting and developing students' social commitment. Although Eyler and Giles restricted their study to the impact of CBL over a single semester, their background work with students with greater CBL experience suggests that a single course is not enough to transform many students' social perspectives.[69] This resonates with common sense about the nature of human moral development. It is all the more reason, given the significant success of CBL in the short run, to promote the continued and increased offering of CBL courses throughout departments and universities. It is only by creating an atmosphere steeped in deeper social analysis and commitment that students may be motivated for social change.

For better and worse reasons, the temptation to use CBL is a great one for the Catholic educator. On the one hand, CBL in all its forms is undeniably effective in commanding students' attention and interest. Furthermore, CBL of all kinds seems proven in its ability to make students aware of the scope and human face of social problems. But to stop at these results is to sell both

Catholic social teaching and CBL short. Even worse, a less-reflective appropriation of CBL threatens to undermine the methods and goals of both
Catholic social teaching and traditional CBL. It is only by seriously focusing
on substantive moral values and by doing so in an inductive manner that students' and teachers' moral development are truly served well. When practiced effectively and conscientiously, CBL offers a way to realize both the
pedagogy and the ends of Catholic social teaching. Likewise, at least in
Catholic academia, Catholic social teaching provides a means to restore CBL
to its original and great promise.

## NOTES

1. This chapter uses the term *community-based learning* instead of the more
common *service learning* or *experiential learning*. The term *service learning* is
avoided because of its potential to denote activity wherein community organizations
are the passive recipients of students' charity. This is opposed to learning in which
the clients and employees of community organizations are in a sense "co-teachers,"
actively enriching the students' learning with their own lessons and gifts. Likewise,
the term *experiential learning* is avoided since it may connote a vision of students
who are going to study situations and realities that are "outside of" their prior range
of experience. This assumption about prior experience may be erroneous. The term
*community-based learning* avoids these pitfalls. (I am grateful to Todd David Whitmore and the deliberations of the Conference on Teaching Catholic Social Teaching
[University of Notre Dame, August 2001], for these observations.)

2. For example, over 72 percent of university students in community-based learn-
ing (CBL) courses evaluate them as above average. See Maryann J. Gray, Elizabeth H.
Ondaatje, and Laura Zakaras, *Combining Service and Learning in Higher Education*
(Santa Monica, Calif.: RAND, 1999), 7.

3. John Dewey, *Experience and Education* (New York: Collier Books, 1938).

4. Janet Eyler and Dwight E. Giles Jr., *Where's the Learning in Service-Learning?*
(San Francisco, Calif.: Jossey-Bass, 1999), 7–8.

5. Eyler and Giles, *Where's the Learning?* 195.

6. D. A. Kolb, *Experiential Learning: Experience as the Source of Learning and
Development* (Englewood Cliffs, N.J.: Prentice Hall, 1984).

7. See Eyler and Giles, *Where's the Learning?* 195.

8. Timothy Stanton, Dwight Giles, and Nadinne Cruz, *Service Learning: A Movement's Pioneers Reflect on Its Origins, Practice, and Future* (San Francisco: Jossey-
Bass, 1999).

9. Stanton, Giles, and Cruz, *Service Learning*, xv–11.

10. Stanton, Giles, and Cruz, *Service Learning*, xv.

11. This demonstrates another downside of the term *experiential learning*. While
it is not inevitable, the concept of "experiencing" often evokes an image of mere observation.

12. See Joseph Kahne and Joel Westheimer, "In the Service of What? The Politics
of Service Learning," in *Service Learning for Youth Empowerment and Social
Change*, ed. J. Claus and C. Ogden (New York: Peter Lang, 1999), 25–42, esp. 37–38.

13. Stanton, Giles, and Cruz, *Service Learning*, 2.

14. Stanton, Giles, and Cruz, *Service Learning*, xi–xvi.

15. Or change in whatever area is studied. This chapter presupposes the use of CBL in courses considering social issues, but the pedagogy is of course not limited to any particular discipline.

16. Eyler and Giles, *Where's the Learning?* 131.

17. Eyler and Giles, *Where's the Learning?* 131.

18. Kahne and Westheimer, "In the Service of What?" 38.

19. John Paul II, *Encyclical Letter Sollicitudo Rei Socialis*, n. 38, in *Catholic Social Thought: The Documentary Heritage*, ed. D. J. O'Brien and T. A. Shannon (Maryknoll, N.Y.: Orbis Books, 1992).

20. John Paul II, *Sollicitudo Rei Socialis*, n. 39.

21. John Paul II, *Sollicitudo Rei Socialis*, n. 35.

22. John Paul II, *Sollicitudo Rei Socialis*, n. 43.

23. Todd David Whitmore, "Practicing the Common Good: The Pedagogical Implications of Catholic Social Teaching," *Teaching Theology and Religion* 3, no. 1 (2000): 3–19.

24. Whitmore, "Practicing the Common Good," 16.

25. *Gaudium et spes*, n. 4, quoted from Whitmore, "Practicing the Common Good," 11.

26. See Whitmore, "Practicing the Common Good," 14.

27. See John Paul II, *Sollicitudo Rei Socialis*, n. 41.

28. Whitmore, "Practicing the Common Good," 5–6.

29. John Paul II, *Sollicitudo Rei Socialis*, n. 3.

30. John Paul II, *Sollicitudo Rei Socialis*, n. 3.

31. See Whitmore, "Practicing the Common Good," 5–7.

32. Paul VI, *Octogesima Adveniens*, nn. 3–4, in O'Brien and Shannon, *Catholic Social Thought*.

33. John Paul II, *Sollicitudo Rei Socialis*, n. 41.

34. John Paul II, *Sollicitudo Rei Socialis*, n. 41.

35. For example, does speaking of the special dignity of human beings ever work to disprivilege the dignity of the rest of God's creation? Furthermore, there is nothing pedagogically or theologically wrong—and perhaps everything right—with discussing even the most obvious of fundamental principles. Especially if students do not believe in the dignity of all women and men, this is the logical place to begin discussion.

36. John Paul II, *Sollicitudo Rei Socialis*, n. 1

37. I am greatly indebted to Margaret Pfeil for her work on the Catholic social tradition as a *living* tradition that students rightly advance through a mutually critical correlation of community-based learning and Catholic social thought. See "Experiential Learning in Service of a Living Tradition," in *Theology and the New Histories*, ed. Gary Macy (Maryknoll, N.Y.: Orbis Press, 1999).

38. Eyler and Giles, *Where's the Learning?*

39. Gray, Ondaatje, and Zakaras, *Combining Service*, 1.

40. Eyler and Giles, *Where's the Learning?* xv.

41. Eyler and Giles, *Where's the Learning?* xvii.

42. Eyler and Giles, *Where's the Learning?*

43. Eyler and Giles, *Where's the Learning?* 60.

44. Eyler and Giles, *Where's the Learning?* 98.

45. Eyler and Giles, *Where's the Learning?* 129–50.

46. Eyler and Giles, *Where's the Learning?* 133.

47. Eyler and Giles, *Where's the Learning?* 135.

48. Eyler and Giles, *Where's the Learning?* 149 and 136.

49. Eyler and Giles, *Where's the Learning?* 136.

50. Eyler and Giles *Where's the Learning?* 157ff.

51. Eyler and Giles, *Where's the Learning?* 162.

52. John Paul II, *Sollicitudo Rei Socialis*, n. 39.

53. Eyler and Giles, *Where's the Learning?* 142, 23–34.

54. Eyler and Giles, *Where's the Learning?* 141.

55. See, for example, Keith Anderson, "Ida, the Subway Station, and Thinking about Learning," *Religious Education* 89, no. 4 (1994): 493–501.

56. See Eyler and Giles, *Where's the Learning?* 141.

57. Eyler and Giles, *Where's the Learning?* 141.

58. Eyler and Giles, *Where's the Learning?* 137.

59. Eyler and Giles, 175–77. See also, Kahne and Westheimer, "In the Service of What?" 37.

60. Eyler and Giles, *Where's the Learning?* 189.

61. Eyler and Giles, *Where's the Learning?* 137.

62. Eyler and Giles, *Where's the Learning?* 136.

63. Eyler and Giles, *Where's the Learning?* 135.

64. Gray, Ondaatje, and Zakaras, *Combining Service*, 9.

65. Gray, Ondaatje, and Zakaras, *Combining Service*.

66. Eyler and Giles, *Where's the Learning?* 137.

67. Eyler and Giles, *Where's the Learning?* 189.

68. Eyler and Giles, *Where's the Learning?* 137.

69. See Eyler and Giles, *Where's the Learning?* 135.

# 6

# Moral Theology for Real People: Agency, Practical Reason, and the Task of the Moral Theologian

*David Cloutier*

## WHAT'S THE "USE" OF MORAL THEOLOGY? FROM GUIDANCE FOR CONFESSORS TO GUIDANCE FOR LIFE

Recent histories of moral theology all tie the development of the discipline, particularly in postmedieval times, to the task of the confessional.[1] As a discrete discipline, "moral theology" does not really appear until postmedieval times. Even for Aquinas in the thirteenth century, there is no discrete task of "moral theology" or "Christian ethics" in the *Summa*. Prior to the rise of the so-called moral manuals, theological reflection on the Christian life was not separated from the tasks we now assign to "systematic theology" or to "spirituality" or to "liturgy." Servais Pinckaers links the rise of the manuals to the (certainly admirable) establishment of the modern seminary system by the Council of Trent but notes that the manuals significantly distorted moral reflection due to their approach to the subject. Pinckaers notes that the "four foundation stones" of the manuals were "human or free action, law, conscience, and sin."[2] These topics composed what became known as "fundamental moral theology," while the evaluation of particular cases then followed in "special moral theology." This approach makes sense when one looks at the specific task the manuals were to perform: assisting priests in hearing confessions and, particularly, in the standardization of confessional practice. But beyond that task, the Tridentine paradigm fostered a focus on isolated acts, a minimalistic approach to the moral life, a focus on sin, and ultimately an anthropology caught between freedom and law.

The tools of our discipline have been forged in this furnace, and even though the usefulness of the furnace itself has been in question for at least fifty years, we have still been puttering about with the same tools. Even before the council, much significant work (now somewhat neglected) was done by various figures who attempted to tinker with the furnace and shape some new tools, but it was the twin events of the council itself and the subsequent controversy over the teaching of *Humanae Vitae* that provoked a quarter century of contentious disciplinary renovation.[3] The council instructed moral theology to become more nourished by the Scriptures and to show forth the nobility of the Christian vocation of all the faithful.[4] In tandem with the renewal afoot in the discipline itself, the council's instruction formally recognized the limitations of the manual tradition, particularly its tendency to center the moral life on law. The issuance of *Humanae Vitae*, then, brought the situation to a paradoxical fever pitch, because for many the encyclical "contradicted" this renewal. Some of the tools of the tradition, particularly the notion of "conscience," were used to batter the encyclical itself, and quite quickly, a new paradigm of moral theology—best known as "revisionism"—came to the fore.[5] Other forms of renewal were also taking place, in the work of diverse younger figures such as Pinckaers and Germain Grisez, who were just as critical of the manualist tradition but took different paths of constructive renewal.[6]

In all of these cases, the previous orientation of the discipline to the practice of confession falls away quite rapidly. The work no longer takes the manual form, the writing is no longer wholly directed to the education of priests in seminaries, and the topics considered move far beyond the status of laws and the responsibilities for sins. But if moral theology was no longer centered on confessional practice, what function did it serve? Though there is not always clarity on this issue, I would argue that one crucial characteristic of postconciliar moral theology, which is now presumed, is that *moral theology seeks to provide action-guiding wisdom for living the Christian life as a whole, that its primary task is in terms of the formation of agents.* Put another way, moral theology shed its orientation to the confessional and entered into being a discipline concerned much more broadly with guiding and developing the practical reasoning ability of Christians and not simply their ability to understand and account for their sins.

Perhaps the best characterization of this turn is provided in a review of generally antiproportionalist responses to *Veritatis Splendor* as a drift toward moral theology done in a "sapiential mode."[7] This label characterizes the way in which other moral theologians have across the board recharacterized the task of the discipline. Germain Grisez openly avows that his revision of Thomism arises out of a perception that moral theology "needs a forward-looking perspective. Its primary orientation should be toward preaching, teaching, and counseling, to assist the faithful in living full and rich lives in

Jesus."[8] Proportionalism comes about largely in pastoral response to *Humanae Vitae*, and the issue of contraception acted as the representative of a larger task of revising long-standing moral norms that had come to appear as arbitrary and ungrounded.[9] But more broadly, liberal revisionists claimed that "the renewed moral theology . . . focuses on the total human vocation of living in response to God's self-communication to us in creation, in history, and most fully in Jesus."[10] Anne Patrick's work in developing a thorough understanding of conscience particularly fed by literature culminates in a conviction that "we must also grow more confident and competent in the skills of practical moral reasoning and acting."[11] Examples could be multiplied almost infinitely; the point is that the task of moral theology (as well as its practicioners) changed radically.

The tools of the discipline, however, have not always changed with this turn to the sapiential task. This chapter tries to provide an explanation of why we have in our midst a new and exciting furnace (thanks to all, both "liberal" and "conservative" who have worked in the last two generations) but some very inadequate tools with which to work on it. To extend the metaphor to its breaking point, I am not at all sure the furnace has been *installed* in the household that is the church, but it certainly has been *delivered*. However, it is uninstalled because various parties have not developed the tools to install it and have engaged in a fair amount of unproductive fighting over the tools that are closest at hand.

A moral theology that actually hopes to heat the house—that is to say, to provide energy for present-day Catholics to reason wisely about their lives and their world—*must start by adequately characterizing the challenges to moral reflection that the People of God actually face.* This chapter seeks to accomplish two purposes as part of such a reformulation of moral theology as sapiential. The first purpose is to argue how presently available moral theologies tend to mischaracterize the actual challenges facing ordinary Catholics. Since they mischaracterize the problem, it is not surprising that their solutions are also inadequate. To be sure, they provide *partially* illuminating accounts, but their focus is so much on overcoming certain mistakes perceived in other moral theologians (i.e., supposedly invidious accounts of rules) that their picture of "the problem" does not really reflect what is faced by the person in the pew. Consequently, their solution is not accepted.[12] Subsequently, the second purpose is to develop a more adequate picture of the problem, to open the way to better constructive work on solutions. In developing this picture, I rely on the recent work of Alasdair MacIntyre, who has provided a nuanced picture of the challenges to practical reason in today's world, one that also seems to match up well with the characteristics exhibited by my students and my fellow parishioners.[13] To conclude, I gesture at certain constructive pathways of teaching and research that follow naturally from MacIntyre's account.

## THE BOOSTERS AND THE KNOCKERS: MISCHARACTERIZING
## THE PROBLEMS OF ORDINARY CATHOLICS

So, then, the first task: how do current options in Catholic moral theology mislead us about the problems facing ordinary Catholics?[14] To steal a phrase from Charles Taylor, Catholic moral theology is divided between "boosters" and "knockers," each of whom fails to assess the promise and the peril of the present situation accurately.[15] The boosters are clearly the proportionalists. While their general endorsement of changing with the "signs of the times" has gotten considerably less triumphant since the sixties, they remain convinced of at least two things: that *Humanae Vitae* is wrong and that rules in general should be nuanced by various factors, especially when facing inevitable situations of conflict. Thus, their constant target is any form of legalism—which normally means the application of moral rules without regard for what they have termed the "principle of totality."[16] Legalism involves an uncritical (and, according to proportionalists, physicalist) adherence to and application of moral rules, particularly in the areas of sexual and medical ethics.[17] Proportionalists are often in direct reaction against their own preconciliar formation and the church that they witnessed at that time. The continued presence of John Paul II in the papacy has allowed legalism to remain the enemy, as is evidenced in some reactions to *Veritatis Splendor*. Their assumption is that today's students have the tendency to accept rules as absolute and exceptionless.

A recent article laments, "Where have all the proportionalists gone?" and it seems quite obvious to me that they are "gone" because their system addresses an enemy that barely exists.[18] Not a single one of my students approaches the moral life in straightforwardly legalist fashion. While some still recognize the importance of rules, none of them seem to be averse to questioning one or another church teaching, nor do they appear to accept such teaching without wanting an explanation of it. Insofar as the proportionalists are mounting *a criticism of the manualist tradition*, they are correct to attribute to it a sort of "legalism." But, both as a characterization of recent defenses of certain moral teachings and *as a characterization of the problem facing Catholic practical reason today*, the charge of legalism is very unconvincing.

The nascent strength of the knockers in this debate has undoubtedly to do with their more convincing choice of an enemy, relativism. *Veritatis Splendor* begins its third section by stressing the central theme of the unbreakable relationship between freedom and truth and offers the following assessment:

> Pilate's question: "What is truth" reflects the distressing perplexity of a man who often no longer knows who he is, whence he comes, and where he is going. Hence we not infrequently witness the fearful plunging of the human person

into situations of gradual self-destruction. . . . The saving power of the truth is contested, and freedom alone, uprooted from any objectivity, is left to decide by itself what is good and what is evil. This relativism becomes, in the field of theology, a lack of trust in the wisdom of God, who guides man with the moral law.[19]

The knockers, particularly in response to the years of strength of the proportionalists, are convinced that the real problem in contemporary Catholic practical reason is not that they follow rules too strictly but that many Catholics cannot follow them at all and so are headed for "gradual self-destruction."

While recent nonproportionalist work in moral theology displays a rich variety and sophistication, giving the lie to any charges that these moral theologies merely seek to "return" to some ostensibly preconciliar state, they nevertheless remain centrally concerned with the defense of absolute moral norms. For example, in the introduction to his *Introduction to Moral Theology*, Romanus Cessario seeks to place his project within the "current climate," saying, "Because of the shaping forces active in contemporary culture, insisting on the perennial validity of norms for human conduct, especially those precepts that, because of their necessary relation to fostering the good of the human person, allow for no exception, has generated a challenging project."[20] The (perhaps unwitting) implication here is that, despite the complexity of Cessario's subsequent presentation, the driving purpose of contemporary moral theology lies in the defense of norms in a climate that is fundamentally hostile to the idea of rules—that is to say, a climate of "relativism." As evidence for this hostility, Cessario cites an article by Alan Wolfe, in which he summarizes that "most Americans want to decide for themselves what is right, good, and meaningful."[21] Cessario then quickly transitions to a concern over false Enlightenment notions of absolute freedom or autonomy that are incompatible with Christian teaching about God and the human person. Thus, following the central argument of the middle chapter of *Veritatis Splendor*, a false notion of absolute freedom, popularly characterized by Wolfe, is made out to be the central difficulty faced by contemporary moral theology.

An "exaggerated conception of human freedom" is a concern, one made even more pressing by the fact that such exaggerated arguments about autonomy are prominent in some proportionalist moral theology.[22] Such conceptions are to be countered by an account of "the truth about the good," for "only truth allows us to overcome the sterility of subjectivism and relativism."[23] In nonnormative ethics, "independence from truth coincides with the demand of a will related to no one and to no thing, because it recognizes no one and no thing prior to its decisions."[24] Hence, Cessario's "realist" moral theology "proceeds on the basis of convictions about the human being,

about the world, and about being that depend on objective truth as its foundation."[25] If an absolute conception of freedom is in fact the contemporary dis-
ease, it is a firm assertion of "truth" ("objective" truth) that will counter it.[26]

The knockers are closer to the truth of the matter, to be sure. The challenge of running an undergraduate moral theology class is not convincing
students that they can disagree with rules but convincing them that moral
theology can be a "class"—that is to say, we can actually learn something
about how to think about the moral life that is not "just opinion." However,
note that the antiproportionalists' characterization of the problem (like the
proportionalists' characterization) is directed by seizing upon an agent's *approach to moral rules* and particularly that narrow set of moral rules called
"moral absolutes."[27] From this attitude toward moral absolutes, antiproportionalists quite rapidly conclude that those who reject moral absolutes are
suffering from relativism and threatening to fall into an abyss of nihilism.

But here is where things get interesting, for although my students may not
be "legalists," they are also very bad candidates for nihilism.[28] To be sure, nihilism can have a "human face," but my students are far too well-formed to
be relativists, and Nietzsche's notion of absolute freedom attracts no more
than a handful of them.[29] As R. R. Reno argues in a very illuminating article,
their relativism is *dogmatic*. It consists in certain slogans in which the students do not actually believe.[30] Moral philosophy may be constantly preoccupied with a search for *foundations*, but despite their inability to articulate
foundations, my students do not lack moral convictions, as can be demonstrated to them quite quickly. They all, for example, regard rape as wrong.
The issue of rape is a very helpful example because it not only defuses the
question of whether any act is "wrong" but also the question of whether any
sexual act can be said to be "wrong."

Moreover, even beyond obvious issues such as rape and slavery, most students operate out of some strong moral convictions. Here the analysis of un-
philosophical commentators such as Wolfe, combined with an ivory-tower
analysis of the errors of proportionalism, gives a misleading picture of the
state of morality in the public at large, or at least the public that retains some
degree of connection to the church. Wolfe takes at face value the rejection of
authoritative rules rather than recognize it as a *slogan*, and consequently
Cessario (and others) propose quickly that many persons possess an absolute notion of their own freedom. The alarmist language is misplaced, both
because in reality absolute freedom is an impossibility for human persons
and because most people do not even regard such freedom as desirable.[31]
For example, the conviction that sex should be private and consensual is *not*
a relativistic belief at all but a strong claim about the nature and goods of sexuality. Furthermore, a large number of students who dissent from the teaching against premarital sex believe that "casual sex" is wrong. The students articulate their defense of this position *not* in proportionalist terms but in terms

of the goods involved in sexuality. The distinction, present in both language and practice, is not one a relativist, committed to the absolute freedom of the individual, would hold.[32]

What approach to moral rules is going on here, if it is neither legalist nor relativist? We can grasp the social roots of their approach to rules by looking at some other concrete examples. American society, particularly American teenagers, functions with civil laws that set a certain age requirement for the use of alcohol and tobacco. For many teenagers, these become very much a day-to-day concern. If typical statistics are used as a guide, the majority of American teenagers act in violation of one or both of these rules. For many of these, doing so is routine and repeated. What are we to make of this? Presumably, many of these teenagers who violate these rules regard them as somehow mistaken or at least mistaken if taken as absolutes. Many might regard the use of alcohol or tobacco by a ten-year-old with substantial suspicion but would not necessarily do so if a sixteen-year-old is involved. Does that mean it is merely the particular choice of an age that is contested? More likely, it is a sense that choosing *any* particular age as absolute is mistaken. They may regard such choices as somehow personal, linked to an ability to use these products "responsibly" or at least an ability to make an informed choice that one can own as one's own. They may regard the rules as appropriate, even when breaking them, as doing the best possible job of setting some sort of necessary boundary, even if the boundary is in reality much more fluid.[33]

Here it should become clear that, while the students are clearly not legalists, they still regard rules as having force. Students who in practice dissent from the tradition's teaching on premarital sex generally do not regard the teaching as "too strict." Why? They say they appreciate the need to set a strong limit in order to prevent gross violations. I dub this the "speed limit approach" to moral rules, and the students find this description quite attractive. People routinely drive five to ten miles per hour over the limit, but the limits are necessary so that people are less inclined to drive one hundred miles per hour (which is generally regarded as "wrong"). Indeed, the switch away from a limit of fifty-five miles per hour in the eighties and nineties involved a recognition that it was not desirable to set limits that people found too low. Nevertheless, the newer limits continue to be regarded with the same sort of "leeway," just a more manageable one. Perhaps the best way to get a sense of this is to name it the "guideline" approach. Moral rules act as *necessarily cautious guidelines*. My eggs may have a date stamped on the package, but we all know that such dates are "conservative." So too are these moral guidelines. The twenty-one-year drinking age is "conservative." Note that this approach to moral rules indicates that my students, as a whole, are not under the sway of illusions about their (or anyone's) absolute freedom— rather, they tend to approach rules as providing a sort of flexible wisdom that indicates a loose but nevertheless present moral order.[34]

This is not, I think, a wholly bad thing—it indicates to me that my non-rule-abiding students are neither relativists nor proportionalists but have made a basic discovery that moral action requires *phronesis* and the virtue of prudence. They have begun to learn to "make the transition from accepting what we are taught by those earliest teachers to making our own independent judgments about goods."[35] This is crucial for how moral theology is to go about doing its thinking and teaching and serving. It suggests further why many of the debates in moral theology at present are not at all helpful. To some extent, my students have progressed beyond the moral theologians, or perhaps it would be better to say that they have never needed to get stuck in the conceptual debates of theologians, because they have not been corrupted by the language of the debate. What is important is to figure out what sort of "moral theory" is in fact helpful in developing the students as successful moral agents. They are doing ethics all the time—perhaps not well, but they are doing it.

## RECOVERING PRACTICAL REASON:
## ASSESSING THE PROBLEMS OF ORDINARY CATHOLICS

So why, then, are certain slogans of a relativistic and entirely subjective morality appealing? What ordinary Catholics lack, I argue, is the capacity to adequately reflect on or reason about their convictions. Thus, the second purpose of the chapter is now possible: if the situation ordinary Catholics find themselves in is more complicated, can we find a more adequate assessment of their problems? What people lack is an ability to understand themselves as *capable of the task of reasoning practically about these convictions.* This is the deficiency that a more sapiential moral theology has to address, and it is a deficiency that largely tracks the "flight from authority" that drives the relativistic bent of contemporary culture as a whole.[36] In this section, I draw on the recent work of Alasdair MacIntyre in order to provide a better characterization of the problem than that given by "legalism" or "relativism." Following this analysis, I conclude with some constructive paths for the discipline in light of the improved characterization of the moral "signs of the times."

In a recent essay, MacIntyre characterizes the situation hindering our ethical reflection as one of "moral thoughtlessness." In such a situation as ours, he notes that everyday people tend to embody a paradoxical combination of "moral dogmatism" and "moral indeterminacy"—either moral complexity is ignored in favor of easy assertions and slogans, or moral complexity and diversity is so evident and overwhelming that no position is held with conviction.[37] MacIntyre's initial picture explains to us why both the boosters and the knockers regard their picture of the problem as accurate. The boosters are arrayed against the advances of the moral dogmatists, while the knockers see the advancing enemy as the state of moral indeterminacy. But MacIntyre helps us to see *both* forces as present and problematic; thus, thoughtlessness appears in both legalist and relativist garbs, sometimes even within the same person.

What is the source of such thoughtlessness? An inability to approach rules properly such that it might be remedied by proportionalist or antiproportionalist accounts? Quite the contrary, for MacIntyre warns that, most often, such competing "modern moral theories" only make the situation worse. Theories (like proportionalism) that portray prudence as some sort of weighing come in for the harshest criticism in this chapter. Faced with a decision whose moral weight we cannot avoid, we will engage in a process of "weighing," which is seen, in an abstract example, in attempts to resolve cases in which rights and utility make competing claims. These metaphors of weighing and balancing, omnipresent in parish, neighborhood, and state, are particularly insidious, according to MacIntyre: "How is this metaphor to be understood? What plays the part of the scales that provide some measure of weight and balance? . . . The short answer is: there are no such scales. . . . And the mind which allows thought to terminate with this metaphor disguises this fact from itself. What is also disguised is the nature of the nonrational influences that are at work in the making of such decisions—the influences concealed by the metaphor."[38] Thus, "balancing" conceals the extent to which the actual decision is dependent on forces that are not rationally available to us. The result: "moral thoughtlessness." In another essay, MacIntyre warns that acquaintance with competing Kantian theories is not necessarily better, since in such a case the person will find oneself involved in the irresolvable debates of modern moral philosophy and most likely end up cynical about any resolution to those debates. This will sound familiar to many who teach our subject in the classroom.[39]

The central problem here is assuming that moral reflection is primarily or foundationally about rule following, which continues to be assumed in debates in moral theologies, despite disavowals of preconciliar legalism on both sides. Insofar as moral theology is *not* about explaining and clarifying rules and rule following, it has often been hazy about what it is in fact about.

MacIntyre offers the following alternative to a rule-based account of our moral crisis: moral thoughtlessness arises from the fact "that individuals without being adequately aware of it are molded by forces at work in their social environment, so that their judgments express uncritically attitudes that they've never had an opportunity to make genuinely their own. They don't exhibit bad character so much as lack of character."[40] It is important to note here that, while MacIntyre is clear that the primary concern is with forces *external* to the self, these forces most often appear (in deliberation) as competing desires *within* the self, whose external ancestry is concealed. This inability to acknowledge and discriminate among desires, then, is the crucial component of the loss of moral agency. And "the knowledge needed for moral agency . . . is the knowledge of how to discriminate among the various objects of attention *presented to us by our desires*."[41] The aim "of course" is not to rid oneself of external influences (that would be "impossible") but rather "to make one's desires truly one's own, by making them, so far as possible, responsive only to those influences to which it is for the agent's good to be responsive."[42]

Hence, the central problem: *an inability to understand and order desires.* While rules play a part in ordering desire, they do not play a foundational role. This picture makes much better sense of the presence of both convictions and relativistic slogans among my students than "legalism" or "relativism." But why is ordering desires (a fundamental task of virtue) such a difficult and arbitrary-seeming task to us? That is, why is it "thoughtless" instead of rational? This question seeks the deeper roots of the problem.

MacIntyre, throughout his work, attributes the problem to *both* deficiencies in our moral language and thinking *and* failures in sociocultural ways of life. In *After Virtue*, the picture is famously bleak. The theoretical and social deficiencies are so linked that there appears no viable way forward (except for St. Benedict). The "plain person" is basically assumed to be emotivist, caught between a personal sphere of arbitrary ends and a public sphere of utilitarian effectiveness.[43] In the absence of an embodied tradition of the virtues, such an agent cannot recover a teleological account of the good life that functioned centrally in premodern moral reflection. Such an account, though the province of philosophers, was always embodied somehow in social practices, narratives, and traditions and therefore allowed the agent to understand him- or herself in terms of virtue. However, in the absence of such an embodied tradition, all we can do is wait for another St. Benedict. The average person is largely (if not totally) subject to the social systems in which he or she is enmeshed. The only possibility is to go off and found new (or recovered) social practices.[44]

This picture, as MacIntyre has implicitly admitted, is too dark and stark. He has not so much repudiated the picture as much as added significant detail and nuance to the basic problem. He has maintained an approach that attends to interlocking theoretical and social difficulties but explains those difficulties in more three-dimensional ways, thus allowing for much more insight into what might actually be done here and now by a discipline such as ours.[45]

I will first outline the philosophical difficulties and then develop the social problems. Theoretically, the problem remains one of the lack of teleology. Without some notion of the telos of a human person and a human life, the project of ordering desires breaks down, and we are faced with the problem of "criterionless choice."[46] Properly speaking, without the ability to name (however provisionally) an ultimate good to which no other intermediate goods can be compared, the "integrity of my practical reason" is lost.[47] However, unlike in *After Virtue*, where the decidedly extreme voices of Weber (sociologically) and Kierkegaard (subjectively) represent what happens in the face of the loss of teleology, MacIntyre now holds that both social practices and the agent himself or herself continue to exhibit a fundamentally "proto-Aristotelian character."

What this means in actuality is that the person will end up being "a particular kind of divided self, exhibiting that complexity so characteristic of and so prized by modernity."[48] This narrative of the divided self is extremely helpful in dislodging the picture of the confusion of the ordinary Catholic as rooted either in relativism or legalism. The confusion actually comes about because agents generally approach their lives in fundamentally Aristotelian ways but, when faced with the inevitable difficulties of conflicting desires and multiple goods, lack the language and the social practices to confront these problems rationally, in a way that is consistent with the Aristotelian conception of life and action as ultimately meaningful. Modern moral theories, once again, make the problem worse because they cannot articulate the intrinsic connections between rules, virtues, and the human good.

But, needless to say, Aristotelian language and reflection on the notion of ultimate good will not solve our problems. Every moral theory still presupposes a sociology.[49] Yet, parallel to the theoretical nuance above, MacIntyre paints a less monolithic picture of the social structures in which the agent struggles. In recent works, he names three social conditions that disable rational reflection on desires and convictions. I will, all too briefly, articulate these and display their interconnection.

The first is the way modern social structures encourage a practical rationality that "abstracts human beings from certain aspects of their beliefs and circumstances."[50] To "think for oneself" is to be ready to hold any and all allegiances at arm's length, to have "been able to or been compelled to free [oneself] from any fixed identity which would impose a standpoint."[51] Such a person "is the individual who is potentially many things, but actually in and for him or herself nothing."[52] Hence, commitment is minimized so as to maximize the choice of goods, but with commitment minimized, genuine choice among desires becomes more and more arbitrary, since commitments, though revisable, nevertheless could give direction to choice. What we call a "commitment" (whether chosen or ascribed or some combination) plays a crucial part in naming (however partially and provisionally) an "ultimate good" not subject to calculation and ordering.

However, the rhetoric of the socially uncommitted and "free" self conceals the second characteristic: the extent to which social roles and identities continue to form (and *deform*) practical reason.[53] To be able to attend to those roles *faithfully* but *critically* (especially within some sort of bureaucratic system), we require something that contemporary social structures systematically exclude: the ability "to understand [agents'] moral identity as to some degree distinct from and independent of their social roles. To understand oneself thus is to understand that one's goodness as a human being" is *not simply a matter of being good at one's roles* and indeed may sometimes require the questioning and criticism of those roles.[54] But one cannot learn this skill and have one's own views subjected to scrutiny and revision unless there is a social space in which relationships and shared practices are not simply governed by one or another *role* but are engaged substantively "in respect of the human virtues"—which is to say, the conception of the human good *qua* human, not simply *qua* social role.[55] Thus, ostensibly "free" from role-dominated behavior, the agent is in fact even more trapped in it, precisely because it becomes invisible. MacIntyre asks, "Are there types of social structure that preclude the existence of such milieus, so that the very possibility of the exercise of the powers of moral agency might be threatened?"[56] Predictably, the answer is yes, such a social structure is characterized by "compartmentalization," which goes beyond the normal ascription of roles in society and "does so by the extent to which each distinct sphere of social activity comes to have its own role structure governed by its own specific norms in relative independence from other spheres."[57] Characteristic of compartmentalization is a serious insulation of spheres (so as to prevent conflicts from breaking out), and the reinforcement of such insulation insofar as there is no social "milieu" in which communal critical reflection can go on about the human good *qua* human.[58] In the case of such social structures, there is no venue in which to even *engage* the questions practical reason must take up.[59]

The third, and perhaps most crucial, social failure is our inability to recognize and practice our ongoing interdependence as practical reasoners. In his most recent book, *Dependent Rational Animals*, MacIntyre pays special attention to the *vulnerability* of our ability to reason practically. Some of this vulnerability has to do with the fact that practical reason is an embodied activity, and therefore we are dependent insofar as our bodies pass through various states. But "the question 'Why should I do this rather than that?' becomes from an early age inescapable and it is characteristic of human beings."[60] This is the question of ordering desires. Therefore, we are dependent upon others—and therefore vulnerable to their failures—in our ability to develop the ability to discriminate among our own desires and to discriminate among the good and bad advice of others, from which we can never become totally independent at any stage.

The crucial work of the rest of the book develops the delicate and very vulnerable process in which the ability to reason practically comes to maturity. MacIntyre focuses particularly upon the importance of parents' ability to both direct the child authoritatively and at the same time slowly develop the ability of the child to make more independent decisions about goods. He offers a detailed narrative of childhood development in which the really crucial stages of development are the ability to discriminate among desires and influences in a number of ways.[61] However, such development does not go on in a social vacuum, nor does it "end" at some determinative point when we achieve moral "maturity." Thus, the parents in the aforementioned description, as well as the adult child, "continue to the end of our lives to need others to sustain us in our practical reasoning."[62] The reason is that, just as we are subject to physical vulnerability as adults, we continue to be subject to both "intellectual" and "moral error," from which "the best protections are friendship and collegiality."[63]

It should be evident that such an ongoing process means that we are dependent upon others (and others upon us) "within a network of relationships of giving and receiving in which, generally and characteristically, what and how far we are able to give depends in part on what and how far we have received."[64] Thus, for our moral agency, we are dependent upon social relationships that can embody "the virtues of acknowledged dependence," including the crucial recognition that our giving and receiving are most often asymmetrical and incommensurable. And, of course, just as we can acknowledge positive dependence, we should also recognize that we are subject to failure as practical reasoners insofar as we become dependent on others who cannot give us what we need and insofar as we live within social relationships that do not in fact embody the virtues of acknowledged dependence.

We have come quite far in characterizing the real problems constituting moral disempowerment. We have a portrait of the moral agent, naturally Aristotelian yet torn by many desires and forces that he or she cannot name effectively or reason about critically and that are embedded in certain social structures that disable both genuine personal commitment and the critical examination of such commitments in the light of the meaning of life as a whole, as well as make invisible and/or absent networks of acknowledged dependence. The explanatory power is substantial: it explains why characterizing the problem as relativism or legalism would be attractive, why modern moral theories are so unhelpful, and why agents might be tempted to give up on moral reasoning entirely.

## THE TASKS OF SAPIENTIAL MORAL THEOLOGY

MacIntyre's work allows us to draw some substantive conclusions about the future of the discipline, and I will name three. First, MacIntyre focuses in on the realm of ordering desires. He offers a picture of the moral life not as a sort of shutting down of desires but of a gradual ability to order them. Thus, if the virtues are to be placed in some sort of developmental order, some sort of temperance becomes the prerequisite for justice, courage, prudence, and love. This focus on ordering multiple desires is promising in two ways. First, it suggests that the "raw material" for the moral theology classroom is readily available in the form of what we want, and it suggests that we need not focus (as rules so often do) on the fact that we want things that are bad for us but that we want a whole bunch of things, and the crucial question is how we decide what we want. Rowan Williams, in an analysis that substantiates and enriches MacIntyre's portrait, explains that

> real choice both expresses and curtails freedom—or rather it should lead us further and further away from a picture of choice that presupposes a blank will looking out at a bundle of options like goods on a supermarket shelf. . . . It is more or less in the nature of the beast [advertising] that the "choices" here put before us are presented to an abstract will or personality, to nobody-in-particular; they address, of course, bundles of instincts, fears and desires, sometimes the instinct or prejudice of a group or class, but never a person with a history or a specific kind of vulnerability.[65]

Both children and adults lack an appreciation of the significance and commitments involved in choice because they are taught that choice is not a skill that is learned over time. By narrating choice in terms of competing desires, we can surface both the analogy to shopping and the ways in which ordering desires is obviously much more difficult than picking a breakfast cereal. Williams's account suggests another reason why ordering desires is an excellent place for the moral theologian to begin teaching. MacIntyre is convinced that a major problem for most "plain persons" (and for us moral theologians!) is our inability to name the forces that produce certain desires in us. Ordering desires should not remain at a level that presumes desires are self-evident and given but explore how they are constructed. What is alarming about students is the extent to which they are unaware of how shaped they are by economic and social forces, particularly the forces of the marketplace.[66]

The "methods" of moral theology developed by proportionalists and antiproportionalists alike pay remarkably little attention to the question of ordering desires. There are already substantial signs that moral theologians are recognizing the need to shift in this direction.[67] These works have tended to focus, however, more on the question of the formation of desire, rather than the ordering of desires, which explains their inability to build a bridge to reflection on particular moral problems.

Second, MacIntyre claims that there is an intrinsic and ineradicable Aristotelian (teleological) shape to the way in which "plain persons" think about the moral life. Moreover, although we may be shaped by social practices that distort this vision, even to the extent of having a false picture of what has been described as the "dispersed self,"[68] even social practices themselves exhibit this tendency toward Aristotelianism. This is a very convincing claim. I ask students, at the beginning of the semester, to describe what a "good human life" looks like. Most students find this question perfectly understandable and are able to respond to it with some sort of picture. (They are not necessarily as able to figure out what to do with competing claims here, but this gets things into an interesting situation rather quickly in the classroom.) Ineradicable teleology provides a type of "natural law" basis with which to begin moral inquiry, evidently consistent with classical ethics and with Thomas. Again, moral theology has made something of a start in this direction.[69] What remains somewhat obscure in recent work is how Christians might specify the telos, particularly in light of discontent with the history of individualist and otherworldly eschatology that has characterized Christian theology. Much fruit might be borne by more vigorous and focused debate on this question of specification.

The third area for constructive work is perhaps the most difficult and yet also the most crucial. Ordering of desires ultimately depends on teleology, but the plausibility of teleology ultimately depends on developing and reflecting upon integrated forms of life that render the notion of an ultimate good (for the person and in general) comprehensible. Thus, moral theology must develop an ability (and the tools) to reflect on particular practices and social milieus and must acknowledge its own dependence on the existence and fostering of such practices. Perhaps the confessional should not be the central practice within which Christians understand the moral life, but the discipline has been slow to articulate concrete alternatives. Where can ordinary Catholics find a social space (not necessitating a new St. Benedict) where plain persons can examine their actions and commitments not *qua* role but *qua* human person? This seems to me to be a promising account of what our classrooms might attempt to be. Hopefully, in the long run, parishes or other forms of local Christian community can be spaces where this sort of examination can go on. How can we recognize and foster the dependence always already present in our moral reflection and convictions? Here, the antiproportionalist concern about "autonomy" finds its real solution in examining dolphins and children rather than foundationalist claims about "truth."[70] The notion of the autonomous individual too often implied in strong claims about conscience can and should be overcome by a richer claim about dependence than simple reference to the magisterium.

Of course, I would echo MacIntyre's skepticism about the extent to which *teaching* moral theology is transformative of practice. As he notes, "Moral debate is . . . not primarily between theories as such, but rather between theories that afford expression to rival forms of practice."[71] But perhaps attention to concrete forms of life can take priority over attention to isolated moral questions, since such questions always occur within forms of life, and it is by attending to the "argument" embodied in the practice, rather than to the "correct" theoretical standpoint, wherein we will find the stuff of ethics. Therefore, reflection on issues such as cloning, abortion, and euthanasia should not be cut off from the question of the place of such activities within a form of life. As teachers, we should be thrilled that we do not have to get our nonphilosophical students deeply entrenched in theoretical debates but can and should approach such debates from the standpoint of communities of practice. However, perhaps more troublingly, MacIntyre's warning should make us concerned about the nature of the college and university communities (not to mention parishes) that shape and direct the everyday practices of both us and our students. Such things as the pervasiveness of professional education, the "creep" of gnosticized and private approaches to religion and spirituality, the continued presence of unconsidered and institutionally endorsed slogans of self-determination and pluralism, the standards of bureaucratic efficiency so often characteristic of institutional politics, the tendency of faculty politics to mirror that of an "interest group"—all these are much more problematic. If we are to do good work as teachers (and, I might add, as researchers and colleagues), we must struggle with our own communities of practice.

Young, post–Vatican II moral theologians find ourselves uneasily "between" the boosters and the knockers but perhaps that much more able to recognize the real possibilities and perils present in the students we teach and the church we serve. I have tried to articulate the challenges for our discipline as well as indicate what new tools we might develop in the years ahead. What I have dubbed the "sapiential turn" in moral theology promises us a way past the often bitter debates of the past decades but also charges us with a rather ambitious mission for the discipline. If we are able to assist in warming God's household in what may turn out to be a dark cultural winter ahead, we will truly be able to say to Christ the words of the faithful disciple: "We are useless servants; we have done what we were obliged to do" (Luke 17:10).[72]

# NOTES

1. See John Mahoney, *The Making of Moral Theology* (Oxford: Clarendon Press, 1987), and John A. Gallagher, *Time Past, Time Future: An Historical Study of Catholic Moral Theology* (New York: Paulist Press, 1990).

2. Servais Pinckaers, *The Sources of Christian Ethics*, tr. Sr. Mary Thomas Noble (Washington, D.C.: CUA Press, 1995), 259–67. See also, Pinckaers, "The Recovery of the New Law in Moral Theology," trans. Hugh Connolly, *Irish Theological Quarterly* 64 (1999): 3–15.

3. For a helpful overview of some of these figures, such as Tillmann and Haring, see Gallagher, *Time Past*, 162–83. On the reaction to *Humanae Vitae*, see Mahoney, *Making of Moral Theology*.

4. *Optatam Totius*, sec. 16.

5. This loosely connected group of thinkers included the Europeans Knauer, Fuchs, Janssens, and Schuller; and the Americans McCormick and Curran as the most prolific writers. Though somewhat methodologically eclectic, the theories of proportionalism and the fundamental option tended to be their main innovations. What these theories have in common is the attempt to provide a systematic basis for evaluating and criticizing extant moral teaching (hence the term *revisionism*) by offering a vision by which acts and agents could be guided and evaluated. In this chapter, I largely use the term *proportionalism* to refer to this movement—certain thinkers (such as Haring and Curran) do not place proportionalism so centrally in their proposals, but they share to a significant extent in shaping their moral theology over against the same "legalism" that shapes proportionalism.

6. For Pinckaers's early and trenchant criticisms of the manualist tradition, see the articles collected in *Le Renouveau de la Morale: Etudes pour une morale fidele à ses sources et à sa mission présente* (n.p.: Casterman, 1964). In this collection of articles, mostly from the 1950s, Pinckaers anticipates (often in a richer form than later efforts by more prominent revisionists) the necessity of a historical approach to moral theology ("L'utilité de la méthode historique"), the criticisms of an obligation-based morality ("Morale de l'obligation et morale de l'amitié"), and the debate over understanding the object of the act in Aquinas's theology ("Le rôle de la fin dans l'action morale selon Saint Thomas"). Germain Grisez, in introducing his major work, plants himself firmly in the same position, criticizing the "rationalism" and "legalism" of Tridentine moral theology in some detail. See Grisez, *The Way of the Lord Jesus*, vol. 1, *Christian Moral Principles* (Quincy, Ill.: Fransciscan Herald Press, 1983), 12.

7. See Christopher J. Thompson, "Moral Theology in a Sapiential Mode: *Veritatis Splendor* and the Renewal of Moral Theology," *Thomist* 65 (2001): 465–73.

8. Grisez, *Way of the Lord Jesus*, 18.

9. The teaching on contraception continues to shape the perceptions of both sides of this debate. From the revisionist side, see Richard McCormick, "Killing the Patient," and Bernard Haring, "A Distrust That Wounds," both in *Considering Veritatis Splendor*, ed. John Wilkins (Cleveland, Ohio: Pilgrim Press, 1994); and from the antiproportionalist side, see Christopher Kaczor, "Proportionalism and the Pill: How Developments in Theory Lead to Contradictions in Practice," *Thomist* 63 (1999): 269–81.

10. Richard Gula, *Reason Informed by Faith* (New York: Paulist Press, 1989), 29–30.

11. Anne Patrick, *Liberating Conscience: Explorations in Feminist Moral Theology* (New York: Continuum, 1996), 208.

12. This is not the only difficulty in these positions, but it is one that I think is crucial for figuring out what moral theologians should teach. Timothy O'Connell, in the introduction to his recent book, provides a very honest and powerful account of how his careful teaching of the basics of revisionist moral theology "had not made contact with those levels of the students where they truly lived." See O'Connell, *Making Disciples: A Handbook of Christian Moral Formation* (New York: Crossroad, 1998), 2.

13. My reliance on MacIntyre here is, to some extent, a matter of convenience. Other moral philosophers, such as Philippa Foot, Bernard Williams, and Jeffrey Stout, would also prove valuable and largely (though not completely) supportive of the conclusions I draw here about practical reason, though perhaps Stout and Williams might be more positive about the possibilities of the situation. The lack of attention

paid to these philosophers by Catholic moral theologians is a lacuna that must be addressed by future work in the field; it would appear that recent work in the field is often (though not always) less informed by careful attention to and critical use of moral philosophy.

14. In this chapter, the phrases *ordinary Catholic, plain person,* and *my students* will be used largely interchangeably. My students at the College of St. Benedict–St. John's University are predominantly from the upper Midwest, almost all white, and represent a mix of rural and suburban regions. It is not fair to call them "homogenous," but the character of the upper Midwest certainly makes them appear more homogenous than the populations at Carleton and Duke. They exhibit many of the same traits and viewpoints that are shared in the broad majority of American teenagers, though their particular experience and formation has made them somewhat more parochial and more sturdy morally than the teens explored in books such as Patricia Hersh's *A Tribe Apart* (New York: Fawcett Columbine/Ballantine, 1998). They are, by and large, representative of the Catholic churchgoing public in terms of their moral thinking and practice, perhaps with a somewhat greater tendency to certain slogans of relativism (which I attribute to the media and to generational formation by the media and the educational system).

15. Taylor, in his *The Ethics of Authenticity* (Cambridge, Mass.: Harvard University Press, 1992) uses the labels to characterize the two sides in the debate among cultural critics between those who regard modern liberal society as truly a pinnacle of human culture and those who regard the development of individualism, instrumental reason, and the like as deeply threatening to genuine human culture. Taylor claims that "the nature of modern culture is more subtle and complex" than either side realizes, so he attempts to offer a way forward that is not simply a tradeoff or balancing of the two. This is analogous to what I hope to do in this chapter: characterize ordinary modern moral thinking as more complex than either side seems to think and then offer a way forward that is *not* a form of "mixed consequentialism," an ill-defined halfway house between proportionalists and antiproportionalists. On "mixed consequentialism," see Charles Curran, "Utilitarianism and Moral Theology," in *Moral Norms and the Catholic Tradition: Readings in Moral Theology,* no. 1, eds. Charles Curran and Richard McCormick, (New York: Paulist Press, 1979) 341–62; and Curran, "A Methodological Overview of Fundamental Moral Theology," in *Moral Theology: A Continuing Journey* (Notre Dame, Ind.: University of Notre Dame Press, 1982), 35–61.

16. On totality, see Mahoney, *Making,* 309–21.

17. However, Martin Rhonheimer has responded that the true "physicalists" are the proportionalists. See "Intentional Actions and the Meaning of Object: A Reply to Richard McCormick" *Thomist* 59 (1995): 279–311.

18. Aline H. Kalbian, "Where Have All the Proportionalists Gone?" *Journal of Religious Ethics* 30 (2002): 3–22. Kalbian's article unwittingly illustrates the way in which defenses of proportionalism are determined by the construction of a certain sort of "enemy." Kalbian is concerned to defend not proportionalism itself but something she calls "the spirit of proportionalism" (7), which involves a more "holistic," "particularistic" approach to moral theology. She constructs this alternative over against something called "traditional moral theology" (17), which is not specifically defined but apparently holds a purely physicalist account of human action and a "static" account of human nature. This straw man is equivalent to what I have here termed *legalism.*

19. *Veritatis Splendor*, sec. 84. Similar characterizations appear in *Evangelium Vitae*, secs. 19–20 and (with more justification, considering the subject matter) *Fides et Ratio*, secs. 81–84.

20. Romanus Cessario, OP, *Introduction to Moral Theology* (Washington, D.C.: CUA Press, 2001), xii.

21. Cessario, *Introduction to Moral Theology*, xiii. See also, Wolfe's more extensive study that develops this same general view of current American morality, *Moral Freedom: The Impossible Idea That Defines the Way We Live Now* (New York: W. W. Norton, 2001).

22. Martin Rhonheimer offers an exhaustive cataloging and strong critique of the notion of autonomy in moral theology in his *Natural Law and Practical Reason: A Thomist View of Moral Autonomy*, tr. Gerald Malsbary (New York: Fordham University Press, 2000).

23. Livio Melina, *Sharing in Christ's Virtues: For a Renewal of Moral Theology in the Light of Veritatis Splendor* (Washington, D.C.: CUA Press, 2001), 60.

24. Melina, *Sharing in Christ's Virtues*, 61.

25. Cessario, *Introduction to Moral Theology*, xvii.

26. Note here that it is false to assume that "truth" simply means an assertion of authoritative rules. All antiproportionalists worth reading concur in the dangerous appearance of nominalism in manualist moral theology. "Truth" means rather assertion about the nature and destiny of the human person. It is not only the overt defenders of *Veritatis Splendor* who seek grounding for moral theology in a normative anthropology. See also, Benedict Ashley, "What Is the End of the Human Person? The Vision of God and Integral Human Fulfillment," in *Moral Truth and Moral Tradition: Essays in Honor of Peter Geach and Elizabeth Anscombe*, ed. Luke Gormally (Dublin: Four Courts Press, 1994), 68–96; John Kavanaugh, *Who Counts as Persons? Human Identity and the Ethics of Killing* (Washington, D.C.: Georgetown University Press, 2002); Jean Porter, "Basic Goods and the Human Good in Recent Catholic Moral Theology," *Thomist* 57 (1993): 27–49; and (in a very dialogical way) Lisa Cahill, *Sex, Gender, and Christian Ethics* (Cambridge: Cambridge University Press, 1996).

27. Also like the proportionalists, they are most formed by their *opposition* to a school of Catholic moral theology. The driving force in many antiproportionalists is precisely to refute proportionalism, which may be a necessary task but is also a limited one.

28. The charges of a sort of nihilism are exaggerated when it comes to proportionalist moral theologians as well. Herbert McCabe, no proportionalist, notes that *Veritatis Splendor* "wastes a good deal of time" combatting this position of supposed absolute autonomy "since it would be hard to find any Catholic moralists who do suppose (as Richard Hare and the early Existentialists used to) that human morality is exactly like football, a human artefact invented some time ago." See Herbert McCabe, "Manuals and Rule Books," in Wilkins, *Considering Veritatis Splendor*, 64. These exaggerated criticisms from the knockers have made it too easy for the boosters to come back and reply that the criticisms are false.

29. For a great examination of nihilism lurking behind today's world, the movie *American Beauty* should be watched with interest. However, its exaggerations, at least in relation to most of my students and most people who go to church every Sunday, should also be noted.

30. R. R. Reno, "American Satyricon," *First Things*, no. 116 (October 2001): 35–41.

31. Wolfe's own analysis notes that, for example, a *New York Times* poll found that 86 percent of respondents said that "if they got married today, they would expect to be married for the rest of their lives." See Wolfe, *Moral Freedom*, 41. Bellah's classic *Habits of the Heart* (Berkeley: University of California Press, 1985) remains the best sociological analysis of the actual moral difficulties of ordinary persons.

32. This exploration indicates that, rather than insist on a foundational approach to moral teaching that begins with the assertion of abstract (and highly contested) metaphysical truths about anthropology, it is more pedagogically effective to recognize that, in their own convictions and practice, students already acknowledge a certain sort of moral order and they can be taught to become more articulate about it—and critical about it—by examining these *extant* convictions. Aquinas follows Aristotle in this approach by beginning with a dialectical discussion of human happiness and *then* proceeding to an analysis of human action and virtue.

33. An interesting side note here would be to consider whether this approach to rules tends to set up a relationship of "bad faith" between those in authority and those bending them. The fact that even many members of the clergy feel obliged to bend and/or avoid certain rules seems to indicate a problem with notions of authority that are related to the issues I raise here. I thank Aimee Burant for pointing this problem out to me.

34. McCabe's distinction between manuals and rule books is helpful. He claims that "the encyclical *Veritatis Splendor* is, in great part, an attack on those who want to read the rule book as though it were a training manual by those who want to read the manual as though it were a rule book." See McCabe, "Manuals," 63. It is not a sign of *relativism* to read the rules more as a training guide, though McCabe agrees that extending this logic of the training manual to all moral rules will mislead us.

35. Alasdair MacIntyre, *Dependent Rational Animals: Why Human Beings Need the Virtues* (LaSalle, Ill.: Open Court Press, 1999), 71. This does not automatically make them proto-proportionalists, I would hasten to add. That such a thought might occur to a reader indicates how thoroughly the discipline is stuck in an unfortunate polarity.

36. The phrase "flight from authority" is explicated by Jeffrey Stout. The claim here that young Catholics' practical reasoning displays little difference from that of the overall culture is an interesting and important one. Though they may hold somewhat different views on certain issues (e.g., abortion), the reason is not because they have been schooled in any other sort of practical reasoning; hence, they are peculiarly vulnerable to those who call their convictions into question. However, generalizations should not be taken as anything more than generalizations; the fine recent book by Dean Hoge and colleagues, *Young Adult Catholics* (Notre Dame: University of Notre Dame Press, 2001), indicates this diversity in creating five "categories" of young Catholics, though it does not contain a lot of empirical data on moral questions.

37. MacIntyre, "The Recovery of Moral Agency?" in *The Best Christian Writing 2000*, ed. John Wilson (New York: HarperCollins, 2000), 112–15. Bellah's *Habits of the Heart* is filled with examples, but a key one that illustrates MacIntyre's characterization is the attitudes toward marriage exemplified by evangelicals on the one hand and secular inhabitants of a therapeutic approach to romantic relationships on the other (85–112).

38. MacIntyre, "Recovery of Moral Agency?" 116–17.

39. MacIntyre, "Plain Persons and Moral Philosophy: Rules, Virtues, and Goods," in *The MacIntyre Reader*, ed. Kelvin Knight (Notre Dame, Ind.: University of Notre Dame Press, 1998), 136–52, here 145–46.

40. MacIntyre, "Recovery of Moral Agency?" 117. Thus, the culmination of modernity's desire to free the individual from forces of tradition and oppression in order to "think for oneself" is a deeply ironic disempowerment of the individual who is no longer able to name and order the manipulative forces to which he or she is subject.

41. MacIntyre, "Recovery of Moral Agency?" 118. Italics added.

42. MacIntyre, "Recovery of Moral Agency?" 119.

43. Alasdair MacIntyre, *After Virtue*, 2nd ed. (Notre Dame, Ind.: University of Notre Dame Press, 1984), chaps. 1–8. The category of "plain person" functions in MacIntyre somewhat technically; I am following his usage from the later essay "Plain Persons and Moral Philosophy," noted earlier, in which "plain person" evidently refers to any agent and not only to agents uncorrupted by modern moral philosophy and practices.

44. Moreover, as some critics of *After Virtue* noted, MacIntyre's defense of Aristotelian virtue is surprisingly "liberal" insofar as it does not escape from the tendency to portray the moral agent as faced with a "choice" between traditions.

45. In fairness, it should be noted that even the 2000 vintage MacIntyre is capable of Benedict-like insights. He offers a trenchant conclusion to his essay, after he has investigated various actual practices or forms of life: "The recovery of moral agency depends . . . upon what type of practice it is in which we and others find ourselves engaging, and not on what type of theoretical standpoint we adopt. Moral theorizing does, of course, have distinctive and valuable functions, but there are times at which it may have the effect of distracting us from our practical responsibilities. And perhaps this is one of those times. Perhaps what I should have learned from my own theorizing in this lecture, and elsewhere, is no longer to give such lectures. And what you should have learned is to no longer to listen to them" (MacIntyre, "Recovery of Moral Agency?" 136).

46. MacIntyre, *After Virtue*, 39–50.

47. MacIntyre, "Plain Persons," 151.

48. MacIntyre, "Plain Persons," 147. MacIntyre provides a rich defense of the continued Aristotelian assumptions of philosophical enquiry in his lecture "First Principles, Final Ends, and Contemporary Philosophical Issues," reprinted in Knight, *The MacIntyre Reader*, 171–201 (see esp. 197).

49. MacIntyre, *After Virtue*, 23.

50. MacIntyre, "Practical Rationalities as Forms of Social Structure," in Knight, *The MacIntyre Reader*, 130.

51. MacIntyre, "Practical Rationalities," 135.

52. MacIntyre, "Practical Rationalities," 135.

53. An aside: once again, MacIntyre's discussion here avoids one-sided characterizations of a moral problem. Our culture, at one and the same time, discourages identity-determining commitments and discourages reflection on action in non-role-driven ways. Thus, MacIntyre agrees (and disagrees!) with both those who claim that people need to "break free" of the modern, robotic world *and* those who claim that the modern world is robotic and empty because people are too preoccupied with keeping themselves uncommitted.

54. "Social Structures and Their Threats to Moral Agency," *Philosophy* 74 (1999): 320. This analysis has particular relevance to the moral problems raised in recent financial scandals.

55. MacIntyre, "Social Structures," 321. In "Recovery of Moral Agency?" MacIntyre similarly suggests that the problem is primarily one of practice and notes that the "thoughtlessness" of public debate is amplified insofar as "it is very rare indeed . . . that there are opportunities for ordinary citizens, for plain persons, to engage together in systematic and extended inquiry into the issues posed for them by debate" (115).

56. MacIntyre, "Social Structures," 321.

57. MacIntyre, "Social Structures," 322.

58. MacIntyre, "Social Structures," 324. It seems hard to avoid the inference that at least one of MacIntyre's reasons for converting to Roman Catholicism is his feeling that, whatever its dysfunction, the church continues to think of itself in this way.

59. Elsewhere, MacIntyre applauds the academy for the rigor in which it engages views in critical exchange, noting that it has achieved exactly the sort of "intellectual public" that the Enlightenment sought but "with a large absence of decisive outcomes and conclusions," which was not what the pillars of the Enlightenment thought would happen. The lack of agreement means that the social world, needing to act, ignores the academy, whose disagreement is "not without practical significance," for "it renders the academic community generally politically impotent except in its provision of services to the private and public corporations." See MacIntyre, "Some Enlightenment Projects Reconsidered," in *Questioning Ethics: Contemporary Debate in Philosophy*, eds. Richard Kearney and Mark Dooley (London: Routledge, 1999), 245–57.

60. MacIntyre, *Dependent Rational Animals*, 67.

61. MacIntyre, *Dependent Rational Animals*, 81–95.

62. MacIntyre, *Dependent Rational Animals*, 96.

63. MacIntyre, *Dependent Rational Animals*, 96.

64. MacIntyre, *Dependent Rational Animals*, 99.

65. Rowan Williams, *Lost Icons: Reflections on Cultural Bereavement* (Harrisburg, Pa.: Morehouse, 2000), 32.

66. That is not to say that it is hard to surface an awareness of this. Indeed, after viewing a video about advertising directed to teens and reading the broad analysis of consumerism presented by John Kavanaugh (*Following Christ in a Consumer Society (Still)* [Maryknoll, N.Y.: Orbis Books, 1991]), students quickly recognized how deeply they themselves and their world were shaped by these forces.

67. For example, William Spohn's *Go and Do Likewise: Jesus and Ethics* (New York: Continuum, 1999) and Timothy O'Connell's aforementioned *Making Disciples* go a large step in this direction, and they are complemented by the precise attention to social structures found in Michael Warren's *At This Time in This Place* (Harrisburg, Pa.: Trinity Press International, 1999). The neglected work of Herbert McCabe recognized this decades ago; see the ethics essays in *God Still Matters* (New York: Continuum, 2001).

68. This notion is described by Robert Wuthnow in relation to contemporary trends in attitudes toward religion in *After Heaven: Spirituality in America Since the 1950s* (Berkeley: University of California Press, 1998), 162. While the dispersed self

has a toehold in our society (and in ourselves), Wuthnow's characterization does not, I think, reflect the sturdier self still possessed by many faithful Catholics.

69. See, for example, Jean Porter, *The Recovery of Virtue* (Louisville, Ky.: WJKP, 1990), and "Basic Goods and the Human Good in Recent Catholic Moral Theology," *Thomist* 57 (1993): 27–49, as well as Ashley's aforementioned "What Is the End?" Overall, Servais Pinckaers's strong argument to return to eudaimonism serves as a programmatic statement for such a turn; see "Amour et devoir: Une réponse à la question de l'eudémonisme," *Nova et Vetera* 64 (1989): 179–97, and "Antinomie du devoir et du bonheur?" *Nova et Vetera* 64 (1989): 98–114.

70. Some antiproportionalists would undoubtedly allege that I (along with MacIntyre) have failed to make truth strong enough, because it is thus made dependent not on strong metaphysical claims but rather on general metaphysical claims about animality, vulnerability, and childhood development. Thus, the slide into relativism is not prevented. But again, why is relativism so evident a danger? I would reply that the problem here is not that MacIntyre or myself are social relativists but that the antiproportionalists find it necessary in their moral theory to articulate and make effective anthropological claims somehow prior to their "embodiment" in any social reality. MacIntyre is clear here and elsewhere that what he is doing is not antimetaphysical, but he refuses to open up a space where anthropology or metaphysics can be considered apart from community.

71. MacIntyre, "Recovery of Moral Agency?" 120.

72. I am grateful to Aimee Burant and Jana Bennett, who provided many helpful comments on a draft of this chapter.

# 7

# Intimacy with God and Self-Relation in the World: The Fundamental Option and Categorical Activity

*Darlene Fozard Weaver*

God created us for intimacy with him. This claim ought to direct moral theological reflection on acts and persons. Josef Fuchs, for instance, says that contemporary moral theology must "explain that man is called personally in Christ by the personal God."[1] And John Mahoney notes the "regular bid on the part of some [post–Vatican II] writers to consider the morality of individual actions not just in themselves but as they enter into a total continuity and pattern of the individual's moral history and life."[2] Moral theology is crucially concerned with the person's relation with God and, hence, the place of her personal acts in that relation. What is the import of particular choices and actions for one's relationship with God? What is the relation between the objective rightness or wrongness of particular actions and the person's subjective moral goodness or badness, that is, her orientation toward or against God? How do particular actions affect growth in or erosion of personal relation with God?

This chapter takes up these questions by forwarding a constructive theological account of our relation to God, the source of freedom and value, as a call to intimacy with him in all that we understand, undergo, and do. Key to this account is the fact and manner of human self-relation. The crucial fact of self-relation is that the person comes to herself as she responds to others, the world, and, just so, to God. The person becomes aware of herself, understands herself, and fundamentally determines herself in and through her encounters with and responses to others, the world, and God. The manner of self-relation encompasses her interpretive, evaluative, and embodied self-determination as a creature who reflexively fashions herself in and as a response. That is, the person takes up and negotiates who she is in and through these encounters and responses in the full and embodied range of her understanding, valuing, and acting in the world with others. Put differently, the person's self-relation is the juncture of "transcendental" and "categorical" freedom—that is, the person's founding and finding response to God with her whole heart and the embodied expression and self-fashioning of this response in the world that God has made.

I explore the inextricable connection between the person's self-relation and her relation with God by reflecting on the intimacy God wills to share with us. This reflection helps us to understand better and move beyond an impasse in recent debates between Pope John Paul II and proportionalists concerning the relation of the fundamental option (the person's basic orientation toward or against God) and particular decisions and actions.[3] As we will see, John Paul argues that the free choice of particular sorts of actions determines the will of the agent who performs them and, thus, that *what* the agent chooses to do may crucially determine her fundamental option. Proportionalists stress that we cannot determine what an agent chooses in performing some action without attending to the totality of her intentions and the morally relevant circumstances and that the objective rightness or wrongness of that action does not tell us whether the person acted with a subjective good or bad motive. Hence, for proportionalists, the import of particular actions for the fundamental option depends importantly on what is going on *in* the choosing of those actions. Even so, they argue, transcendental freedom—and so the person's fundamental option—cannot be reduced to her particular choices and actions. This chapter navigates this debate, seeking to retain insights from both sides while also arguing that neither side adequately renders the dialectical relation of the person's response to God, her fundamental option, and her free involvement with the creaturely goods God gives. I argue that the *reflexive* character of human self-relation, as it is intimately bound up with our homeward movement toward intimacy with God, allows us to understand better how human acts, *in* the choosing of *what* is chosen, are (1) more engaged with our fundamental option than proportionalists allow or can explain but (2) less regimented to it by *what* is chosen than the pope imagines. My aim is to bring the God-relation into clearer and closer contact with the person's moral willing and acting. With respect to the fundamental option, this means that attention is due to the fact that it both expresses itself in particular choices and actions and is always being made in them.

I

To appreciate what is at stake in this particular debate about the fundamental option, and since the point of reflection on persons and acts is to understand better and orient ourselves in faithful responsiveness to God's self-offer, let us begin by considering the intimacy that God wills to share with us. Both sides of this debate need to be tested against whatever insights we might uncover regarding intimacy with God, and our way beyond this debate needs to be adequate to them.

God's presence, as St. Augustine described it, is "more inward than my most inward part and higher than the highest element within me."[4] It is writ within my self-relation. More intimate than the person's self-presence is the presence of God. It is not as though the person stands before God unrelated and makes a decision about whether to take up a relation *to* God. This would deny God's immanence and suggest a sovereign self-possession that the person, as a creature, does not have. Rather, the person's self-relation, situated as it is within and vis-à-vis God's self-offer, depends on and always already involves relation with God. Because God creates us for intimacy with him, God's self-offer, as an invitation, precedes and bears our response to it. This primordial and inextricable connection between self-relation and relation with God means that our exercise of freedom, in its particulars and as a whole, is always responding to God's desire for intimacy with us and, thus, that the person experiences the gain or loss of God in her self-relation.

Intimacy consists in the mutual indwelling of persons, a participation in, belonging to, and possession by one another. Intimacy involves the self-gift of persons who are different. Genuine intimacy does not obliterate this difference but makes it a gift to be received, welcomed, and revered. It requires dependence in freedom—we are free when we embrace our dependence on others to be who we are, at least to make an offering of ourselves to them. It also requires freedom in dependence—we are intimate when we learn to be dependent in a way that preserves freedom. Intimacy with God is an utterly gratuitous possibility, as is all intimacy. In creating us for intimacy with him, God "depends" on us in order to be the God he has freely willed to be. This does not mean that there is anything about us that requires God's self-offering but rather that God's sovereignty and transcendence expresses itself in the divine willing of immanent self-communication. Since God establishes our freedom, it is realized and fulfilled in dependence on him. Intimacy with God is possible for and as creatures of the God who made us to know and love him.

Intimacy has a constitutively historical or narrative character. It is possible only between and among persons who are bearers of freedom and, as such, negotiate relations in history as they forge histories with others. The mutual self-presence of intimacy is possible by virtue of and takes its shape and tenor from the history or story of approach and withdrawal, communion and alienation, availability and evasion that persons weave together. The "always already" of God's self-offer comes to us in creation and covenant; in the person, death, and resurrection of Jesus; and in the gift of the Spirit. It is encountered and mediated in our experience of and personal histories with God, others, and the world. So, intimacy with God involves coming to know more directly the history of God's saving love as one's own history.

As a mutual self-gifting intimacy cannot but be particular. Because relation with God is writ into the person's self-relation and because intimacy is constitutively historical, the self-gift persons make is not the offering of a self that is finished or independent. The self that is given emerges in the relationships she negotiates for better or worse. The person is made by them in her making of them. In intimate relations our very selves are at stake. Intimacy cannot be exacted or demanded—when it is, we surely experience only a counterfeit of it—though it exacts and demands everything. The particularity of any intimate relation encompasses who we are; it is not a sharing of part of ourselves but the whole of ourselves. Yet it begets something new, transforming us into ones we could not be without giving ourselves to a particular other and without receiving this particular other as a gift. Intimacy with God, then, requires one to love God with one's whole heart, mind, and strength (Matt. 22:37), and just so requires her to make herself as one receiving and ever more made by God's self-offer.

Because intimacy is this free self-gift of particular persons in history, who make a history, it is never finished or episodic, however many moments might be decisive for the relationship. There is a certain provisionality to intimacy. It is polarized toward ever greater degrees, toward a fullness that is not finally possible in this world. Intimacy with God cannot but be incomplete short of the beatific vision. And because this intimacy is with a living God, it beckons us continually toward an ongoing conversion. At every moment God invites us into deeper intimacy. The provisionality of intimacy with God arises from, rather than qualifies, the fidelity or steadfastness of God's self-offer. And, of course, this provisionality is due to our freedom to accept or reject God. Our particular free choices can honor, deepen, and substantiate intimacy with God or betray, evade, and diminish it. Sin and weakness and fear, human finitude and incompletion, and the person's plurality and complexity all make intimacy provisional. But this provisionality does not mean that our choices can be undone; although we remain free (albeit in varying degrees), since intimacy is constitutively historical, these choices matter and persist.

Because God creates us to know and love Him, we can speak properly of God as the source of freedom and value. God's intimate presence in the depths of our self-relation founds our freedom and founds it for the sake of deeper intimacy. The God who is the source of our freedom is also our highest good, the true end of our freedom. We can only encounter God's desire for intimacy in the gift of our creatureliness (and we see it manifest supremely in the Incarnation). We know that God affirms the goodness of creation and wills its good in him. As our creator and as our highest good,

God is the source of value. We make intimacy with God and others in a world laden with divine gifts given for the sake of the divine self-promise. Indeed, our experience of and response to God's self-offer are mediated by the objective goods and values that compose our lives. So, our intimate involvement in and with this world is always also an involvement with the God who gives it and loves it and us.

This brief excursus on intimacy with God highlights the inextricable connection between the person's self-relation and relation with God. The person responds to God in and through the full range of her creaturely existence in the world. Because intimacy with God is necessarily historical, particular, and provisional, the person's moral willing and acting fashion a response to God that is always in the making and is always meant to be a movement into deeper intimacy. And because God is both the source of freedom and value, we cannot separate the person's self-relation, her response to God, and her involvement in a world thick with goods and values. By and large, fundamental option theory elucidates these insights in an account of human freedom's relation to God as its source and end. But we will see in the following sections that proportionalist deployments of the theory insufficiently attend to the reflexive character of human acting while the pope renders it too punctually.

## II

This section introduces fundamental option theory and debates about it between John Paul II and proportionalists. Proportionalists distinguish between the objective rightness or wrongness of particular acts and the subjective goodness or badness of the person's motive (whether or not she strives to love God as best she can). John Paul takes this distinction as evidence that proportionalists separate particular actions from the fundamental option, such that what the person chooses, a concrete behavior, has no bearing on the fundamental option. Proportionalists argue that the pope misunderstands the fundamental option as an act; he fails to appreciate the athematic character and irreducibility of transcendental freedom. These respective charges concern, on the one hand, the way particular actions not only express but constitute the fundamental option and, on the other hand, the fact that the fundamental option, as the total self-determination of the person in response to God, is irreducible to any particular act.

Fundamental option theory emerged in dogmatic theology but has considerably influenced moral theology. Karl Rahner, drawing on Jacques Maritain and Joseph Maréchal, developed the idea of the fundamental option by investigating the conditions for the possibility of revealed truths, like the Incarnation. In doing so he set the stage for moral anthropology on the terms of God's self-communication. Knowing what we know of God, what can we say about ourselves as creatures who have received this gracious revelation? Rahner argues that the human person has a receptive potential for it—we are created as ones who can receive God's self-communication.[5] God is our true end, highest good, the fulfillment of our aspirations and longings.

The fundamental option articulates this recognition of God in an account of human freedom. Because God is the source of our freedom and its ultimate orientation, freedom is basically and always a freedom vis-à-vis God.[6] It has a transcendental depth or dimension. It consists in more than freedom of choice; it is a capacity to decide about ourselves in response to God's self-offer. This means that transcendental freedom is not reducible to particular categorical choices or to their sum total—the transcendence of freedom eludes such a complete objectification.[7] Yet, as bodily, social, historical, and finite creatures, we only experience the transcendental ground and orientation of freedom categorically, that is, as spirits in the world. Transcendental freedom "as the freedom of the subject about himself and towards himself and from himself as a single whole . . . is not a freedom which lives behind a merely physical, biological, exterior and historical temporality of the subject. Rather, it actualizes itself as this subjective freedom in a passage through the temporality which freedom itself establishes in order to be itself."[8] The fundamental option refers to the unity and interpenetration of transcendental and categorical freedom. Transcendental freedom expresses itself in and is irreducible to categorical freedom. Categorical freedom is the constitutive medium of transcendental freedom. If we limit freedom to the categorical choices of objects, we cut short its reach and may overlook its unity, which abides through the individual and disparate choices we make. If we disassociate transcendental freedom from these categorical choices, freedom becomes an abstraction and we risk denying the unity of the person as an embodied spirit in a world endowed with value, who reflexively fashions herself in and through these choices.

The theory has prompted analyses of moral acts that, despite differences, basically insist that if we are to understand the moral meaning of acts we must consider them in light of the fundamental option, that is, the present direction of a freedom that is yet unfinished.[9] This is quite evident in proportionalist uses of the theory. Klaus Demmer, for example, argues that individual decisions are "interpretations" and "ratifications" of the person's fundamental option.[10] Similarly, Franz Böckle calls them "constitutive signs."[11] According to Böckle, while the fundamental option can only be expressed and actualized in categorical choices, the person "can neither understand himself as a whole nor fail as a whole by means of an individual decision."[12] Thus, we cannot say that the choice of some categorical object necessarily posits a negative fundamental option. Josef Fuchs insists that acts manifest only a part of the person and "never touch more than a rather small area of the full horizontal reality of the individual, or of humanity, or of the subhuman world."[13] Fuchs argues that we can and should distinguish the moral status of the person, as one fundamentally open or closed to God and so good or evil, from the rightness or wrongness of her acts, that is, their "fittingness" to "the good of the person and of his world."[14] Because freedom is a unity, there is no separation between goodness and rightness.[15] But morality is really about persons, not "actions as such."[16] Goodness disposes us to seek and to realize what is right. Wrong behavior does not "directly involve" goodness or salvation, for "one who does what is unfitting, but does this in error or in good faith can be morally good and can be saved in his relationship with God."[17]

There are several important, interrelated moral theological insights in fundamental option theory. First, it emphasizes the relational character of grace and salvation, and it befits a developmental understanding of the moral life as growth in (or the erosion of) relation with God and others. It thereby helps to account for erratic and mistaken actions and behaviors, the existential possibilities and limits of the person as an acting subject, and so forth. Second, the theory stresses the unity and history of the person's freedom. The person is an acting subject; she has a totality and complexity that underlies, abides in, and absorbs her particular acts. Thus, we ought to avoid construing the moral life atomistically, that is, as a series of discrete acts. Third, the person's fundamental option, as a transcendental and so athematic self-determination in relation to God, eludes complete and fully conscious objectification. The ineffability of her fundamental option prompts an appropriate agnosticism about the relation of any of her particular acts to it. This agnosticism, when appropriate, can express a faithful recognition of God's sovereignty, our finitude, and the open texture of human freedom. Finally, fundamental option theory is particularly amenable to the relations between the moral and spiritual life. The person has the task of integrating her individual choices with her basic decision, of engaging in an ongoing conversion.[18]

This tensive relation between transcendental and categorical freedom is the great merit of fundamental option theory. Nevertheless, recent debates about persons and acts suggest that it might be deployed to better effect. In his 1993 encyclical *Veritatis Splendor* Pope John Paul II affirms the fundamental option as a self-determining response of faith to God's self-offer but worries over certain formulations or deployments of the theory wherein the distinction between the fundamental option and deliberate choices of concrete kinds of behavior can tend to appear as a separation.

> Particular acts which flow from this option would constitute only partial and never definitive attempts to give it expression; they would only be its "signs" or symptoms. . . . There thus appears to be established within human acting a clear

disjunction between two levels of morality: on the one hand the order of good and evil, which is dependent on the will, and on the other hand specific kinds of behavior, which are judged to be morally right or wrong only on the basis of a technical calculation of the proportion between the "premoral" or "physical" goods and evils which actually result from the action. . . . The properly moral assessment of the person is reserved to his fundamental option, prescinding in whole or in part from his choice of particular actions, of concrete kinds of behavior.[19]

Proponents of fundamental option theory, particularly proportionalists, offer rejoinders. Thomas Kopfensteiner, for instance, says the theory posits "no such separation between goodness and rightness or person and act." By suggesting that it does, the pope fails "to appreciate the interpenetration of the transcendental and categorical levels of action."[20] This failure leaves him, and others who worry about such a separation, open to the charge that they remain in the grips of a reductive neoscholastic analysis of acts. And, says Kopfensteiner, these folks are the ones who are prey to a culpable demarcation between the subjective and objective dimensions of the moral life, inasmuch as their focus on the phenomenal structure of the act fails to attend to the human subject. Josef Fuchs says that because the fundamental option and specific choices "happen on different levels of the same person," it is "just not possible for us to examine the core of our person from the outside so as to establish whether we are fundamentally good or evil . . . [though] we can to some extent conclude by a conjecture based on our actions." Moreover, "it is not as easy for a good person to change his or her fundamental option as it would be to swap morally good particular actions for morally bad ones," though individual decisions and actions "can nevertheless gradually bring a person to a point at which he is now committed to the contrary of his previous direction and disposition. When this happens, his fundamental option is reversed."[21] The pope's failure to appreciate the necessarily athematic character of the fundamental option leads him to suggest it is "a precise, definite, determinable *act*" and to assume that we can morally judge persons on the basis of their free and conscious acts.[22] So, he sees a split or dissociation in the positions of his interlocutors that simply is not there. Fuchs argues that it is "precisely because the fundamental option and moral choices are on different levels, [that] the theory stresses rather their mutual relationship and interpenetration."[23] The problem is how to relate acts "to the ethical status of the person as a whole, which is on another level."[24]

Of course, the pope also thinks the problem is how to relate the acts of the person to her fundamental self-determination before God. But, for him, this means the fundamental option "*is always brought into play through conscious and free decisions. Precisely for this reason, it is revoked when man engages his freedom in conscious decisions to the contrary, with regard to morally grave matter.*"[25] This passage gives the lie to rejoinders that say that the pope fails to appreciate the interpenetration of the fundamental option and particular choices, though he may render it in too tight and punctual a fashion.

Proportionalists, for their part, are right to say they do not separate the fundamental option from individual choices or acts, though as a reply to *Veritatis Splendor* this insistence is unhelpful. The worry that the fundamental option drags attention away from the person's social and historical situation and from her particular acts is common and persistent among both detractors and proponents of the theory.[26] It places on those sympathetic with the theory the task of better articulating the interpenetration of transcendental and categorical freedom. How can we avoid, on the one hand, a reductive analysis of acts that locks the fundamental option into them and, on the other, a more nuanced analysis of acts that implies a separation of the fundamental option from them? We need to consider more directly some of what the pope and proportionalists say about moral acts.

## III

Recall that the following insights emerged in our initial consideration of intimacy with God. Self-relation and relation with God are inextricably connected such that we experience and respond to God's self-offer in and through the full range of our creaturely existence. Because intimacy is historical, particular, and provisional, our actions disclose and negotiate, express and constitute who we are in relation with God. The meaning of any particular act for our self-determining response to God depends on the history and future of that relationship, even as it contributes to the loss or gain of intimacy with God. The reason is that God is the source and end of human freedom and the source of those goods and values God gives for the sake of our creaturely good in intimate relation with him. Since our free actions are self-determining or reflexive, our involvements with creaturely goods are always also involvements with God. With these points in mind we can consider further the debates between John Paul II and proportionalists regarding the import of particular actions for the fundamental option. We will see that John Paul understands this import in terms of what the person chooses when she acts—the object of her act—and its order or disorder in relation to the human good and to God. On the basis of this account, the pope judges that proportionalists separate particular actions from the fundamental option. Proportionalists think the pope prematurely judges persons' wills on the basis of their acts (thus they charge him with "physicalism"). Proportionalists construe the import of particular actions for the fundamental option in terms of distinctions between rightness and goodness, intention and motive. These distinctions permit an understanding of persons, acts, and relation with God that is more attentive to the historical, particular, and pro-visional character of intimacy with God than the pope's argument allows. Yet, they also show how porportionalists undercut the reflexivity of human acting, and so distance particular acts from the person's response to God, be-cause proportionalists do not allow or explain how the objective rightness or wrongness, order or disorder, of particular acts redound upon the person as a creature growing in or eroding intimacy with God in and through her in-volvements with the goods God gives.

In *Veritatis Splendor* John Paul II's worry about the fundamental option becomes clearer in his subsequent discussion of the moral act. He argues that human acts, insofar as they are deliberate choices, morally define the person and that the morality of acts depends on the relation of these free choices to the person's good and to God. "Activity is morally good when it attests to and expresses the voluntary ordering of the person to his ultimate end and the conformity of a concrete action with the human good as it is ac-knowledged in its truth by reason. If the object of the concrete action is not in harmony with the true good of the person, the choice of that action makes our will and ourselves morally evil, thus putting us in conflict with our ulti-mate end, the supreme good, God himself."[27] The pope repairs to the tradi-tional fonts of a moral act (intention, circumstances, and object) in order to argue that, while intention and circumstances matter, they are insufficient for morally judging a concrete choice. "*The morality of the human act depends primarily and fundamentally on the 'object' rationally chosen by the delib-erate will.* . . . In order to be able to grasp the object of an act which speci-fies the act morally, it is therefore necessary to place oneself *in the perspec-tive of the acting person.*" The object is "the proximate end of a deliberate decision," a "freely chosen kind of behavior" that "determines the act of will-ing on the part of the acting person."[28] It must be capable of being ordered to the person's good; such an act is therefore capable of being ordered to God and is ordered thus by the will through charity.

Some acts are "intrinsically evil," that is, incapable of being so ordered.[29] They cannot be justified by a good intention or anticipated good conse-quences. The pope therefore rejects a thesis he finds in some moral theories, that we cannot identify deliberate choices of specific acts as evil "*apart from a consideration of the intention for which the choice is made or the totality of the foreseeable consequences of that act for all persons concerned.*"[30] John Paul thinks this thesis is characteristic of proportionalism. According to him, proportionalism suggests that "concrete kinds of behavior could be dis-cerned as 'right' or 'wrong,' without it being thereby possible to judge as morally 'good' or 'bad' the will of the person choosing them."[31] Proportion-alism tends to separate the fundamental option from the person's particular choices "when they expressly limit moral 'good' and 'evil' to the transcen-dental dimension proper to the fundamental option, and describe as 'right' or 'wrong' the choices of particular 'innerworldy' kinds of behavior: those, in other words, concerning man's relationship with himself, with others and with the material world."[32]

Proportionalists contest the pope's presentation of their arguments.[33] Several note that no one wishes to deny what the pope affirms.[34] The encyclical does sometimes misrepresent proportionalism, for instance, in its charge that proportionalists separate the fundamental option from particular acts. Nevertheless, it poses a challenge to anyone seeking to construe the relation of persons and acts. John Paul repeatedly returns to the capacity of acts to be ordered to the human good, and thus to God as the final end of the person, and says, "Clearly such an ordering must be rational and free, conscious and deliberate."[35] His sustained focus on the deliberate choice of particular acts and on the voluntary ordering of the person to God indicates his principal concern: whether particular sorts of intentional involvements with goods respond fittingly to God, who made us and wills our good in Him as the creatures we are.

In their responses to *Veritatis Splendor*, proportionalists run past the pope's challenge in large part because, to them, the way the pope casts it embodies an unacceptable physicalism that regards acts apart from our moral willings. The physicalism that proportionalists discern in the encyclical (and in the magesterium's moral teaching on sexual ethics) suggests one can morally evaluate an act on the basis of the act "in itself," that is, as a physical occurrence, without knowing the person's intention or considering all the morally relevant circumstances and consequences. Moreover, as the pope seems to suggest, we can morally evaluate not only the act but the will of the person who performs it insofar as the act is freely chosen. Physicalism seems either to imply a picture of acts "out there" in the world, shorn of persons who are acting subjects within them, or to collapse persons into particular acts as though the acts are totally determinative of the person and of her relation to God.

Charles Pinches has argued recently that the charge of physicalism does not stick to the pope's argument in *Veritatis Splendor*. Since the pope speaks of the perspective of the acting person and of the will's involvement in the person's choice of particular actions, he clearly does not mean to be physicalist.[36] John Paul does acknowledge the charge of physicalism and suggests that it arises from a modern tendency to oppose freedom and nature.[37] In fact, following Martin Rhonheimer, Pinches argues that it is the proportionalists who are physicalist.[38]

Whatever the verdict on physicalism, proportionalists are manifestly concerned with the relation of persons and acts and with the person's relation to God. But their arguments fall short of the challenge *Veritatis Splendor* makes. The reason is not that they separate the fundamental option from particular choices but that in their formulations of the theory, and subsequently, in their analysis of moral acts, they do not attend sufficiently to the reflexive character of acting. Their arguments tend to emphasize the irreducibility of transcendental freedom to its categorical objectifications. This undercuts the reflexive or constitutive character of those objectifications for the fundamental option and, just so, distances them from the person's response to God, who at every moment calls her into deeper intimacy in and through her categorical, creaturely existence. We can see this distancing by moving from claims proportionalists make about particular acts back to claims they make about the fundamental option.

Proportionalists insist that if we are to morally evaluate an act, we must consider it in its totality. They are not saying, as the encyclical wrongly states of them, "that *morally wrong actions (ex objecto)* can be justified by the end [but] that an action cannot be judged morally wrong simply by looking at the material happening, or at its object in a very narrow and restricted sense."[39] We cannot know the object of a given act, what the agent chooses in her choice to perform it, unless we consider not only the material happening but the agent's intention and the morally relevant circumstances.[40] Sometimes the agent's intention crucially determines the object. By way of example, Richard McCormick draws a distinction between masturbation for sperm testing versus for self-pleasuring. Says McCormick, "They are different because of different reasons for the act, i.e., different goods sought and aimed at different intentions. Intention tells us what is going on."[41] (Note that, though McCormick is surely correct, his point does not settle whether the agent's intention in, say, masturbation for sperm testing is an intentional involvement with the desired goods, presumably procreation, that responds fittingly to God.) Sometimes circumstances crucially determine the object. For example, in an act in which one person kills another, it is not "a mere circumstance that the killer is an authorized executioner and the victim is a duly convicted criminal."[42] Proportionalists do not quarrel with the claim that there are intrinsically evil acts, acts that are always wrong by virtue of their object, "*if the object is broadly understood as including all the morally relevant circumstances.*"[43] Like the pope, proportionalists are concerned with what the person chooses in her acting. For them, this requires consideration of the act in its totality.

But even once we have considered an act in its totality, we are only yet in a position to speak of the act's rightness or wrongness, its order or disorder with reference to the human and common good. According to Fuchs, "rightness of conduct is not directly related to the personal morality of the human person, i.e., to his moral goodness, but refers as such to the good of the human being (of mankind) in his horizontal dimension."[44] Goodness disposes her to seek to identify and realize right behavior, to incarnate her goodness, but inevitable failures in this discernment and realization do not circumscribe the perennial possibility of being good.[45] The distinction between goodness and rightness helpfully forestalls premature moral judgments about persons on the basis of their acts. The person sometimes acts mistakenly but in good faith. Note, however, the movement from goodness to rightness but not back from rightness to goodness. If the question that concerns us is the import of some act for the person's God-relation, any answer must wait because "rightness of conduct is not directly related to" personal morality, which concerns the person's response to God.

We are not without help, however, because we can consider a distinction some proportionalists draw between motive and intention. "Goodness pertains to the former, rightness to the latter."[46] Rightness, says James Keenan, "has two realms: the executed act (choice) and the agent's reason for acting (intention)."[47] From here we can go some way in discerning how it is or is not ordered to the human and common good. But this will not tell us the agent's motive. Motive "explains [one's] fundamental disposition," that is "whether one moves oneself out of charity or benevolence to realize oneself or one's acting rightly." What's more, "moral goodness depends solely on the motivation of the person."[48] This is more helpful. Goodness tells us something about the person's response to God in this decision and action, and rightness tells us something about its fittingness to the human good. Again, note the movement from the person's goodness to rightness but not from rightness back to goodness. Rightness in conduct may express, manifest, incarnate goodness. Wrongness in conduct, if accompanied by a good motive, signals, perhaps, error on the person's part, or limitations of existential or innerworldly varieties, or disorder in the person because of a vice like greed. It does not alter, or evidently even touch, her motive.

This is all the more evident when we link the person's response to God in a given act to the fundamental option. The fundamental option (and so the person's relation to God considered most properly) is not separate from her choice in acting. Indeed, the choice may express it. Then again, it may not. Whatever the case, a particular act is a partial expression and actualization of transcendental freedom. This means that it is probably insufficient to revoke or reverse the fundamental option unless it "attain[s] to the same nonconceptual level."[49] And, in any event, her fundamental option is inaccessible to her since it is necessarily athematic.

Proportionalists rightly insist that the person is required to integrate her choices, actions, and relations with her fundamental option for God.[50] Categorical choices are partial exercises of the one total freedom the person has and is. Joseph Selling suggests actions carry the fundamental option, and Böckle calls acts constitutive signs of it.[51] The picture they give is one wherein actions ferry the fundamental option into the categorical realm. But the emphasis falls on the fundamental option as expressing itself in particular actions. The ferry ride, as it were, does not appear to make a return trip. Emphasizing the irreducibility of transcendental freedom to its categorical objectifications undercuts the reflexivity of the person's acting, which effectively distances her response to God from the particular choices she makes in acting. Moreover, inasmuch as the rightness/wrongness of particular acts does not directly affect goodness, it is unclear how they affect the person's growth in or the erosion of her God-relation or her future capacities to respond fittingly (i.e., to act rightly and with good motives) to God. Given the reflexive character of acting, categorical freedom is not simply a realm of partial appearances of transcendental freedom but its constitutive medium.

John Paul II's argument in *Veritatis Splendor* faces difficulties of its own. The pope argues that the correct identification of the object of a moral act is sufficient for morally evaluating it and the person's will, insofar as the act is freely chosen.[52] He notes that factors may limit the person's subjective guilt. But he nonetheless gives the impression that in deliberate choices of specific acts persons act with relatively unified wills; in this way he may eclipse the complexity of the person as an acting subject. Proportionalist distinctions between intention and motive speak to the multiple, conflictual character of human willing. An adequate account of the will's participation in any freely chosen act must acknowledge our diverse and sometimes contradictory intentions, our blindness and self-deception, the subconscious needs, fears, and desires that motivate us, that operate in and on our freedom, the influence of social mores and relational particularities that shape the individual agent's existential limits and possibilities. Inasmuch as John Paul implies a tidier picture of our interior lives, he renders the link between our fundamental self-determination before God and our choices of concrete behaviors too tightly and neglects the disparate character of our wills.

Certainly John Paul recognizes that as persons work out their self-relation, they make choices that reverberate in, indeed that can decisively affect, their relation with God. Yet, the pope's approach to moral acts is also overly punctual or episodic. He is right to alert us to the way certain sorts of actions are definitively important for the person's self-determining response to God. I doubt that John Paul believes the person can change her fundamental option willy-nilly in the course of a day. Yet his argument fails to account for the historical, narrative structure of human freedom, the gradual relational shifts between God and an individual that may precede his choice of a particular act. Concrete actions are not merely signs or symptoms of the person's God-relation—they are also determinants of it—but their moral meaning does reside in this particular historical mix. In short, John Paul rightly attends to the will's involvement in the person's choices but may overplay its determination by these choices given the historicity, particularity, and provisionality of any act as it transacts our relations with our selves, God, and others in the world. He risks subsuming the person, and hence her response to God, into her acts, rather than locating her acts in the person's complex and historical self-relation as this fashions a response to God.

Neither side separates the person's response to God from her involvement in a world thick with goods and values. Proportionalists, nevertheless, stress the former in a way that burrows it into the person. By undercutting the re-flexivity of the person's acting, they do not address sufficiently the way those actions bear on her response to God. John Paul II, for his part, stresses our involvement in the world in a way that absorbs, even locks in the person's response to God. He thereby constricts self-relation, and so the fundamental option, to particular acts. Neither the proportionalists nor the pope render adequately the dialectical relation of the person's response to God and her involvement in the world.

## IV

At its best, fundamental option theory affords us a kind of poetry for appre-hending the fact that God is closer to us than we are to ourselves. Good po-etry succeeds inasmuch as it breaks language out to spark an appreciation of our affective and spiritual depths, while at the same time rooting language in the possibilities and perils of our everyday activity in the world. But various deployments of fundamental option theory can constrict such appreciation and undercut the significance of our embodied life and living. Reflection on intimacy with God permits a more dialectical account of the person as an act-ing subject responding to God in and through her involvement in the world.

Because God is closer to us than we are to ourselves, the person's experi-ence of and response to God's self-offer are inextricably bound up with her self-relation, encompassing her free self-understanding and responsiveness to others and the world prior to, in, and beyond any particular acts she per-forms. The very springs of agency—freedom, reason, and desire—are always already set within her relation to the God who made her, who meets her in particular circumstances and in a world marked by the distorted relations of sin. Accordingly, her growth in or resistance to intimacy with God is not con-fined to explicit acts and endeavors to respond to God, for example, in prayer. It occurs in all of her (self-)interpretation, in what she considers, neg-lects, and takes for granted; in all she chooses and apprehends, seeks and avoids; in all she accomplishes and omits; in all her responses to what she un-dergoes. This intimate and inextricable connection between self-relation and relation to God captures the interpenetration of transcendental and categori-cal freedom. Transcendental freedom underlies and *infuses* her choices such that her fundamental option, as the present orientation or direction of tran-scendental freedom, *expresses* itself in this full range of free interpretive, eval-uative, and responsive activity. It also *marinates* in the breadth and com-plexity of her categorical self-relation. Because the person's activity is reflexive or self-constituting, she *fashions* her response to God in it.

Intimacy with God is possible for and as a creature of God. Given the inextricable connection between self-relation and relation to God, in her exercise of freedom the person must order herself to God, her highest good, and her acts ought to be ordered to her human good as a person in a community of persons, a point both the pope and proportionalists make. Proportionalists tend to emphasize the person's ordering of values associated with the human good in the rightness of intention and execution of acts. The pope tends to emphasize the conformity of free and rational acts with the human good as an order of goods. As we have seen, they differ on the import of particular actions contrary to her good for her fundamental option. The historicity, particularity, and provisionality of intimacy with God captures their respective insights and clarifies the relation of the fundamental option and categorical activity.

Intimacy with God occurs in history. The person encounters and responds to God's call to intimacy in her relations with others and the world. The respective histories she makes there are part of the one history that is hers and hers with God. The fundamental option expresses itself and takes shape in these overlapping stories. Yet, the meaning of any act comes clear only within this narrative context. It remains open to reinterpretation in light of future information and insight, especially the more truthful perspective conversion brings. And in some sense its meaning awaits the completion of the story. This does not mean, however, that we are unable to reach reliable descriptions or understandings of acts until then. Indeed, our endeavors in this regard are part of the history we make with others and God and are accountable to them. Though we cannot consciously grasp the fundamental option, we can conjecture about it based on our actions, as Fuchs says. Intimacy with God requires such conjecture in the form of prayerful and open inquiry into the "state of the union." It also enables such conjecture and purifies it of self-deception and scrupulosity.

The particularity of intimacy with God emphasizes that the person's acts are *her* acts. Whatever the reach of any instance of categorical choice, the person responds to God as the one she is, has been up to now, *and* as one called to become herself more authentically. Her free activity expresses her fundamental option or discloses something of the relationship she and God have made thus far. In this activity she continues to make this relationship and so contributes something to the fundamental response she fashions. Intimacy with God heightens our sense of the particularity of any act and its relation to a person's fundamental option. This particularity emphasizes rather than qualifies the person's obligation to consider how her acting bears on the God-relation by considering the wisdom, experience, norms, and exemplars of her community.

The provisionality of intimacy relativizes the meaning of particular acts inasmuch as the person remains free to accept or reject God. It heightens their meaning because they bring about something new for her God-relation, which matters and persists precisely because the person fashions her response to God with her life. Growth in intimacy includes moments of marvel and delight as we welcome the gift the other makes of himself and as we come to discover who we are, in and as the other's delight shows us to ourselves. Because intimacy is polarized toward ever greater degrees, growth in it also includes acute pangs as we apprehend its incompletion, and wrenching challenges as we confront (and are confronted by) obstacles to it. These obstacles include more than explicit and fairly discrete choices against intimacy's demand to deepen; they include a variety of implicit terms or conditions we bring to the relationship, the inertia of patterns of relating, the distorted images we project onto the other. Growth in intimacy with the living God confronts us with such obstacles, inviting and challenging us in each moment to accept the grace that enables our ongoing conversion. Each moment in an intimate relation is both expressive of it and an opportunity to fashion it further.

Because God is the source of freedom and value, our creatureliness is an encounter with the goodness of God's work and with the harm and muddle that violations of it beget. It sets parameters within which intimacy with God is possible. This is why both the pope and proportionalists are concerned with *what* the person chooses in her acts, and its order to the human good. Because God wills deeper intimacy with us in and through our choosing, a theologically adequate understanding of persons and acts concerns itself not only with what is chosen and its order to the good but what is going on *in* the choosing. Proportionalists help us to appreciate that more is going on in the choosing than the pope's argument in *Veritatis Splendor* shows. The pope, for his part, helps us to appreciate that whatever is going on *in* this willing and choosing is yoked to *what* is chosen, given the person's unity as body and spirit. I have suggested that proportionalists risk undercutting our moral willing as it fashions a response to God while the pope risks constricting it.

Reflecting on intimacy with God has shown that transcendental freedom not only expresses itself in particular choices in acting but plays out in the springs and full range of the person's activity. In the choosing of what is chosen, the person engages her fundamental option as the present direction or orientation of transcendental freedom. It informs her self-understanding, reason, and desire, all of which influence the way she presents any decision to herself, considers the expectations and norms of her community, seeks, avoids, or violates particular goods. The choosing is a new and deliberate categorical interpretation and self-disposal that may substantiate or redirect the fundamental option; without fully expressing or determining it, the choosing necessarily affects the fundamental option because of the unity of transcendental and categorical freedom and the reflexivity of the person's activity. Intimacy with God indicates why and how what goes on in her choosing of what is chosen expresses and fashions her fundamental option. In and through her free involvement in a world thick with goods and values, the person responds to God, the source of her freedom and of the goods and values her moral willing orders and is ordered by. Because the person responds to God in and through the full range of her creaturely activity, she experiences the loss or gain of God in the transcendental depths and categorical breadth of her self-relation. Since intimacy is the mutual indwelling of persons, since it is a participatory belonging to and possession by the other, the person shares in or alienates herself from God's life with her own. The God she encounters and to whom she responds in the world is the God in whom she lives and moves and has her being.

## V

God created us to know and love him and wills our acceptance of the divine self-offer at every moment and for eternity. I have attempted to locate, and to recalibrate thereby, the tensive unity of personal freedom in its transcendental and categorical dimensions within this basic claim about the divine–human relation. Reflecting on the intimacy God wills with us enriches our understanding of the person's innermost, fundamental response to God precisely by binding it more closely to her categorical freedom. It brings the person's response to God into clearer and closer contact with her acting than proportionalist deployments of fundamental option theory have done, without falling prey to the constrictive account John Paul II offers in *Veritatis Splendor*. Because God is the source of value, our disordered and disordering involvements with creaturely goods do more than signal a need for integration and conversion; they contribute to the loss or gain of God in the intimate depths of self-relation. They touch our response to God. Because God is the source of freedom, which in this world is always unfinished, this "touch" is neither an embrace nor a grip but an imprint. The experience of our loss or gain of God in our self-relation is always also an experience of God inviting us into deeper intimacy.

## NOTES

1. Josef Fuchs, "Moral Theology According to Vatican II," *Human Values and Christian Morality* (Dublin: Gill and Macmillan, 1970), 8. I thank William Mattison and Maria Malkiewicz for inviting me to participate in the Notre Dame conference that gave rise to this volume. Several reviewers of this book, the conference participants, and Bill offered helpful feedback on this chapter. I thank them all for their comments. I am grateful to Mark Begly and William Werpehowski for discussing the work with me and for their feedback on the manuscript.

2. John Mahoney, *The Making of Moral Theology* (Oxford: Clarendon, 1987), 318.

3. Some readers of this chapter have questioned the "usefulness" of fundamental option theory. The usefulness of any theory, concept, or claim is shown if and inasmuch as it dialectically exposes problems and points a way beyond them. Here I offer the following: First, fundamental option theory has considerably influenced Catholic moral theology. Second, debates about it center on a crucial problem vexing contemporary moral theology—the relation of persons to their acts. In particular, contemporary Catholic ethics displays an unfitting agnosticism about the import of particular sorts of actions for the person's God-relation. This insufficiently theological treatment of moral acts couples with a breakdown in the social contexts that help us to name truthfully the ends that we seek and actions by which we seek them, and it results in a real practical inability to understand our own and others' behavior. Third, fundamental option theory has a resolutely theological center of gravity—something we may appreciate more by way of its spiritual suggestiveness than its philosophical methodology. Its basic insights—that God is closer to us than we are to ourselves, that God is the source and end of our agency and of the goods of creaturely life, that we are meant for embodied communion—challenge going accounts of and beliefs about persons, the world, and the moral life. For these reasons, critical consideration of the fundamental option is important for understanding and moving constructively forward in moral theology. A full argument on these matters will appear in my forthcoming book on persons and acts.

4. St. Augustine, *Confessions*, trans. Henry Chadwick (Oxford: Oxford University Press, 1991), 43.

5. That is, grace presupposes and perfects nature. See Karl Rahner, *Foundations of Christian Faith: An Introduction to the Idea of Christianity*, trans. William V. Dych (New York: Crossroad, 1993), 132 and 218; and Karl Rahner, *Hearer of the Word* (New York: Continuum, 1994).

6. Karl Rahner, "Theology of Freedom," *Theological Investigations*, vol. 6 (Baltimore: Helicon, 1969), 180.

7. See, for example, Rahner, "Theology of Freedom," 186. See also Rahner, *Foundations*, 95–97.

8. Rahner, *Foundations*, 94.

9. Fundamental option theory has played an important role in Catholic theologies of sin, developed against neoscholastic tendencies to emphasize sins—that is, to construe sin and the moral life chiefly in terms of particular acts. See, for example, Josef Fuchs, SJ, *Christian Morality: The World Becomes Flesh* (Dublin: Gill and Macmillan; Washington, D.C.: Georgetown University Press, 1987); Franz Böckle, *Fundamental Moral Theology*, trans. N. D. Smith (New York: Pueblo, 1980); Mark O'Keefe, "Social Sin and the Fundamental Option," *Irish Theological Quarterly* 58, no. 2 (1992): 85–94.

10. Klaus Demmer, *Shaping the Moral Life: An Approach to Moral Theology* (Washington, D.C.: Georgetown University Press, 2000), 51.

11. Böckle, *Fundamental Moral Theology*, 108.

12. Böckle, *Fundamental Moral Theology*, 110.

13. Fuchs, *Christian Morality*, 116–17.

14. Fuchs, *Christian Morality*, 107.

15. Fuchs, *Christian Morality*, 26. See also, James F. Keenan, SJ, *Goodness and Rightness in Thomas Aquinas's Summa Theologiae* (Washington, D.C.: Georgetown University Press, 1992).

16. Fuchs, *Christian Morality*, 21.

17. Fuchs, *Christian Morality*, 111.

18. Mark O'Keefe, OSB, *Becoming Good, Becoming Holy: On the Relationship of Christian Ethics and Spirituality* (New York: Paulist, 1995), 47–48.

19. Pope John Paul II, *Veritatis Splendor*, 65. See also, reservations about the fundamental option in *Persona Humana* and *Reconciliatio et Paenitentia*.

20. Thomas R. Kopfensteiner, "The Theory of the Fundamental Option," *Christian Ethics: An Introduction*, ed. Bernard Hoose (Collegeville, Minn.: Liturgical Press, 1998), 130.

21. Josef Fuchs, "Good Acts and Good Persons," *Considering Veritatis Splendor*, ed. John Wilkins (Cleveland, Ohio: Pilgrim, 1994), 23–24.

22. Fuchs, "Good Acts and Good Persons," 24.

23. Fuchs, "Good Acts and Good Persons," 24.

24. Fuchs, "Good Acts and Good Persons," 24.

25. Pope John Paul II, *Veritatis Splendor*, 67.

26. See Johann Baptist Metz, *Faith in History and Society: Toward a Practical Fundamental Theology*, trans. David Smith (New York: Seabury, 1979). See also, Charles Curran, *Directions in Fundamental Moral Theology* (Notre Dame, Ind.: University of Notre Dame Press, 1985), 87–89.

27. Pope John Paul II, *Veritatis Splendor*, 72.

28. Pope John Paul II, *Veritatis Splendor*, 78.

29. Pope John Paul II, *Veritatis Splendor*, 80.

30. Pope John Paul II, *Veritatis Splendor*, 79.

31. Pope John Paul II, *Veritatis Splendor*, 75.

32. Pope John Paul II, *Veritatis Splendor*, 65.

33. See, for example, Richard McCormick, "Some Early Reactions to *Veritatis Splendor*," *John Paul II and Moral Theology*, Readings in Moral Theology 10, ed. Charles E. Curran and Richard A. McCormick, SJ (New York: Paulist, 1998), 20.

34. See, for example, Richard McCormick, "Killing the Patient," in Wilkins, *Considering Veritatis Splendor*; and Charles Curran, "*Veritatis Splendor*: A Revisionist Perspective," in *Veritatis Splendor: American Responses*, ed. Michael E. Allsopp and John J. O'Keefe (Kansas City, Mo.: Sheed & Ward, 1995).

35. Pope John Paul II, *Veritatis Splendor*, 73.

36. Charles R. Pinches, *Theology and Action: After Theory in Christian Ethics* (Grand Rapids, Mich.: 2002), 63–69. See sections 75 and 78 in *Veritatis Splendor*.

37. See Pope John Paul II, *Veritatis Splendor*, 46–48 and 78.

38. See Martin Rhonheimer, "'Intrinsically Evil Acts' and the Moral Viewpoint: Clarifying a Central Teaching of *Veritatis Splendor*," *Thomist* (1994) and "Intentional Actions and the Meaning of Object: A Reply to Richard McCormick," *Thomist* (1995).

39. McCormick, "Killing the Patient," 18. See Pope John Paul II, *Veritatis Splendor*, 79–82, where the pope suggests that proportionalists think morally wrong actions can be justified by good intentions. See also James Gaffney, "The Pope on Proportionalism," in Allsopp and O'Keefe, *Veritatis Splendor: American Responses*; Curran, "*Veritatis Splendor*: A Revisionist Perspective," in Allsopp and O'Keefe, *Veritatis Splendor: American Responses*; Bernard Hoose, "Circumstances, Intentions and Intrinsically Evil Acts," *The Splendor of Accuracy: An Examination of the Assertions Made by Veritatis Splendor*, ed. Joseph A. Selling and Jan Jans (Grand Rapids, Mich.: William B. Eerdmans, 1994).

40. Louis Janssens, "Teleology and Proportionality: Thoughts about the Encyclical *Veritatis Splendor*," in Selling and Jans, *Splendor of Accuracy*; and Joseph A. Selling, "The Context and the Arguments of *Veritatis Splendor*," in Selling and Jans, *Splendor of Accuracy*.

41. McCormick, "Some Early Reactions," 18.

42. Jean Porter, "The Moral Act in *Veritatis Splendor* and in Aquinas's *Summa Theologiae*: A Comparative Analysis," in Allsopp and O'Keefe, *Veritatis Splendor: American Responses*, 283. Porter is not a proportionalist, but proportionalists have made appreciative use of this essay.

43. McCormick, "Killing the Patient," 19.

44. Fuchs, *Christian Morality*, 108.

45. Fuchs, *Christian Morality*, 108–9.

46. Keenan, *Goodness and Rightness*, 13.

47. Keenan, *Goodness and Rightness*, 14.

48. Keenan, *Goodness and Rightness*, 14.

49. Fuchs, "Good Acts and Good Persons," 25.

50. Fuchs, *Christian Morality*, for example, 150–53.

51. Selling, "Context and the Arguments."

52. See Pope John Paul II, *Veritatis Splendor*, 72.

# 8

## Economic Beatitude, or How I Learned to Stop Being Miserable and Love Economic Ethics

*Kelly Johnson*

Economic ethics does not have a reputation for being delightful. In fact, economics was christened "the dismal science" in Malthus's day, and although much of present-day economics attempts to avoid being either gloomy or delightful by being merely mathematic, its concern with how to produce and distribute in a world of endless desire and scarce resources means the story is always tragic. Insofar as ethics is, as some would have it, a matter also of making decisions that always rule out some good as well as create some good, it too is implicitly tragic. Those of us who work in both fields would seem to be people who derive some pleasure out of an endless study of misery. What sex appeal economic ethics offers has to do with studying power relations, direct and more subtle, well-intentioned and perverse. There is a kind of delight in that, but it is more akin to sadomasochistic eroticism than to Christian holiness.

But Christian economic ethics is, as all Christian ethics must be, fundamentally about happiness. In fact, it is, as I will claim that all Christian ethics must be, about plenty and delight, declared and demonstrated in the face of economic tragedy. Christian ethics is a comic discipline, and therefore it can only be a strange bedfellow to the tragic world of modern economics. But bedfellows they are, and more. Christians create, perpetuate, adapt, and resist modern economic systems; we critique not from an impartial distance but from within. We who want to teach the good news are tied in intellect, affect, and body to a world that takes starvation for granted.

My aim in this chapter is not to resolve that conflict but rather, first, to explore it in more detail, showing how Adam Smith's thought has shaped the rhetoric of stewardship and some of our deepest habits about property; second, to point toward what we can call Eucharistic solidarity as a richer direction for thinking about property; and third, to suggest how moral theologians might cultivate the prudence we need to speak truthfully about Christian ethics for ourselves and for our students.

## THE PROBLEM: THE TRAGIC MORALITY OF SCARCITY

Economics textbooks commonly begin with an ontological claim stated as a matter of fact: goods are scarce.[1] The world does not provide enough for all to have all of their desires met. Of course, this ontological claim is a function of an appended anthropological claim: humans have insatiable desires, and therefore no matter how much the world produces, humans will still find its goods scarce. This grim assertion, made briefly and as a matter of fact, situates the discipline of economics within a tragic narrative. No matter how well intentioned we may be, we will not come to a peaceable distribution. Someone will have to be the loser.[2]

This idea has a deep hold on our habitual understanding of property. We need look no further than our reaction to beggars. One of the sources of our anxiety when someone asks us for our spare change is the endless line of requests that we imagine will follow. How many more will approach me if I give to this one, and how will I ever distinguish fairly among them? How will I draw limits to protect myself from them? The necessity to answer yes or no to such a request leaves us with a visceral sense of economic tragedy.

While we could trace this thrilling tragedy to many sources and usefully spend a great deal of time doing so, I want for the moment to consider just one possibility: the moral anthropology of Adam Smith, in which strangerliness is morally normative. The economic studies that trace themselves back to Adam Smith are rooted in certain fundamental presuppositions, such as the efficiency of economy of scale and the division of labor (which implies the advantageousness of a wealthy capitalist class, even if they are not trustworthy), as well as the confidence that God's providence means that we do not have to be good to have a robust society. Scarcity, the matter with which we are chiefly concerned here, did not have in Smith the horrific significance it would gain in the generation of Malthus and Ricardo, but this is not to say that it was absent. Smith's thought is marked by an anthropology that digs a deep grounding for scarcity. For Smith, morality as well as economics is a matter of negotiations between strangers to find an equilibrium point.

Like his friend Hume, Smith thought a great deal about people's isolation from each other's inner sensations. *The Theory of Moral Sentiments*, in fact, used this as the basis of an entire moral theory. We are isolated in this way, but we also sympathize with each other, imagining how it would be to be the other. In imagining how the other experiences the world, we begin to imagine how the other sees us, and in this we first really consider ourselves. The observer becomes our mirror. We are, in this sense, constituted by our ability to sympathize with others. Our sympathy, however, never affects us with the intensity that the other actually experiences, so one who suffers must work to moderate his expression of pain, adapting it to my ability to sympathize. Knowing we are utterly alone in our sensations, we must not ask for more sympathy than others can give. One could say that in Smith's world sympathy is scarce. A wise person must calculate how much to bid so as not to appear desperate or beggarly, for to do so would drive away all sympathy. The notion, then, that negotiated exchange among isolated economic players is a universal and innate tendency in all persons is hardly new when Smith presents it as the famous "propensity to truck, barter, and exchange" in the *Wealth of Nations*. Nor is his hope to demonstrate that the good society can thrive even given these constraints. Rather, the isolation and stranger-liness that constitute our moral lives require our personal dignity and a capacity to imagine the other's feelings. Though we cannot touch each other in truth, we are structured so that we must continually interact, economically and morally, to our own and each other's benefit.[3] That interaction, however, does not include any real sharing. In spite of our being constituted by social relations, we are, and are well-off being, strangers to each other.

Though Smith is more generous and optimistic than many of his philosophical descendents, this anthropological commitment to strangerliness remains fundamental in economics. In consequence, dependence is degrading, for it requires that one person ask another to enter into her pain and treat it as his own. Such true fellow-feeling is impossible. This is so much so that Smith wonders at the anguish of commoners when their king falls. As the suffering is only his, Smith explains the widespread distress as a function of their sympathy for the enormity of his change of fortune. He does not allow, or even apparently consider, that the fall of the king *is* a calamity for the people who have identified with him. Such sharing of fate is alien to his thought.

From this fact, a kind of morals can emerge. To ask for fellow-feeling is to ask for what others cannot give. Deliberately to expose one's suffering to "weak" persons (Smith's term, not mine) in an attempt to increase their sympathy is to pervert reality for the purpose of manipulation.[4] The dignified person must disguise his suffering.

The result of this move is to make poverty intrinsically morally disadvantageous, not because of the temptation to theft, the loss of leisure for worship, or potential damage to self, others, or the common good, but because the poor person cannot be frank with others. If she lets the whole truth of her need be seen, she is unjustly demanding not only a sympathy to which she has no title but a sympathy that cannot be given. The noble person will attempt to conceal the depth of her suffering. Where a sympathetic observer notices poverty, he must not acknowledge the sight, which would increase the moral disadvantage of the poor person. Thus for all of Smith's warm appreciation for human social life, we see that real communion is impossible, as is, incidentally, a moral role for the poor. In the push and pull of economic life, no room can be found for frank trust or for genuine common cause. As discrete bodies, we are always affecting each other, but we cannot be members of one another.[5]

In present-day Christian economic reflection, this moral anthropology gets an unexpected new lease on life, particularly in the description of ownership as "stewardship of blessings given by God." The rhetoric of stewardship is plagued with difficulties, most notably, that when we hear possessions called *God-given blessings*, we may forget to ask, "Who says these things are blessings or that they are given by God?" It is salutary to note that just this kind of argument—about a "sacred trust"—was used in the antebellum South to describe and implicitly justify ownership of slaves.[6] Those matters aside, this language is troubling because it implies a version of Smith's moral strangerliness. For example, the Christian steward faces numerous appeals, a world full of needs. She is concerned and involved, but her role is carefully circumscribed. She must make tragically prudent choices in an attempt to hold back the horror of poverty. In these choices she is fundamentally alone, although other Christians similarly responsible for property will offer her counsel and many recipients will eagerly await her decisions. She alone will face judgment for her use of resources. While her moral calling requires her to continually engage with others, her calling and her activity are hers alone, as in the title of the 1992 bishops' letter on stewardship, entitled "Stewardship: A Disciple's [singular] Response." And those to whom she may give are also alone, standing on the other side of an abyss awaiting her decision. Stewardship issues a call to act for the good of others, but it does so in such a way that giver and receiver do not seem to be of one body anymore than Smith's sympathetic observer can be.

This separation is not simply a failure to name the common body we are made into in Christ. It does not merely divide; it grants moral superiority to one side. The standard stewardship appeal concerns not some commonality binding people together. It emphasizes rather the virtue of those who have been "blessed" in sacrificing themselves for others, others whose lack of wealth leaves them unable to share in this moral adventure, except insofar as they conceal their need and attempt in a limited way to share in the role of the blessed wealthy person. Everyone has to be known as someone who has something to give, not in the sense that the church must be willing to receive different and difficult charisms, but such that no one is in the immoral position of needing and receiving.[7]

Among conscientious Christians, then, the question of Christian economic ethics typically ends up focusing on what the wealthy person ought to do to avoid and/or reduce poverty. Stewardship campaigns and social justice committees alike share this concern, although typically from different angles, the one looking at giving and the other at moderation of economic systems. This is our usual way of confronting the tragic question of scarcity: we stage a courageous battle to hold back the evil of poverty. I do not say that such aims are cowardly or mediocre. On the contrary, tremendous energy and sacrifices have been poured into this battle. But I will say that insofar as we think this is the characteristic Christian economic ethic, we are mistaken. Our Scriptures, our longer history, the lives of the saints, and indeed the "social encyclicals" point us in other directions, in particular toward a plenitude announced in the heart of suffering, at the cross.

## THE STRANGE COMEDY OF CHRISTIAN PLENITUDE

John Milbank has attempted to out-Nietzsche Nietzsche by claiming that Christian virtue can be called immoral because it surpasses heroic morality in a shocking way. The heroic always requires the existence of its enemy. One can only light a candle if the world is dark, or die to save the city if barbarian hordes are attacking the fragile walls. One can only be generous within a world of scarcity, against the backdrop of poverty. (Mother Teresa is said to have dreamt that the angels told her she would not be happy in heaven because there are no slums there.) Contrary to this tragic morality, Milbank reminds us of the "notes" of Christian morality: Gift, End of Sacrifice, Resurrection, Plenitude, and Confidence. Christian faith is not a candle in the darkness but the discovery that we stand in full daylight.[8]

Here we see the crux of Christian delight. David conquers Goliath, and the walls of Jericho fall because, before God, assertions of human strength are like a child's attempt to box with the rain. The loaves and the fishes, like the manna and quail of the desert, are not rations to sustain a few out of the many who are hungry but evidence of an order of such plenty that hoarding is made nonsense. Consider the grimly comic prophecy of Israel eating quail until it comes out their noses (Numbers 11:18–20). If the story turns from farce to vengeance, it is only because the participants missed the comedy of divine providence. Seen in this light, even the massacre of the innocents becomes a kind of horrific slapstick, Herod lashing out violently and with complete futility against the appearance of his rival. The wailing in Ramah is real and terrible, but the joke is on Herod. The resurrection itself is, after all, the great joke on death, when God turns the table to reveal that tragedy is not the final word. What appears on Friday as the all-too-familiar tale of a doomed, courageous hero showing dignity as he goes down with the ship, turns out on Sunday to be the bursting of the very bonds that make such courage necessary. In *Piers Plowman* the harrowing of hell features a version of *Christus victor* soteriology in which Jesus plays Satan's trick back on him—he who stole humans in the disguise of a serpent now has them stolen back when God comes for them in their own form. On the principle of "an eye for an eye," Satan's guile is itself beguiled, and he has to drink the cup he prepared for others.[9]

This characteristically Christian comic turn of the tables is salutary for economic ethics, which so tends to concern itself with lack and death that it forgets to listen for and expect the eschatological punch line. Of course, the divine sense of humor may strike us as excessive and even grisly, when not hidden altogether. We may trust in plenitude and resurrection, but we still see grave, debilitating lack and death. How many people starved today? Hope, along with faith, passes away, leaving only charity in the End. But we do need hope and faith, and it is often enough of a fight simply to maintain them.

Given all this, the category of plenitude is at face value dangerous nonsense. Whatever is right about it, it cannot mean turning a blind eye to the misery of millions or proclaiming an escape into a kind of plenitude of grace that has nothing to do with adequate intake of calories. Milbank's eagerness to overtake Nietzsche leaves him rather short on this explication, for Christian plenitude is no more an escape from poverty than resurrection is from death.[10] That is to say, Jesus's followers may proclaim plenitude as a reversal of poverty but a reversal they expect to find only by passing through poverty somehow rather than by escaping from it. I have often thought that Milbank's comments on plenitude should have as an illustration a portrait of Benedict Labre, the eighteenth-century French saint, who was a homeless beggar and a pilgrim. His extreme poverty left his face cadaverous, his clothes ragged and lice-infested, but in canonization hearings one witness after another attested to his joyful expression and his radiant peace, in which several of them claimed to have seen the very image of Christ.

> Whereas, in moral sacrifice, the parts are given up for the whole, passions for the intellect, and heroes for the city, in Christian sacrifice, as Kierkegaard says, the whole itself—the person and the city together—are *absurdly* given up, *not* for any higher gain, but for or *as* the receiving back of themselves as a gift from God which is same-yet-different.[11]

The great Christian affirmation of resurrection is confident martyrdom—taking the horror of murder and passing through it in a way that does not affirm murder but transforms the act so that God's mercy and victory show up in it more strongly than ever. Even as the murder is a horror and an anguish, the beauty of martyrdom exceeds those evils. In the same way, the great Christian affirmation of plenitude is joyful voluntary poverty. It takes on the horror of hunger and physical precarity, even sickness and early death, pass-ing through them in a way that does not affirm poverty but transforms it so that God's mercy and victory show up more strongly than ever within it. The triumph and the plenitude of the cross are nothing if they cannot proclaim that the story of creation is a comedy there, in its most tragic places.

Perhaps a better example is the story of the rich man who asks how to in-herit eternal life (Mark 10:17–31). When the man claims to have followed all the commandments, Mark says, "Jesus looking upon him loved him." As a gift to this one he loved, he offered the one thing lacking to him, an invita-tion to leave all and become a disciple. It is an invitation to one who wants to stop measuring out devotion in teaspoons, who wants to be free to love God. It was, apparently, too much freedom for that man to accept, although he himself knew it to be a good gift, for we are told he went away sad. Those who had accepted it and reminded Jesus of their offering are assured of their reward and of their share in the cross.

Nothing in this story speaks of the obligation of the wealthy to make effi-cient use of their wealth to end suffering, nor does it speak of self-destructive asceticism; avoiding fraud, murder, adultery, and theft are necessary first steps, but they are not the real issue. The crucial matter is an invitation to be free from fear through faith, from despair through hope, from pride through charity. Or, to be more specific, to be free from the habits of comfort and control that separate us from our brothers and sisters. Using the Acts 2 as a hermeneutic aid, we can say that the rich man was invited into the commu-nity that would be fully constituted with the gift of the Spirit, able to call nothing their own but to be of one heart and mind, dedicated to the prayers and the breaking of the bread, in which it is obscene for one to claim a right to a portion while another goes without. That is, this law-abiding but sad man was invited into the Eucharistic community. The economic question for wealthy Christians, which is to say for most of those we are and those whom we teach, is not how to do good with our wealth. It is how to live in Eu-charistic solidarity with our brothers and sisters in Christ, free from the ethic of strangerly sacrifice that makes such commonality impossible. Only that kind of solidarity can offer a fundamental alternative to the ethic of scarcity.

## ECONOMIC ETHICISTS AS WAYFARING STRANGERS

If then Christian ethics and classical economic anthropology are at odds in the respects I have mentioned, if the Eucharistic commonality I am pointing toward is rarely articulated and rarely embodied, and if the job of the moral theologian is to assist the Christian community in understanding its calling and following it more faithfully, then we who are called to teach about eco-nomic ethics have two closely linked problems: how to teach and how to live. The two are closely linked because our ability to speak well about Eucharistic solidarity is distinguishable but not entirely separable from our living (albeit imperfectly) in that solidarity so that we begin to know it from the inside. The rest of this chapter consists of suggestions for addressing those two problems.

As we shift then into the matter of the moral theologian's vocation, I have to say that I find it awkward to write about the economic ethics of being a moral theologian. I am, for one thing, new at the profession and only beginning to understand the complexities of it. I am also afraid of being shown to be a hypocrite, of asking too much of my colleagues and friends and family, and of asking too little of the church. I suspect that I am not alone in these fears. After all, determining what an economically ethical life for any Christian or group of Christians in the United States would look like is a nasty problem. Add to that the question of how the institutions in which most of us work, Catholic universities, should be run, and how we ought to participate in them as people committed to solidarity rather than scarcity, and I will tell you, our lives will be easier if we punt this one over to individual conscience. But then, we did not enter this field because we thought invoking "individual conscience" was a sufficient answer. So as a beginning, let me offer three rules of the road to serve as guidelines for discussions about personal economic practice.

First ground rule: In all things charity. This is not a contest to see who can be the most consistent or radical or subtle. It is not about wearing a badge of honor for living in a slum or a mantle of suburban shame. Remember Jesus's first comment to the rich man: "God alone is good." In Christian communities committed to voluntary poverty, this issue can be a big stick with which we beat each other. The question is raised not to castigate but to set free.

Second, and as a corollary of the first, let us agree not to offer guilt-ridden confessions of social location in lieu of a serious consideration of the issue and amendment of life. Living with a bad conscience is not an option. If you think changes must be made, start making them. If you think the changes others advocate are wrongheaded or unnecessary, argue against them. If you cannot make the changes you think you should, find ways to protest, to intercede, to explore, to take even very small steps. The mercy found in confession and penance would be a good place to start and a necessity all along the way. If you are not sure what changes to make, ask for guidance and engage in experiments. But to accept that changes must be made and then to persist in long-faced refusal to address them is bad for our souls, not to mention our scholarly integrity. It will be work and we will make mistakes and suffer the consequences, but let us not make false apologies. God save us from luxuriating in despair.

Third, whatever steps we may take, we do no service to the church if we cease to be scholars, thinkers, writers, and good teachers. I have, and I know colleagues who also have, been tempted to refuse to accept this role of a university professor because of the social and economic status it bears with it. We are employed, those of us lucky enough to get such employment, in universities that produce the knowledge class, managers, and communicators of the post-Fordist economy, including ourselves. Our students who resent their years of study as out of touch with the "real world" have no idea what they are talking about. Universities are the real world. And yet, although universities are enthralled by an economy of scarcity, they do remain uneasy participants, resistant in a notable and useful respect. Study is notoriously inefficient. The scholarly life is all about an ethic of plenitude, and the muscle memory of study simply for the sake of learning is a troublesome blessing for academic institutions. Good scholarship and good teaching remain slow and uncertain, excessive and delighted rather than efficient, based in an internal presumption that the good of learning is itself sufficient rationale. The money and effort expended are not "investments" that must pay off but are well spent simply to fund the good of learning. The ever-increasing demand that educators more efficiently produce student-products suited to the present job market is an incursion into one of the few remaining sites of an ethic of plenitude.[12] But the propensity for that academic life to become merely the leisure of a privileged elite is also a danger. The Catholic university is caught therefore in this very interesting squeeze—how to survive in this economy while continuing to be scholarly rather than merely productive and how to make that same university a site of Christian solidarity rather than a protected sphere of privilege. Lip service notwithstanding, that last question is largely unexplored territory. Here is a problem worth our best efforts and demanding our full commitment. Abdicating the privileges and duties of scholarship will not be an acceptable response.

With those guidelines laid down, we can face our difficulty. The essence of the Christian economic ethicists' position is this: we participate in an economically unjust order, and it is our duty and privilege to oppose it. But we will not oppose it by being drawn into its own fearful and tragic reasoning. It is necessary to us who hold the office of moral theologian to be courageous and inventive in patiently cultivating our talents and sharing our goods, in becoming vulnerable to our neighbors, in speaking frankly to each other about our needs and resources, and in naming and attending to common goods and to the common good. But we are not obligated to fight back the host of monstrous evils we see in the interest of establishing some golden era. The problem with that kind of Pelagianism (in its current, cheerful form, we might call it Haugenism) is its tendency to turn brutal with those who do not fit in, with the fearful or addicted or stubborn, or those afflicted with bad taste. Let the wheat and the tares grow together.

This obligation and invitation to submit our lives to Christian teaching is incumbent on all the baptized, but we who have the charge to be teachers of moral theology must be particularly energetic. If we do not, we will lay burdens on our students that we will not carry ourselves; or, what is more likely, we will not tell our students what Christian economics means, preferring to lay that burden neither on them nor on ourselves.

But here we come to the heart of the problem. It is not only that I am unwilling to lay the burden on them. I do not know and I am not sure that any of us know exactly what that "burden" is, what we ought to teach our students about the comedy of Christian plenitude. When we do not know how to live, how can we teach our students? We know something of the ends toward which we must be oriented: the civilization of love, solidarity, that justice that is not mere equality in exchange but that is rich in mercy, restorative. We certainly know something about unjust means and disordered appetites. But we lack the blueprint that would console us with its certainty.

A blueprint for "building the city of God" would be comforting, but we know that such architecture is mistaken from the outset. Rather, our participation in God's plenitude must mean that we do not fear to admit this lack and to search out our next steps in prayer and common discernment. It may be that we, in our good but peculiar office, are not the holders of the best insights. If we pretend to know all we need, we will not hear the answers that God is offering in our brothers and sisters in, for example, business and social services. I at least will admit to you, in the hope that guidance is forthcoming, that I do not know quite what to do.

Our great and pressing need is for prudence concerning property and business, the skills of good judgment and creative adaptation to always new circumstances. We need to know how, in the face of both astounding cruelty and ostensibly neutral systems that lead good people to participate in evil, to continue to speak of and witness to resurrection and plenty without glossing over the details or making light of the blood shed.

We do have scholarly resources that can help us in this, and they should not be ignored. After all, voluntary poverty, economic sharing, and the problem of defining "superfluous wealth" have a long history. Such work is challenging, but fruitful. What, for example, are we to make of the thirteenth-century debates that eventually decided that confiscation of a necessity in the case of mortal danger was not theft? We, most of us, would concur that the starving man who steals to save his life is not guilty of theft. But what then of the owner of bread who does not give it? Or of the members of a large group ("mob") who decide to act together to confiscate goods pertaining to another group ("owners")? In a world that takes mortal inequality for granted, how can we meaningfully continue this debate?[13] Or again, whatever happened to the usury debate? I would love to see someone take up again the claim that human work, the soil, and animals may be fruitful, but dollar bills cannot be, and therefore no one should profit from mere possession of currency. Is it moral to profit from savings rather than from work? Or rather, could we, as medieval scholars did, articulate a moral distinction between such acts as profiting from investment in a partnership with shared risk and profiting without risk or personal engagement in the work?[14]

Yet these scholarly resources, while significant, are in themselves insufficient. The debate on theft, for example, cannot be usefully joined so long as life-threatening inequality is taken for granted as a fact of our economic lives. We cannot rightly consider whether property is common in time of mortal necessity, because all of our time is of mortal necessity for millions whose suffering has simply become background noise to us. What kind of life would we have to live to be ready to engage in such a conversation, to be ready to be bound and freed by the conclusions we reached? The prudence we need is not just another topic we can brush up on. It is an accumulation of ways of seeing and speaking learned in a certain kind of common life. It requires the possession of certain well-shaped tastes and desires that move us toward an increasingly understood end. Prudence is more properly a matter of training than of simple learning or research. The economically constructed world in which we move trains us, and our students, to save ourselves and our loved ones out of the flood. Who will teach us how to replace fear with confidence?

My own ideas about how we can begin to cultivate the prudence we need are perhaps already evident, but let me spell them out, inchoate as they still are.

## Voluntary Poverty

Not everyone is called to be an activist or to be voluntarily poor à la Benedict Labre or Francis, but that is not to say that no one is so called, and we must encourage those who may have such vocations to pursue them, for we need them. I have said that Christianity delights in nothing so much as inversion, parables, turning the tables; and if we are to gain a sense of the Christian delight possible with regard to possessions, we need the parabolic witness of voluntary poverty. Poverty is misery and evil, but Christianity has fostered a kind of holy poverty that takes that misery and evil on, witnessing confidently to God's exceeding faithfulness and plenty. If we are to learn to see rightly and to love rightly so that we can begin to judge in keeping with the Christian economic comedy, then we need the help of those most committed to witnessing to plenty, those who joyfully refuse to be defeated by poverty.

I am not claiming that poverty is "not so bad." I am saying that Christians have endured poverty in a way that attests to its eschatological reversal. Even as what we see and suffer is destruction, pain, frustration, and perversion, still where sin abounds grace abounds all the more. God's past and future deeds put even these horrors solidly within a story of joy and confidence. This is no "pie in the sky" refusal to face reality. In fact, the faith that defeat and horror are absurdities, that plenitude is the reliable reality, makes escapism less attractive and certainly less useful. The result of such a way of enduring is that we need not exert all of our energy toward avoiding suffering and death. But all of these affirmations of mine ring a bit hollow when the embodiment of them is so rare among us. I do not think that we can understand the delight of Christian economics until we understand better the practice of voluntary poverty, and a practice, by definition, cannot be studied in the abstract.

### Our Houses, Our Selves

This is not a matter that touches only those few who enter into poverty as a religious vocation. All the baptized are called into the community of Acts 2, where goods are shared. We have never entirely lost track of this point—the offertory collection remains the most stable and ecumenical liturgical practice of all. But the collection can become merely ritualized taxation if we do not carefully situate it in the context of Christian sharing, which is to say in the context of Jesus's gift—giving in the Eucharist. Again, I see no short-cut to the cultivation of economic prudence. We will have to go through practices of sharing if we want to know how to do it. For the moment, we must note that if we are to enter into some kind of sharing, we must know others' lives. We must enter into others' houses.

In particular, we, scholars and professionals, must make ourselves vulner-able to Christians who do not share our assumptions about what it is normal to possess, whose definitions of "need" challenge ours. This is not to say that someone in my parish with an income of $10,000 a year necessarily will know what it is right for me to do with the $42,000 that will find its way into an account under my name. I have had some frank and heated debates with acquaintances about the right use of my and their incomes, and the outcome has not often been a union of hearts and minds. The old saying still stands: "The cry of the poor may not be just, but you do not know justice until you hear it." Until we enter into this kind of common life, where we see others' worlds of needs and desires, our judgments will be barren because they will not be about charity, by which I mean the entirely practical and personal su-pernatural upbuilding of the body of Christ.

### Teaching and the Professional-Managerial Class

For those of us who are university teachers or are aiming at such a career, this problem also implicates offices and classrooms. Eugene McCarraher has called attention to the class of Christian social critics, claiming that their membership in the professional–managerial class is not an innocent factor in their work.[15] Our offices, our tools, our long-distance collegial relationships and regular travel to conferences, our familiarity with the life of the profes-sional will tend to inculcate in us an idea of the "normal" that can, to say the least, impede our imaginations and shape our tastes in ways that make economic sharing more problematic and unlikely. Our students hope to follow us into such lives, in which computers and airports feature more significantly than, say, chicken-processing plants and bus stops. In fact, attending university is for our students a hedge against ever having to think much about such things or perhaps an escape from them. Universities represent (and, as good symbols, also are) a ladder to the top of the heap in a world of tragic scarcity.

I am indebted to McCarraher for his insistence on this point, but I do not think he has fully realized how the internal logic of our profession problematizes our place in the professional–managerial class and has given rise to many creative variations on that class. I do spend more time dealing with e-mail than with my neighbors and far more time sitting in an air-conditioned (if aging) car than waiting for the bus. But I am a theologian for the church, which includes all sorts of people, even if I am employed by the university. My audience is not only the professional-minded students of the University of Dayton but also, if usually more indirectly, all the church and particularly the members of my home diocese and my present parish, among whom even the little children often know much more about the streets than I do.

Of course, lawyers and doctors may also find themselves as professionals pushed beyond the professional world. But the challenge of the profession of theology to itself runs deeper than this. As a Christian theologian, I also cannot avoid considering that the poor are blessed, that the last shall be first, and that the word of God to prestigious religious teachers has on occasion been "Woe!" It requires me to expect to share in Ruby Turpin's vision at the end of O'Connor's story "Revelation," in which the "respectable" folk enter into heaven with shocked looks on their faces, as their very virtues are burned away.

Does this internal critique of theology as a profession do any work? That, it seems to me, is up to us. Can we take service learning a different way so that we and our students and our universities become more transparent and vulnerable to those we supposedly "serve"? Could our Catholic universities engage in some actual solidarity rather than merely move up the national educational pecking order? What should we do about the geography of our campuses, which generally reinforces the separation of "normal" (professional-to-be) people and "townies," even when members of each group are Catholics, hearing the same word and sharing the same meal? Many people, I am glad to recognize, are working in theology to advance our field for the good of the church rather than merely to produce commodities that compete for attention on the market of the academy. But if we take this critique of our profession-as-class seriously, we have a long way to go.

I am aware that pursuing any of these matters is likely to lead us into sharp conflict with any number of people, not least among them the minimum-wage workers and unemployed people of our parishes. I am also aware that a fruitful outcome is unlikely without the exercise of wise and beloved pastoral authority, which can be in short supply. Nevertheless, despair is a luxury we cannot afford. We are made for delight, and the hard road of Christian delight takes us in this direction: we need neighborhoods of Christians who care for each other, who can be frank with each other, who know enough about their common good to walk the road toward it together, who are unafraid to be poor together. And we need our universities to be part of such communities. We need ecclesial arrangements that more truly echo Paul's teaching that "as a matter of equality your abundance at the present time should supply their want, so that their abundance can supply your want, that there may be equality" (2 Corinthians 8:14). As scholars, we have disciplined ourselves to be readers and writers; now we must discipline ourselves to be neighbors, distinguishing our justifiable need for quiet time for study from our desire for privacy and tidiness of life. If we are to speak the Christian message of economic plenty as against a world shaped by scarcity, we can only do so from the midst of suffering. No bystander can claim the massacre of innocents as leavened by comedy without committing a cruel cheapening of that pain. The rightful proclamation of delight must come out of sharing in the weeping of Ramah.

This is not a plan for a new program in the church. God forbid. The final "mark of the beast" in Milbank's essay on the immorality of Christianity is *generality*, for the reactionary ethic needs uniformity as a way of imposing order and right on disorder and wrong. Our experiments, our commitments, and our households will be diverse, as our responsibilities and talents and selves are. But that diversity does not excuse us from the wedding feast to which we have been urgently invited.

Michael Novak has quipped, "We are all capitalists now, even the Pope." Actually *most* people are wage slaves within capitalist economies, but the point remains the same. The pressing issue for economic ethics is *not* presently "socialism versus capitalism." One economic system in a multitude of forms exerts an inexorable hold on our imaginations and our lives. Insofar as we understand that system to be at odds with the joy and freedom of the Christian, we are bound to find ways to resist it, to live in it but not of it.[16] The church as a whole and in its particular local communities can, does, and will do this, for we do live together in a comedy, and our happy common End is not simply future. The place to begin to share plenitude is among ourselves, in our parishes, our households, our church. No change we envision for world systems can be more potent than the determination of Christians to define their households and communities in accord with these insights. It is certainly a messy and awkward challenge, and it will cause us a great deal of trouble. It is the place we can hope to find Christian delight and plenitude, and the cross as well.

# NOTES

1. See, for example, Roy J. Ruffin and Paul R. Gregory, *Principles of Microeconomics*, 5th ed. (New York: HarperCollins, 1993), 3; William Baumol and Alan S. Blinder, *Economics: Principles and Policy*, 7th ed. (Fort Worth, Tex.: Dryden Press / Harcourt Brace, 1997), 49.

2. A more modest reading of the principle of scarcity would claim that it merely means that humans must have rational systems of distribution, that not all of us can simply take what we want and expect things to turn out well. This more benign reading, however, could be described fairly as "finitude" rather than "scarcity" to recognize the reality of limits without implying the tragedy of shortage. I draw this suggestion from James Halteman, *The Clashing Worlds of Economics and Faith* (Scottsdale, Pa.: Herald Press, 1995).

3. I do not subscribe to the view that sets *The Wealth of Nations* at odds with *The Theory of Moral Sentiments*. Smith continued to revise *Theory* years after he had written *Wealth*, in no way recanting the earlier work. Indeed, the two are of a piece in taking negotiations among strangers (imagined or actual) to be the fundamental human activity. Genuine friendship and other erosions of individuality are problematic peculiarities.

4. "Persons of delicate fibres and a weak constitution of body complain, that in looking on the sores and ulcers which are exposed by beggars in the streets, they are apt to feel an itching or uneasy sensation in the correspondent part of their own bodies." Smith *The Theory of Moral Sentiments* 1.1.1.3.

5. Smith was, in fact, a generous philanthropist. But that in no way undercuts my point. His own writing indicates that he would see those gifts as a noble negotiation of sympathy. He would honor the needs of others insofar as he could imaginatively enter into them, and he would respect those needy recipients who attempted to moderate the appearance of their distress. But their suffering was not, and could not, be his.

6. See, for example, Eugene Genovese, *A Consuming Fire: The Fall of the Confederacy in the Mind of the White Christian South* (Athens: University of Georgia Press, 1998).

7. This is not to deny that within stewardship campaigns in parishes some real sharing does happen. Grace abounds. Nevertheless, the logic of the approach makes actual sharing, friendship, and recognition of Christ in the poor awkward. For a more detailed treatment of this topic, see my forthcoming book, *The Fear of Beggars: Stewardship and Poverty in Christian Ethics* (Notre Dame, Ind.: University of Notre Dame Press, 2005).

8. John Milbank, "Can Morality Be Christian?" *The Word Made Strange: Theology, Language, Culture* (Cambridge: Blackwell, 1998), 219–32.

9. William Langland, *Piers Plowman*, C-version, transl. George Economou (Philadelphia: University of Pennsylvania Press, 1996), 192–93 (Passus XX, 370–402).

10. Milbank does discuss the way the end of sacrifice actually means that "now at last it is fully moral to give ourselves sacrificially—as the only mode in the fallen order by which we can continue to give—because we now have confidence that this does not cancel out our own existence" ("Can Morality Be Christian?" 230). But he

offers no historical examples to assist us in distinguishing sacrifice from this gift-giving, nonsuicidal end of sacrifice. Such examples, in the concrete, are disturbing and open to dispute.

11. Milbank, "Can Morality Be Christian?" 230.

12. My thanks to David McCarthy for raising this point.

13. A study of these debates is Gilles Couvreur, *Les pauvres ont-ils des droits? Recherches sur le vol in cas d'extrême nécessité depuis la Concordia de Gratien (1140) jusqu'à Guillaume d'Auxerre (+1231)* (Roma: Libreria Editrice dell'Università Gregoriana, 1961). See also *Gaudiaum et spes*, 69.

14. The classic reference work on usury is John T. Noonan, *The Scholastic Analysis of Usury* (Cambridge, Mass.: Harvard University Press, 1957). Odd Langholm has recently made a rich contribution to this history in his *Economics in the Medieval Schools: Wealth, Exchange, Value, Money, and Usury according to the Paris Theological Tradition, 1200–1350* (Leiden, Neth.: E. J. Brill, 1992).

15. Eugene McCarraher, *Christian Critics: Religion and the Impasse in Modern American Social Thought* (Ithaca, N.Y.: Cornell University Press, 2000).

16. I am indebted to Steve Long for this formulation.

# Index

abortion, 133–34

academic culture: Catholic identity within, 45, 60n8, 61nn11–12; history of, 28; lay theologian within, 45, 47, 52, 59, 60n8, 61nn11–12; research/writing for, 47, 52, 62n30; shaping of, 27–28, 41n6; tenure within, 50; values for, 28–29, 30–31. *See also* professionalism

*After Virtue* (MacIntyre), 128–29, 139n40

*aggiornimento* (openness to the world), 2

agorism, 28

St. Alphonsus Ligouri, 12

American Vatican II, 2–3

Arian controversy, 80

Aristotelian tradition, 30, 32, 129, 131, 132, 139n44

Aristotle, 30, 32, 87, 91, 97n8, 98n23, 99n24

asceticism, 32, 34, 42n22, 171

*askesis* (exercises for reflection), 34–35, 37, 43n26

St. Augustine, 16, 78, 85–91, 95–96, 98n17, 98n23, 99n33, 100nn39–40, 100n42, 145

baptism, xi, 52, 71, 173–74

St. Benedict, 128, 133

St. Benedict Labre, 170, 175

Bible: Acts 2, 176; 1 Corinthians 2:4, 86; 1 Corinthians 12, 72; 2 Corinthians 8:14, 178; 2 Corinthians 11:6, 86; John 1, 86, 91; John 3:16, 86; John 10:9, 73; John 14:6, 73; Luke 17:10, 134; Mark 2:22, ix; Mark 10:17–31, 171; Mark 13:11, 86; Matthew 5:48, 86; Matthew 19:16–22, 10; Matthew 22:37, 146; Numbers 11:18–20, 169; Scripture study of, 32, 34, 42n21, 51, 63n36; 1 Timothy 6:20, 88

birth control, xii, 21n30, 120–21, 122, 135n9

bishop, theologian and, 69

Böckle, Franz, 148, 155

Bonhoeffer, Dietrich, 54

Burggraeve, Roger, 46

Callahan, Daniel, 2–3, 4, 5, 7, 20n11, 42n20

canon law, x, 57, 64n55, 68, 70

capital punishment, 38

Carroll, Colleen, 5–6, 21n19

181

# About the Contributors

**William P. Bolan** is currently Visiting Assistant Professor of theology at the University of Notre Dame, where he regularly employs the pedagogy of community-based learning. His areas of expertise include fundamental moral theology, social justice, and the requirements of Christian solidarity. His most recent writing addresses the nexus of Catholic social thought and the work of faith-based community development organizations. He received a doctorate in Christian ethics from Notre Dame in 2004.

**David Cloutier** teaches moral theology at the College of St. Benedict–St. John's University in Collegeville, MN. He received his Ph.D. from Duke University in 2001, writing under Stanley Hauerwas on the relationship of happiness/teleology and renunciation in the Christian life. His areas of interest include sexual ethics, teleology and eschatology in practical reason, and the relationship of scriptural narratives to ethical reflection. His first book, an introduction to Catholic sexual ethics, is forthcoming from Saint Mary's Press.

**Kelly S. Johnson** teaches moral theology at the University of Dayton in Dayton, OH. She was awarded a Ph.D. from Duke University in 2001, where she investigated the intersection of Christian debates on property and exchange with the history of economic analysis. She works principally on the importance of liturgical, ascetical, and ecclesiological studies for what is commonly called social ethics. She is author of *The Fear of Beggars: Stewardship and Poverty in Christian Ethics*.

**William C. Mattison III** teaches moral theology at Mount St. Mary's University in Emmitsburg, MD. He completed his doctorate in 2003 at the University of Notre Dame, where he wrote under Jean Porter on the moral significance of the passions, in particular anger, in the Christian life. His main areas of interest are Thomistic virtue ethics and the theology of marriage/family/sexuality. He founded the New Wine, New Wineskins symposium in 2002 with fellow doctoral student Maria Malkiewicz.

**Margaret Pfeil** teaches moral theology at the University of Notre Dame, where she also earned her doctorate in 2000 under the direction of Jean Porter. Her work focuses on the correlation between social sin and social forms of reconciliation. Among her areas of interest are Catholic social teaching, peace studies, and the relationship between spirituality and moral theology. Together with Michael Baxter and Ben Peters, she founded the St. Peter Claver Catholic Worker House in South Bend in 2003.

**Christopher Steck, SJ,** teaches Christian ethics at Georgetown University, Washington, DC. He received his Ph.D. from Yale University in 1999. His research has focused on fundamental themes in moral theology. His book, *The Ethical Thought of Hans Urs von Balthasar*, was published in 2001 and received the College Theological Society's annual book award in 2003.

**Christopher Vogt** teaches moral theology at St. John's University in New York. He received a Ph.D. in theological ethics from Boston College in 2002, having written his dissertation under the direction of James F. Keenan, SJ. He is author of *Patience, Compassion, Hope, and the Christian Art of Dying Well*, published by Rowman & Littlefield in 2004.

**Darlene Fozard Weaver** teaches Christian ethics at Villanova University. She earned her doctorate in 1998 from the University of Chicago Divinity School, and published a revised version of her dissertation as *Self Love and Christian Ethics* (2002). Her main research interests focus on moral anthropology and moral theory. She is currently working on a book on persons and moral actions.